DAVID BOWIE IS

DAVID BOWIE IS THE SUBJECT

EDITED BY VICTORIA BROACKES
AND GEOFFREY MARSH

V&A PUBLISHING

First published by V&A Publishing, 2013
Victoria and Albert Museum
South Kensington
London SW7 2RL
www.vandapublishing.com

Distributed in North America by Harry N. Abrams Inc., New York
© The Board of Trustees of the Victoria and Albert Museum, 2013
The moral right of the author(s) has been asserted.

Hardback edition ISBN 978 1 85177 737 2
Paperback edition ISBN 978 1 85177 735 8
Library of Congress Control Number 2012948899
10 9 8 7 6 5
2017 2016 2015 2014 2013

Every effort has been made to seek permission to reproduce those
images whose copyright does not reside with the V&A, and we are
grateful to the individuals and institutions who have assisted in this
task. Any omissions are entirely unintentional, and the details should
be addressed to V&A Publishing.

Graphically yours: Jonathan Abbott & Jonathan Barnbrook [BARNBROOK]
Copy-editor: Alexandra Stetter
Index: Hilary Bird

New photography by Richard Davis and Eileen Travell
V&A Photography by V&A Photographic Studio
Colour reproduction, DL Imaging Ltd., London
Printed in Italy by Graphicom s.r.l.

Special thanks to
JPMorgan Chase & Co. | Technology for Social Good
for the use of camera equipment

OPPOSITE: Promotional photograph of David Bowie for *Diamond Dogs*, 1974
(printed 2009) ❋ Terry O'Neill ❋ V&A: E.315–2011

V&A Publishing
Supporting the world's leading
museum of art and design,
the Victoria and Albert
Museum, London

DAVID BOWIE IS AN ABSOLUTE BEGINNER

DAVID BOWIE IS A JOY FOREVER

DAVID BOWIE IS MOVING LIKE A TIGER ON VASELINE

I OPENED DOORS THAT WOULD HAVE BLOCKED THEIR WAY

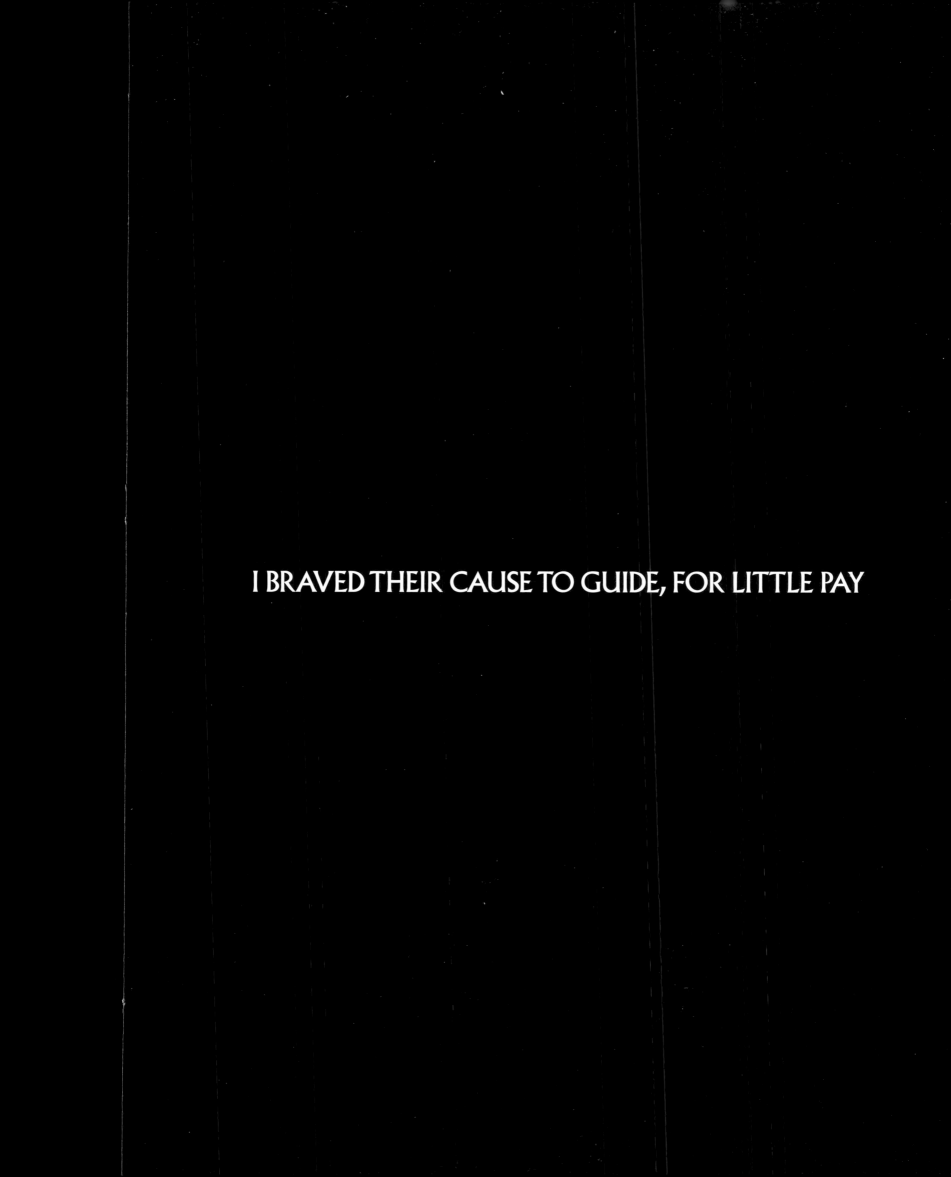

I BRAVED THEIR CAUSE TO GUIDE, FOR LITTLE PAY

DAVID BOWIE
IS WHAT
FOLLOWS

David Bowie has left an indelible stamp on the look, the style, the sound and the attitudes of his time. It is an extraordinary achievement and I am delighted that the V&A is staging the exhibition, *David Bowie Is*. One of the key roles of the museum is to celebrate great design. Bowie is not only one of the great musicians and performers of the last half century, but is also among the great design visionaries. An instigator not just of memorable individual pieces – an album sleeve, a costume, a hairstyle – but of a particular zeitgeist that is uniquely his and yet resonates with enormous numbers of people around the globe.

I felt this impact personally, a teenager growing up in Germany, proud that David Bowie had come to live in my country, in Berlin, where he spent two of his most productive years, and where he created *"Heroes"*, the centrepiece of a triptych of groundbreaking albums. This book attempts to chart the wider significance of Bowie's impact on our cultural life. Frustratingly, of course, no book can fully capture what for many people remains the essence of David Bowie – his music. Fortunately the exhibition is able to fill that gap – delighting not just the eye, but also the ear.

Exhibitions such as *David Bowie Is* could not be staged without the involvement of sponsors, and it gives me particular pleasure to thank Sennheiser GmbH and Gucci for their support. It was clear from the beginning that music was going to be fundamental to the exhibition, but the use of sound in museums is relatively new, and we have much to learn about how to use it to its best effect. Sennheiser know more than most that the enormous rise in the sound quality of consumer goods has increased the public's expectations. Their aim has been to help the V&A to present the music with the same distinction as the physical artefacts, and recreate the sound experience of a real performance. Their financial and technical support has been much appreciated.

David Bowie is a style icon, and one of the most instantly recognizable men on the planet. One of his greatest impacts on our cultural life has been as a proponent of individualism – that we should be what we want to be, look how we want to look, and lead, not follow, without depending always on the views of others. As Brian Eno, Bowie's collaborator, once responded to an over-enthusiastic critic exhorting him to 'do the same thing again', 'If I'd followed your advice in the first place, I'd never have got anywhere.' For over 90 years the House of Gucci has protected and nurtured its founding traditions and values, while evolving into a contemporary global business. They have travelled a distinctive path in an industry that has undergone extraordinary upheaval. Gucci understand, better than most, that *Changes*, rebels, 'Fame', 'Time', pretty things, *"Heroes"*, the 'Speed of Life', 'Fascination' and 'Who can I be now?' are all part and parcel of Fashion.

As well as thanking our sponsors I must also offer my profound gratitude to The David Bowie Archive. Without their extraordinary generosity none of this would have been possible.

MARTIN ROTH
Director, Victoria and Albert Museum

CURATORS' PREFACE

Travelling recently through London, we stopped at the junction of Grove End Road and Abbey Road. Although it was early evening, there were still about thirty people, mostly tourists, milling around taking photos of each other on *that* zebra crossing. Most of them would not have been born on 8 August 1969 when, as David Bowie's first hit 'Space Oddity' crept towards the charts, Iain Macmillan took his iconic photograph of the Beatles. In a single image he anchored not only the group and their studio, but also created a landmark and a metaphor for the cultural journey that the Beatles opened up for people around the world.

For Bowie there is no single equivalent location. The plaque unveiled in 2012 on Heddon Street commemorating the birth of Ziggy Stardust only applies to part of his career, and it came forty years after the event. Besides, central London has changed a lot over the last half-century. The capital's booming status as a world city reflects and proclaims the profound changes that have occurred since Bowie's Soho days.

David Bowie is one of the most important artists of the last fifty years. He is cited as an inspiration by numerous contemporary artists and designers and recognized as one of the most innovative of performers. He has been at the forefront of a revolution in freedom of individual expression and sold more than 140 million albums. It is straightforward to make the case for him as the most significant musician of his generation, but the impact of his music, visual style and public presence has spread further. His influence in the wide arena of performance, fashion, art, design and identity politics continues to shape contemporary culture in the broadest sense.

A vigorous forward-looking spirit was fostered in the decades post 1945 by artists, such as Bowie, who channelled the avant-garde into the populist mainstream without compromising its subversive, liberating power. Bowie forms a link that connects Andy Warhol, Bertolt Brecht, William Blake, Charlie Chaplin, Antonin Artaud, Salvador Dalí, Marlene Dietrich, Philip Glass, Nietzsche, Hollywood glamour, graphic design, platform shoes, film, music, Kurt Weill, Berlin, New York, London, Alexander McQueen, the 2012 London Olympics, Jim Henson, the moon landings, Kansai Yamamoto, Kate Moss and Marshall McLuhan.

Hundreds of thousands of words in many languages have been written about Bowie, from the carefully considered to the intuitive response, and even bitter festering rage. There are already several biographies published, and books continue to be produced that analyse his career in ever-greater forensic detail. No previous book, however, has illuminated and drawn in full on The David Bowie Archive. That exceptional collection, astutely amassed over many years and spanning the entirety of Bowie's career, has set the course for this book and the Victoria and Albert Museum exhibition. Both seek to link Bowie's art and music, through artefacts from costume to film, into the wider cultural narrative represented by the Museum's own collections.

Bowie's music catalogue together with his archive gives us wonderful material for a gallery exhibition, but only partly explain his iconic role and growing status. The remaining parts of the picture lie in the changes in the world around us and with us, his audience.

VICTORIA BROACKES AND GEOFFREY MARSH

When I first discovered David Bowie, as a young girl in Rome, I was electrified by his voice and enigmatic stage persona. From Ziggy Stardust to the Thin White Duke, his fearlessly inventive spirit has stayed with me, and still proves a constant source of inspiration in my own work at Gucci.

This is why I am so proud that Gucci is sponsoring *David Bowie Is*. The exhibition is significant for many reasons, first among which is the chance for an unprecedented look into the personal archive of one of the most influential performers of the past century, and secondly, for the preservation of iconic cultural artefacts, a cause to which Gucci is strongly committed.

Bowie needs no introduction or explanation: his creativity and idiosyncratic authenticity have helped shape everything from contemporary art, music and fashion to popular culture and social conventions. His contribution to the modern world will be felt for decades to come.

I hope that this book sparks your imagination and stimulates you to continue his legacy by challenging yourself to create something that is truly your own.

FRIDA GIANNINI
Creative Director, Gucci

GUCCI

As you can imagine, music is at the very heart of the *David Bowie Is* exhibition, which is dedicated to one of the greatest music and style icons of our times. And as music and sound are the heartbeat of Sennheiser, we are naturally delighted to be providing the audio equipment for this genuinely unforgettable experience.

The Victoria and Albert Museum has very much designed this exhibition as an audio experience. Therefore, you will have the Sennheiser audio guide and sound system that should hopefully fully immerse you in the many sounds of David Bowie. They will also enable you to discover all of the facets of an artist who has continually reinvented both himself and his music. Our sound engineers have used their considerable expertise to assist in the audio design of the exhibition as they are well aware that perfect music reproduction is needed to truly reach the audience.

We sincerely hope that you will enjoy the exhibition as much as we have enjoyed working with the Victoria and Albert Museum on helping put together this extraordinary event.

PAUL WHITING
President, Global Sales, Sennheiser

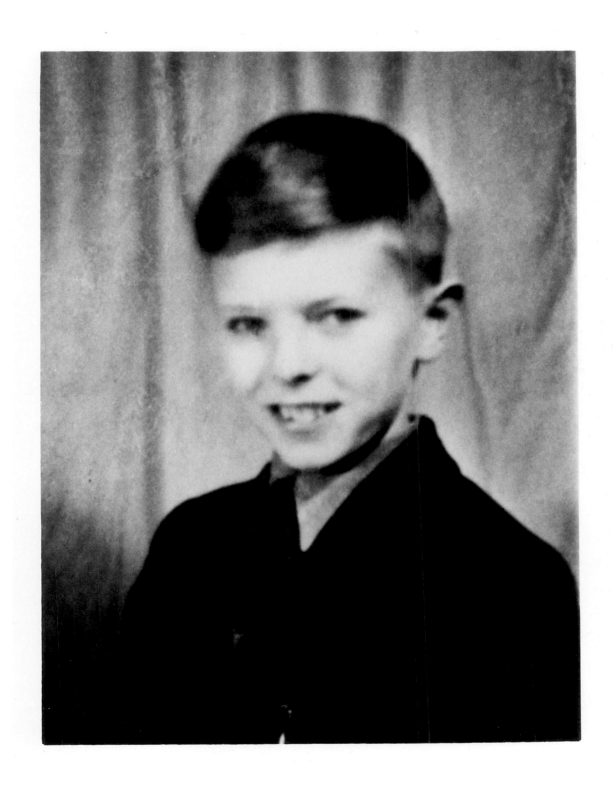

←[4] OPPOSITE • David Bowie aged 10 months, 1947 • THE DAVID BOWIE ARCHIVE

↑ [5] ABOVE • David Bowie aged 6, 1953 • THE DAVID BOWIE ARCHIVE

↑ **[6] ABOVE** ● David Bowie aged 19, 1966 ●
Photograph by Robin Bean ● THE DAVID BOWIE ARCHIVE

→ **[7] OPPOSITE** ● Life mask in resin, 1975 ●
THE DAVID BOWIE ARCHIVE

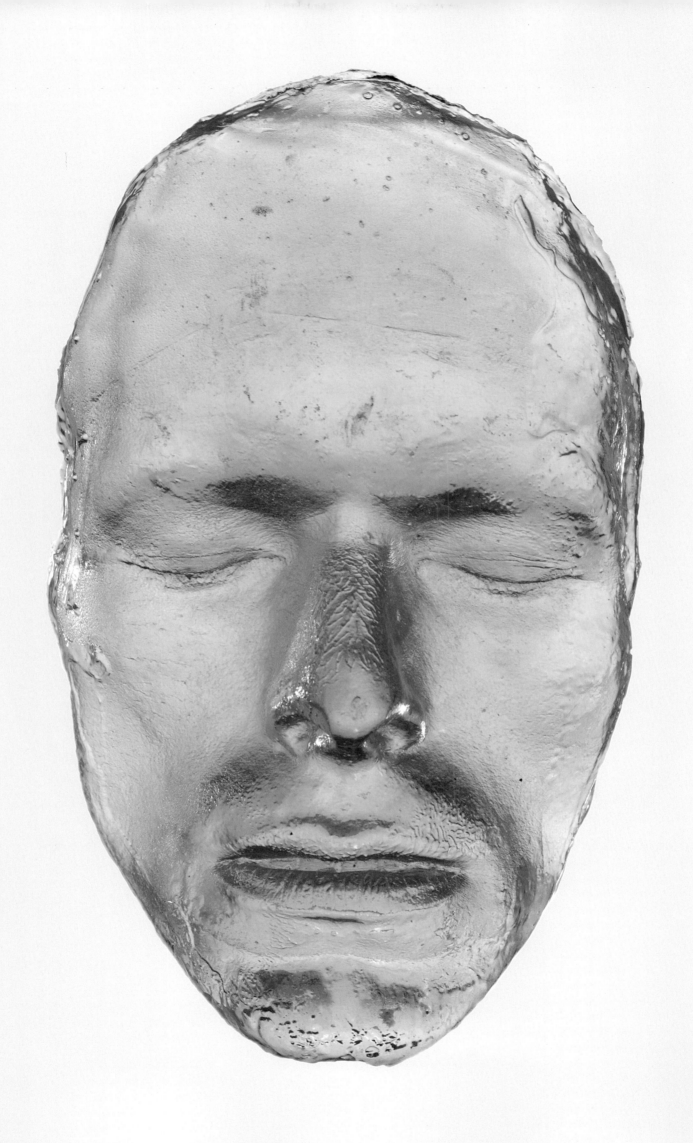

GEOFFREY MARSH

ASTRONAUT OF INNER SPACES: SUNDRIDGE PARK, SOHO, LONDON ... MARS

THE LAST OF ENGLAND
LEAVING THE HOMELAND

Living in lies by the railway line
Pushing the hair from my eyes
Elvis is English and climbs the hills
Can't tell the bullshit from the lies
Screaming along in south London
Vicious but ready to learn
Sometimes I fear that the whole world is queer
Sometimes but always in vain

DAVID BOWIE, 'Buddha of Suburbia', 1993[1]

On 29 March 1974, David Jones 'Bowie', then aged 27 (pl.9), left London, crossed the Channel by ferry and, although he did not know it at the time, abandoned England as his home. Since then, his stays in Britain have been fragmented and Bowie has become a globalized citizen – currently resident in Manhattan. This chapter explores how Bowie began his global journey by travelling through the cultures, textures and streets of post-World War II London. This psychogeography was fundamental to the evolution of his career.

Before 1972, Bowie had spent only a few weeks abroad.[2] Prior to *Young Americans* in 1975, his career had been founded on a powerful personal reaction against England and specifically the values of suburban London – a city that during his lifetime has transformed itself from the bombed-out, soon-to-be ex-imperial capital of 1947 to its current status as one of the three great world financial centres (pls 10 and 11).[3] Bowie's career has paralleled that transformation in terms of globalization, status and recognition. Neither success was inevitable. Both, in the face of intense competition, have used unfettered ambition, deep experience, shrewd marketing and some luck to secure their current position. The Batman-loving Uncle Arthur, Major Tom, Ziggy Stardust, Aladdin Sane and the others were conceived with a British sensibility, but during a period when American influence on Britain remained profound.

THE LONDON OF SUBURBIA

Actually, the suburbs are far more sinister places than most city dwellers imagine. Their very blandness forces the imagination into new areas. I mean, one's got to get up in the morning thinking of a deviant act, merely to make certain of one's freedom. It needn't be much; kicking the dog will do.

You see these suburbs spring up. They represent the optimum of what people want. There's a certain sort of logic leading towards these immaculate suburbs. And they're terrifying, because they are the death of the soul. This is the prison this planet is being turned into.

J. G. BALLARD[4]

Suburbia, a distinctive form of English housing development, has become a world phenomenon. Between 1918 and 1939, nearly four million new houses were built in the UK.[5] Around every town, a tide of red roofs swept across the fields and, swallowing up villages, eventually set into a rigid framework of low-rise Modernist social ambition subverted by speculative free enterprise (pl.11). Over 600,000 of these houses, homes for over two million people escaping inner-city grime, were on the edges of London, doubling the capital's area and creating a tight corset of suburbia.[6] Among these drowned settlements was Sundridge Park – a clump of Victorian villas planted around an eighteenth-century country-house estate, nine miles from the centre of London.[7] Somewhat apart, next to the branch-line railway station, stands a short terrace of 'two-up, two-down' Victorian railway workers' houses. Here at 4 Plaistow Grove, backing on to a pub, David Jones grew up from 1955 to 1967. This street was surrounded by avenues of larger inter-war semi-detached houses – with proper gardens, garages and indoor bathrooms.[8] Apart from being the physical manifestation of the expanding middle classes, this new suburban Britain imposed a rigid code of social, moral and dress conformity.[9] This survived World War II and, arguably, reached its apogee in the late 1950s, when, thanks to a booming economy, the consumer culture of America finally began to infiltrate the households of respectable Acacia Avenues.[10] Over a quarter of the 500,000 boys born in 1947, the peak of the post-World War II baby boom, grew up in these identikit suburbias, and many in the 1960s and '70s came to rail against their perceived blandness. These were the 'precious' babies that would inherit the brave new world for which their parents' generation had suffered, but they were often to show little gratitude. However, few rejected it as vehemently as Bowie, and only a handful broke through to become performance stars.[11] What happened there? What did he see there? What did he think to generate such a powerful reaction? How did home, family mythology, education and Bowie's eventual escape shape his career? Bowie's home life did not match the ideal of the conventional, contented 'two-child suburban nuclear family gathered together around the television' beloved of 1960s advertisers. His parents had four children between them but after 1953, Bowie never lived with his older half-siblings, except for short periods. Mostly, he was effectively an only child, and he has commented on the stresses underlying this situation:[12] 'I think there's an awful lot of emotional, spiritual mutilation goes on in my family.'[13] Although he had friends, he grew up relying on his own company in his backroom bedroom.

'He didn't actually go out very much, but preferred to stay at home,' his childhood friend George Underwood remembers. 'I'd often invite him to a party and he would say, "No, I'm going to stay in, I've got some work to do." No doubt that's why he became so successful.'[14]

Alone in his bedroom, Bowie could let his imagination run free, soaking up ideas and images from books, magazines and records: 'I felt often, ever since I was a teenager, so adrift and so not part of everyone else ... so many dark secrets about my family in the cupboard ... they made me feel on the outside of everything.'[15]

He recalled later:

I wanted to be a fantastic artist, see the colours, hear the music, and they just wanted me turned down. I had to grow up feeling demoralized and thinking, 'They are not going to beat me'. I had to retreat into my room; so you get in the room and you carry that ruddy room around with you for the rest of your life.[16]

Most families have their own mythology, a mix of fact and storytelling that legitimizes their present reality. Throughout Bowie's childhood his father, Haywood Stenton 'John' Jones, had steady employment with Dr Barnardo's Children Homes.[17] However, this quiet and hardworking man had an exotic past. In 1933, as a 21-year-old jazz enthusiast new to London, he had inherited the substantial sum of £3,000.[18] He decided to become an entertainment impresario by investing all this money in promoting the career of his newly met and newly wed wife, Hilda Sullivan – a singer known as 'Chérie – The Viennese Nightingale', who had just fled from the growing political turmoil in Austria.[19]

The result was a financial and emotional disaster. John Jones lost his whole inheritance in a matter of months on a variety of ventures. The last was the Boop-A-Doop, a piano bar located in the Swiss Club (*Schweizerbund*) at 74 Charlotte Street in bohemian north Soho.[20]

As Bowie grew up, the family memory of a European-style nightclub in pre-war Soho and a squandered inheritance must have offered powerful symbols of the exciting and enticing – but also dangerous – opportunities that lay beyond the confines of a small terraced house on the edge of London.

Meanwhile the young David's interest in entertainment increased. In 1956, his father was appointed head of public relations at Barnardo's and began to use leading entertainers of the day to promote the charity's work.[21] As a result, Bowie met showbiz stars, such as Tommy Steele in 1957. His interest in music also grew – his cousin Kristina recalls that Bowie had a tin guitar at an early age and, unusually, a 78rpm record player.[22] At Christmas 1961, John Jones made a significant investment by buying his son a British white acrylic Grafton saxophone, and shortly afterwards an American brass Conn sax.[23] 'I wanted to be a white Little Richard at eight or at least his sax player,' Bowie remembers (pl.8).[24] 'I wanted to be a musician because it seemed rebellious, it seemed subversive.'[25]

Bowie did not, as is often erroneously stated, go to art college, as Pete Townshend, Brian Eno and many other key musicians did in the early 1960s, but his secondary school had a strong arts focus. After passing his 11-plus exam in 1958, Bowie chose the brand-new Bromley Technical High School for Boys in preference to Bromley Grammar School.[26] In his third year his form master and art teacher was Owen Frampton, who developed a progressive, creative syllabus.[27] Bowie's first band, the Kon-rads (including his school friend George Underwood), made their first public performance at a PTA fête on 16 June 1962. Earlier that year, Bowie had been hit in the face by Underwood – a blow that required a couple of months' convalescence and resulted in his distinctive non-matching eyes. Thus at 15, Bowie had an unusual, and unexpected, opportunity to practise his new saxophone – but also to spend time analysing his personal circumstances, thoughts and ambitions.

As Bowie became old enough to begin spreading his creative wings, his half-brother Terry, older by a decade, returned from National Service in the RAF in 1958. Although Terry did not live with David, they spent time together, with Terry introducing him to Beat writing such as Jack Kerouac's recently published *On the Road* (1957), jazz and stories, at least, of visits to the licit and illicit pleasures of Soho clubland.[28]

↖ [8] ABOVE LEFT • Little Richard, 1950s • This publicity photograph has been in David Bowie's possession since the 1950s • THE DAVID BOWIE ARCHIVE

↑ [9] ABOVE • David Bowie at a press conference at the Amstel Hotel, Amsterdam, February 1974 • Photograph by Gijsbert Hanekroot • Getty Images

← [10] CENTRE LEFT • Cyclists on a bombed street in London, October 1944 • Originally published in *Picture Post* (no.1814) in 'London's Bombed Homes: A Defeat On The Home Front' • Photograph by Haywood Magee / Getty Images

← [11] CENTRE RIGHT • Suburban sprawl in south London following the war • Getty Images

← [12] BOTTOM LEFT • The 2i's Coffee Bar, Old Compton Street, London, 1966 • S&G Barratts / EMPICS Archive

← [13] BOTTOM RIGHT • David Bowie performing with the Buzz at the Marquee Club, London, April 1966 • Michael Ochs Archives / Getty Images

REMAKING SOHO AND THE MODERNIST VISION

Bright lights, Soho, Wardour Street
You hope you make friends with the guys that you meet

DAVID BOWIE, 'The London Boys', 1966

Down on my knees in suburbia
Down on myself in every way
With great expectations I change all my clothes
Mustn't grumble at silver and gold
Screaming above central London
Never born, so I'll never get old

DAVID BOWIE, 'Buddha of Suburbia', 1993[29]

1963: Dr Who arrives, John Profumo leaves, Martin Luther King dreams and the UK is barred from the EU. In the summer of that year, a revolution was underway in the UK's popular music. Between January 1962 and April 1963, Cliff Richard and/or the Shadows were at number one for a total of 22 weeks. But as Bowie left school in July, the Liverpool/Epstein/George Martin dynamic began to take over, with 'I Like It' by Gerry and the Pacemakers at the top of the charts,[30] and the group in the studio to record their third number one hit, 'You'll Never Walk Alone'. At the same time, the Beatles were recording 'She Loves You', soon to be their second number one, and the Rolling Stones were just beginning to tour.

At 16, Bowie might have disappeared into a series of dead-end jobs and short-lived south London bands. Fortunately, his art teacher had found him work as a paste-up artist at Nevin D. Hirst, an advertising agency in New Bond Street in London's Mayfair – and Bowie became a commuter, travelling by train to Charing Cross station. Although commentators are often disparaging about this job, it provided Bowie with a regular escape route, out of suburbia and into a creative milieu that was being transformed as London started to 'swing'.[31] Twelve months in advertising also introduced him to current theories on maximizing the effectiveness of mass marketing.

In the aftermath of the brainwashing hysteria of the Korean War, major research was undertaken into methods for manipulating public opinion.[32] Bowie would have had the opportunity to pick up a wealth of ideas about how to influence audiences, in particular; as the ad man in Hitchcock's *North by Northwest* (1959) explains, 'in the world of advertising there's no such thing as a lie. There is only expedient exaggeration.' Combined with his father's experience in PR, Bowie developed a precocious marketing talent.[33] And beyond the agency's walls the job gave him the opportunity to explore more of the West End, from Dobell's Records[34] and the second-hand bookshops of Charing Cross Road to the surviving rag-trade businesses around Berwick and Carnaby Streets.[35]

However, the Soho that Bowie began to frequent seemed to be under a death sentence. Nearly half of central Soho and Piccadilly Circus were slated for demolition as modernist architects, in an unholy alliance with property developers and politicians of both the left and the right, promised to create a Brave New London.[36] Harry Hyams' towering and un-let Centre Point (pl.14), completed in 1965, was to be only the first of over a dozen similar office blocks intended to transform the area.[37] Speculators bought up many of the West End's nineteenth-century theatres for demolition as they offered the large footprints necessary for building skyscrapers.

In 1960, most people would have probably agreed that such redevelopments were a good thing – the physical transformation of central London to match the newly minted welfare state.[38] Modernism offered a progressive vision of orderly and spacious streets with clean and efficient flats, compared to the smells, dirt and immigrants of inner-city slums.[39] Just to the north, the silhouette of the new Post Office Tower (pl.17), built between 1961 and 1964, created a powerful and compelling icon of the 'white heat of technology' promoted by the new Labour government.[40] Harold Wilson offered a vision of a new-look technocratic Britain, a United Kingdom for forward-looking people who wanted to forget about the fading empire.

Despite the tightening noose of demolition, traditional bohemian Soho hung on, just, and four new venues launched new cultural trajectories. On 22 April 1956, the 2i's Coffee Bar was opened at 59 Old Compton Street (pl.12). It became an instant Mecca for musicians and the birthplace of British rock'n'roll, attracting performers such as Tommy Steele, Cliff Richard and the Most Brothers.[41] Two years later, in 1958, the London Hippodrome on Charing Cross Road, the flagship of the Moss Empires' music-hall chain, was gutted and converted into the Talk of the Town, with the aim of providing a Las Vegas-style show and cabaret venue.[42] That same year, Paul Raymond opened his Revuebar, the first British strip club – a development that heralded the rapid growth of sex-related businesses in Soho.[43] Also in 1958, the Marquee Club was founded at 165 Oxford Street. A few years later, the club moved to 90 Wardour Street. On opening night, Friday 13 March 1964, Sonny Boy Williamson, the Yardbirds and Rod Stewart were on the bill. Eight months later Bowie would be playing there, and hosting his Sunday afternoon session, the Bowie Showboat (pl.13), two years later.[44] The move of the Marquee Club reflected the explosive growth of businesses based around pop music. In 1964 Beatlemania went global, and the huge success of the 'British Invasion' of America secured London's position as one of the key music cities of the world. On the back of this breakthrough, fashion, advertising and photography transformed the capital into 'Swinging London' – a success that coincided with a decisive shift towards a youth culture of rebellion against authority,

→ [14] OPPOSITE • David Bowie on a rooftop in front of the newly built Centre Point, September 1967 • Photograph by Mark Hayward

excitement, sexual liberation and permissive legislation.[45] This changing social climate was symbolized by the BBC's creation of Radio I, launched on 30 September 1967, and the Government's reduction of the voting age from 21 to 18 in 1969.

Although accounts of the period tend to focus on the fashions of the King's Road and Carnaby Street, Soho and the surrounding Theatreland retained their role as the vibrant hub of the entertainment world. It was like a village with networks of personal connections, and for a few years Soho became Bowie's second home. It offered a world of opportunity for anyone with the drive to hustle hard. In a few minutes Bowie could walk from the Gioconda Café to the Marquee Club, passing by Saint Martins School of Art, the Astoria dance hall, Les Cousins folk club and Ronnie Scott's. Close by were other music venues, like the 2i's, Flamingo Club, Le Discothèque, 100 Club, Tiles and the Scene. Many of the new music venues, such as Brian Epstein's Saville Theatre (1965), the UFO Club (1966) and the Electric Garden/Middle Earth (1966), opened on the borders of Soho and Covent Garden.

Bowie plunged into the mod music scene, which shaped him 'by instilling an idea of experimentalism, of a true modernism'.[46] By May 1964, he had his first record deal with Decca. His first single, 'Liza Jane' (see pl.61),[47] was released on 5 June 1964, the following day he appeared on BBC1's primetime *Juke Box Jury*[48] and a few weeks later he gave up his advertising job to concentrate on a music career full time. At the age of only 17, major success seemed just around the corner.

And yet, as it happened, that leap proved elusive. For the next five years Bowie grafted his way around the shifting London music scene. The Gioconda Café at 9 Denmark Street, in London's 'Tin Pan Alley', became his unofficial hang-out, with hours passed over cups of tea.[49] It was only five years later, in 1969, that he achieved his breakthrough success with 'Space Oddity'. By then London, youth culture and British society had shifted radically.

Bowie might have had a precocious introduction to Soho's musicland, but London's entertainment industry in the early 1960s was an altogether more impenetrable obstacle for the 'let's get a band together and cut a record' ambitions of a typical suburban teenager. The London Palladium, physically and commercially, still dominated popular entertainment: 'Sunday Night at the London Palladium' was the anchor variety show of Independent Television (ITV), from the launch of commercial television in Britain in 1955 until 1967.[50] The Beatles appeared on 13 October 1963 to an estimated audience of 15 million. The BBC struggled to match the new commercial network's focus on the mass market, but responded with 'The Black and White Minstrel Show', which ran from 1958 to 1978.[51]

The music business was a small world of interconnected managers, investors, publishers, promoters and publicists working around the four main recording companies – Parlophone (EMI), Decca, Phillips and Pye (ATV from 1959). Pop music

was still seen as a short-lived career trajectory, with the lucky or ambitious few cutting through into mainstream entertainment in the form of TV light entertainment shows, West End pantomime or film work.[52]

But outside the small group of closely linked entertainment dynasties, the first wave of pop-group managers, such as Andrew Loog Oldham and Brian Epstein, were struggling to crack open this closeted world and create new business models.[53]

Battling his way into this tight-knit business, Bowie's driving ambition took him a long way.[54] In 1966, Ken Pitt, an experienced showbiz operator, became his manager (a position he held until 1970), and provided a careful guiding hand. Bowie tried a wide range of approaches: writing songs for himself, writing songs for others, or trying to break into films and children's television. In an interview with Radio London at the Marquee in 1966, he spoke about developing a musical with Tony Hatch, adding that he'd 'like to get into cabaret, obviously'.[55]

By late 1966, Pitt had secured Bowie a contract with Decca's prestigious and progressive new Deram label.[56] The variety of Bowie's work was seen as suitable for this new audio approach, and this is reflected in the final choice of tracks on his first LP, *David Bowie*, released on 1 June 1967, the same day as *Sgt. Pepper's Lonely Hearts Club Band* on Parlophone (EMI). Both covers (pls 15 and 16) feature military jackets, but each record's impact was very different.[57] Although it received some positive reviews, Bowie's album was not a commercial success, and he was dropped by Deram. Then, almost immediately afterwards, Bowie's London years were to take a sharp turn towards a new aesthetic.

Ironically, if Bowie had become a commercially successful singer-songwriter at this point, he might still have had a lengthy musical career, but much less overall cultural impact. Looking back, Bowie noted: 'In a way, if anything had happened for me in the mid-60s, I might well have been cut off from an awful lot of influences.'

↑ [15] **ABOVE LEFT** • *David Bowie*, 1967 • Deram

↑ [16] **ABOVE RIGHT** • *Sgt. Pepper's Lonely Hearts Club Band*, 1967 • The Beatles • Parlophone

→ [17] **OPPOSITE** • The Post Office Tower, Maple Street, London, 1969 • Fox Photos / Getty Images

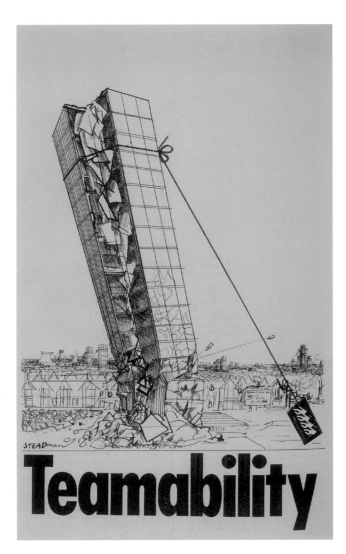

↑ [18] • Cartoon referencing the collapse of the Ronan Point tower, 22 November 1968 • Ralph Steadman • Published in *Private Eye* magazine

If there was unison, it was in reflecting the schizophrenic world of Vietnam, Oxfam, Twiggy, the invasion of Czechoslovakia, the Beatles, LBJ, Che, the Space Race, and trendy figures like Gagarin, McLuhan, Buckminster Fuller, plus James Bondery, acid, GNP, Swinging London, TW3, and the theories of Durkheim, Marcuse, and Laing, with, if you like, Timothy Leary, Wilson-and-Brown, and Marx.

BRIAN ALDISS[58]

The 'fast-forward' London in which Bowie started his career in 1963 lasted only a few short years. At 5.45 a.m. on 16 May 1968, Ivy Hodge, a 56-year-old cake decorator, struck a match to light her gas oven in Flat 90 on the eighteenth floor of Ronan Point (pl.18), a high-rise block in east London, completed earlier that year. The explosion and partial collapse of the tower symbolized, in the UK at least, the end of the Modernist dream of 'villages in the sky'.[59]

While councils, particularly on the left, continued comprehensive housing clearance schemes for a few more years, the growing social problems associated with new estates eventually brought the process to a halt, and it was finally finished off by the Thatcherite attack on the entire principle of council housing.[60]

This was part of a broader reaction against the tenets of modernist social planning, and the growing shift towards an appreciation of the past – alongside restoration and renewal instead of demolition. On a personal level, this development paralleled a swing towards a focus on the self and the individual, rather than grandiose and theoretical strategies for the mass – a shift that was to become fundamental to Bowie's interests.

New directions for artistic exploration were beginning to be defined, notably by J. G. Ballard, writing in Shepperton, far out in London's western suburbia. Bored by traditional science fiction and influenced by the Surrealists, he wanted to explore the ambiguity of private fantasy that might be obscure, meaningless or nightmarish:

> This zone I think of as 'inner space', the internal landscape of tomorrow that is a transmuted image of the past, and one of the most fruitful areas for the imaginative writer. It is particularly rich in visual symbols, and I feel that this type of speculative fantasy plays a role very similar to that of Surrealism in the graphic arts. The painters de Chirico, Dalí and Max Ernst, among others, are in a sense the iconographers of inner space, all ... concerned with the discovery of images in which the internal and external reality meet and fuse.[61]

In stories written between 1966 and 1969, which eventually formed *The Atrocity Exhibition* (1970), Ballard explored ideas of fragmentation – in character, narrative, language and meaning – similar to those promoted by the writer William S. Burroughs and others.[62] Burroughs' impact at this time was considerable, as important movers in the counter-culture took up his interests.[63] His friend Brion Gysin, who was involved with the Surrealists, had developed his 'cut-up' technique in 1959 in Paris, and first published the resulting texts as 'First Cut-Ups' in 1960.[64] A few years later, the artist and activist Jeff Nuttall launched *My Own Mag*, a magazine he produced from 1963 to 1966, which published Burroughs' cut-ups.[65] During this time, Burroughs also experimented with Anthony Balch in film-making, creating a 19-minute short, *The Cut-Ups*, released in 1967.[66]

The same ideas were being explored by others. According to Burroughs, Alexander Trocchi, the Scottish Beat writer, called himself 'the Cosmonaut of Inner Space' at the famous Edinburgh Writers' Conference in August 1962.[67] Burroughs later commented:

> In my writing I am acting as a map-maker, an explorer of psychic areas, a cosmonaut of inner space, and I see no point in exploring areas that have already been thoroughly surveyed.[68]

Artists increasingly wanted to explore these new mindscapes. In September 1967, Bowie appeared in his first film, *The Image*, which was described as 'a study of the illusionary reality world within the schizophrenic mind of the artist at his point of creativity'.[69]

Bowie was also to be strongly influenced by Andy Warhol and his creation of the Factory in New York in the 1960s. In August 1965, Warhol made *Outer and Inner Space*, possibly the first example of video art.[70] Comprising two films projected alongside each other, to evoke the inner and outer selves of his star, Edie Sedgwick, the piece is a forerunner of *Chelsea Girls* (1966, pl.21). In May 1963, *Life* magazine had published 'Long Voyage in Inner Space', an article about Whilden P. Breen, Jr., who was in the middle of five months' confinement in a windowless, soundproof isolation chamber, a NASA experiment to discover the psychological effects of prolonged isolation. On 15 May 1961, President Kennedy had announced the mission to land a man on the moon by the end of the decade.

The artistic investigations of imagination were intertwined with an increasing interest in 'self discovery' and mystical religion, particularly from the East. These were paralleled by an upsurge in interest in 'mystic Albion', associated with Stonehenge, ley lines and the myths of Glastonbury.[71] The past, the distant, the futuristic and the mystic became a vast warehouse of 'old stock', ready to be pillaged to create new identities, whether through buying antiques, wearing costume or ethnic clothes – or stopping inner-city redevelopment.[72] Psychedelic explorations of the self were linked to the rise of drug use to provide new forms of perception, as promoted in Timothy Leary's *The Psychedelic Experience: A Manual Based on the Tibetan Book of the Dead* (1964).[73] Within a couple of years, such ideas were entering the mainstream – for example, Dirk Bogarde's LSD trip in the 1968 film *Sebastian*, set in the British secret service.

Bowie, along with many of his contemporaries, became interested in Buddhism. In 1967, when interest in Eastern religions was at its height, he thought of becoming a monk and, in September of that year, stayed briefly in Scotland at the Buddhist retreat at Eskdalemuir, then at the start of its development.[74] *International Times* magazine was an important conduit for disseminating ideas to a wider audience, who may never have bothered to read original works. Issue 12 (28 April 1967) contained a psychedelic centre spread containing cut-up texts by Brion Gysin (pl.19).

London was convulsing – but David Bowie, who was physically close to the epicentre of all of this activity in the West End, was, until June 1967, still sometimes commuting the nine miles home to stay at Sundridge Park.

Bryon

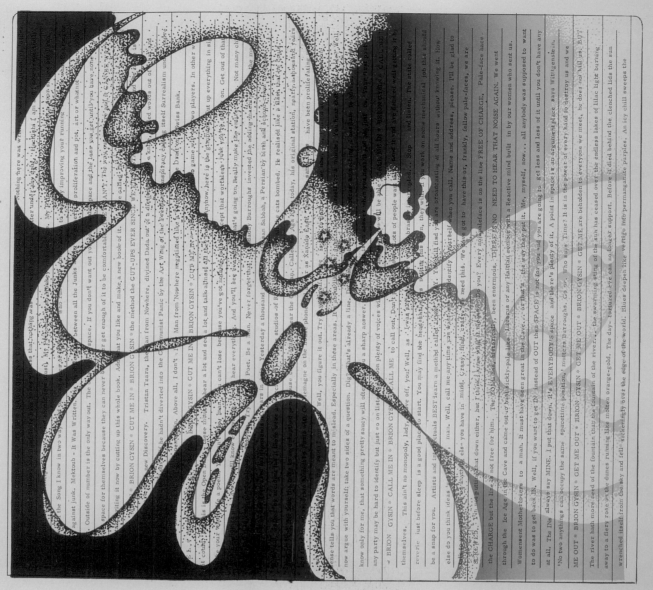

the texts on this page are taken from minutes to go, a cut-up laboratory work put together by william burroughs, gregory corso, brion gysin and sinclair beiles some years ago, but still not on worldwide circulation channels. permission to reprint was given to IT by mr burroughs who provided the words for the first IT cut-up machine-cum-poster, the invisible generation, which was IT no 5.

this is our latest machine, the between the line. like the best machines, it is much too weak to kill a man and much to empty-minded to control him. so proceed without fear. cut around dotted line. then cut up on the thin black lines to make one long continuous strip. you will then have raw materials for a burroughs-gysin-IT fold-in word encounter machine. the rest is up to you - bend it, twist it, wear it thru your nose, paint it, set it alight, push it thru one ear pull it out the other, stick it on the wall, hang it from the ceiling, fly it, float it, read its twists and turns and discover what lies between behind the words...

further complications can be achieved by cutting out the texts by gregory corso and sinclair beiles which appear at the top of most pages of this issue of IT, and are also taken from minutes to go. the resultant strips can then be pasted down in among the gysin-burroughs material on this page. a new strip, perhaps of even greater length, can be produced. of course, this requires that you buy more than one copy of IT ll ... buy six copies and you can cut

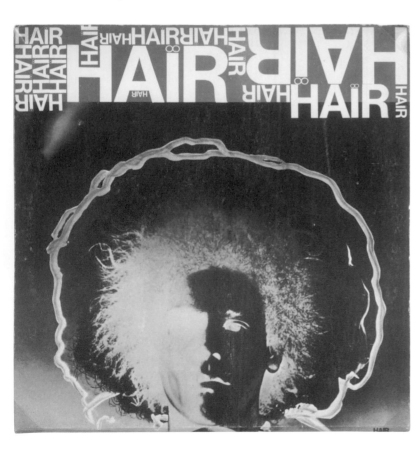

↑ **[19] ABOVE** • 'Minutes to Go' cut up texts by Brion Gysin • *International Times*, Issue 12, 28 April 1967

← **[20] LEFT** • Soundtrack for *Hair!*, 1968 • Recording by the original London cast • Polydor Records

→ **[21] OPPOSITE** • Poster for Andy Warhol's film *Chelsea Girls*, October 1968 (first British showing August 1968) • Designed by Alan Aldridge • Drury Lane Arts Laboratory

TAKING THE STAGE

In 1967, aged 20, Bowie discovered The Stage.

Not the tatty stages, feeble PA systems and basic lighting of the ballrooms and clubs he had toured in previous years. Rather, the vast 'philosophical' stages of theatre thinkers such as Stanislavski, Artaud and Brook, where there is no beginning or end, and the limits are solely those of the deviser – stages that could become any type of space.

The London alternative performance scene took off in the mid 1960s. There were new ideas, new performers, new companies and new venues.[75] In 1966 the American-born Jim Haynes set up the London Traverse Theatre Company with set designer Ralph Koltai, among others, at the new Jeanetta Cochrane Theatre.[76] In 1964, the playwright Arnold Wesker had launched Centre 42 at the Roundhouse, turning a nineteenth-century railway shed into a performing arts venue.[77] Alongside new theatres were 'happenings', including the famous International Poetry Incarnation held at the Royal Albert Hall on 11 June 1965.

There was also an increasing interest in crossing art-form boundaries, and using different types of space to match these new manifestations, often involving multimedia installations. In 1967 Haynes took over an empty warehouse at 182 Drury Lane and established the famous, if short-lived, Drury Lane Arts Lab, where Bowie performed.[78] The Lab included a theatre, cinema, gallery and restaurant, alongside music, an information bank and astrological readings. 'The Arts Lab', Haynes wrote, 'was many things to many people: a vision frustrated by an indifferent, fearful and secure society; an experiment with such intangibles as people, ideas, feelings and communication.'[79]

The following year, the Institute of Contemporary Art (ICA) moved into its new home on The Mall.[80] Across the country, local Arts Labs were started, many eventually morphing into permanent arts centres.

Moving elegantly and enigmatically through this upheaval was the distinctive figure of Lindsay Kemp, mime artist, dancer, actor and total performer *extraordinaire* – at least by his own definition (pl.23). Kemp was using Bowie's music in his show, and the two met in early August 1967 and immediately fell for each other.[81] 'Lindsay Kemp was a living pierrot,' Bowie subsequently said. 'He lived and talked Pierrot. He was tragic and everything in his life was theatrical. And so the stage thing for him was just an extension of himself.'[82] And later, he said of Kemp:

Lindsay was a trip and a half ... He lived on his emotions, he was a wonderful influence. His day-to-day life was the most theatrical thing I'd ever seen, ever. Everything I thought Bohemia probably was, he was living.

Kemp, for his part, was equally taken with Bowie:

I felt a bit like the Virgin Mary, confronted by this vision of the archangel Gabriel, glowing, shining, incredibly beautiful and immediately inspiring.

Kemp's total commitment to his art introduced Bowie to an edgy world of make-up, camp and sexual ambiguity, but perhaps more important was the experience of living as a complete performance.[83] Bowie started training and working with Kemp ('I taught David to free his body,' Kemp said later),[84] and in 1968 he spent several weeks first rehearsing and then performing at venues in London and elsewhere (pls 24 and 25).[85]

Bowie learnt not only to act, but also gained fundamental experience in the power of costume, lighting and sets. He understood increasingly how to work the bond with the audience through characterization, voice and physical expression. On 13 and 14 September 1967 he acted in the short film *The Image*, and received his Equity card on 28 October (pl.22).[86] In 1968–9, Bowie auditioned twice for the musical *Hair* (pl.20) and was an extra in the film *The Virgin Soldiers*.[87] Ken Pitt, his manager at the time, also encouraged him to see mainstream theatre.[88]

Bowie's immersion in performance deepened when he met, and fell in love with, Hermione 'Farthingale' Dennis, a classically trained ballet dancer, in April 1968. Not only was she a supportive partner and musical collaborator with whom he could discuss every aspect of performing, she was also involved in some of the major films of the time, playing an Edwardian chorus girl in the musical film *Oh! What a Lovely War* – a fascinating mix of staging, songs and styles designed to evoke World War I.[89]

By early 1969, his understanding of stagecraft had been transformed. Ironically, it was just at this point that, having been dropped by Hermione, a saddened Bowie retreated to the suburbs, establishing his own Arts Lab in Beckenham in the spring of 1969.[90] Once again, he might have faded into suburban obscurity, but the eventual chart success of 'Space Oddity' at the end of the year finally launched Bowie towards stardom.

Height 5 feet 10½ inches   *Robin Bean 1967*

DAVID BOWIE

Kenneth Pitt Management Ltd.
35, Curzon Street
London, W.1   **01–499 7905/6**

↑ **[22] ABOVE** • David Bowie's entry in casting directory
Spotlight, 1969 • Kevin Cann Collection

↗ **[23] ABOVE RIGHT** • Lindsay Kemp in Soho, *c*.1967 •
THE DAVID BOWIE ARCHIVE

↑ **[24] ABOVE AND** → **[25] OPPOSITE** ◦ David Bowie as a mime, 7 May 1968 ◦
Photograph by Kenneth Pitt, London ◦ Kevin Cann Collection

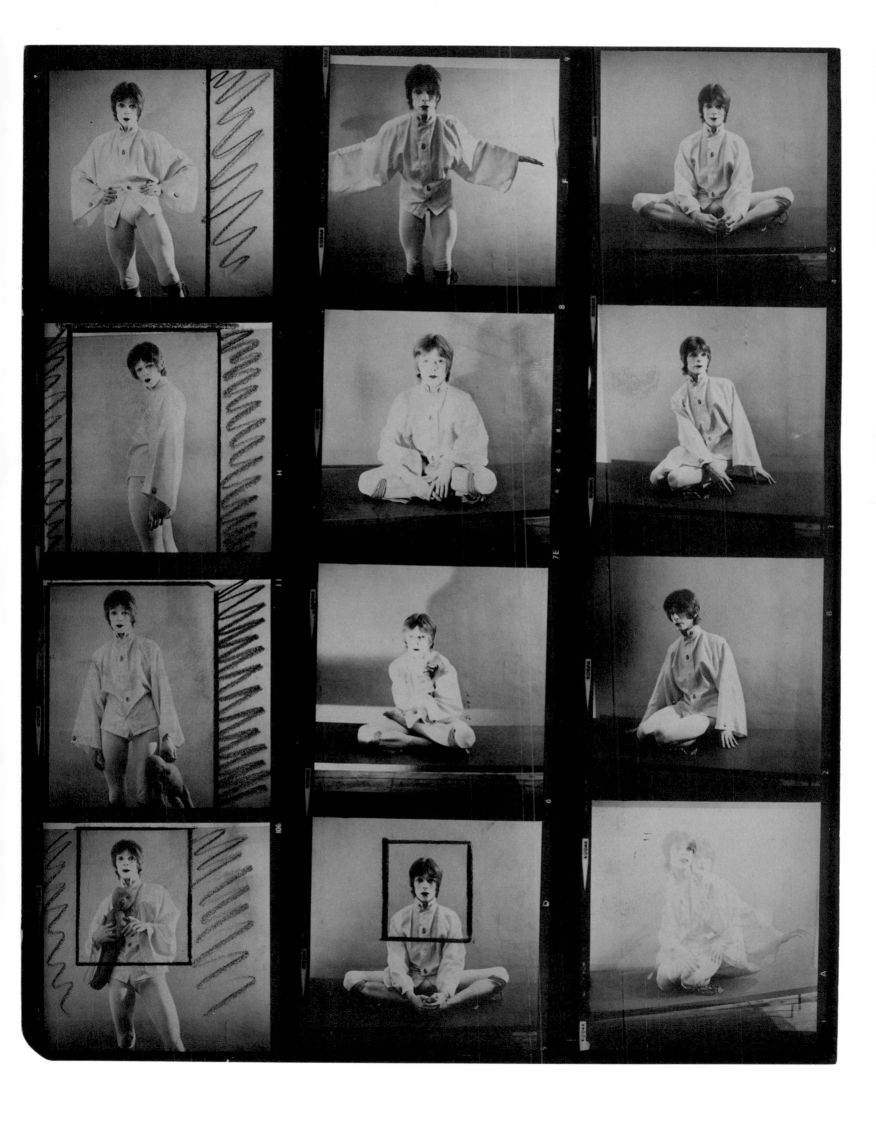

GENESIS: THE APOLLO 8 MISSION
AND SELLING THE EARTH

In 1968, the concept of scientific progress was the dominant practical belief system for most people in the West. The space race, as a symbolic demonstration of technocratic ritual, exerted a massive pull on the public's imagination throughout the decade.[91]

On Christmas Eve 1968, David Bowie's career course cut across that of world history. Apollo 8 became the first manned flight to orbit the moon and return – a journey captured in the 'Earthrise' photograph, taken by NASA astronaut Bill Anders, which has been called 'the most influential environmental photograph ever taken' (pl.26).[92] Viewed across the barren moonscape, Earth is a small blue sphere utterly alone in the vast blackness of space. The answers to mankind's problems were not 'out there' – they existed, if they did at all, within the human race anchored on that tiny speck.

Thirteen days later, on 6 January 1969, *The Times* published a special Apollo 8 insert that included the 'Earthrise' image.[93] Within a week, by 13 January, Bowie had crossed into a new psychoscape and created 'Space Oddity':

For here
Am I sitting in a tin can
Far above the world
Planet Earth is blue
And there's nothing I can do.[94]

In doing so, as Bowie turned 22, he turned off the century's timeline, and set off on his own.[95] In a few words Bowie rejects the triumph of technology, whether western or communist, and speaks instead of a new challenge for humanity. If the individual demands the choice to determine his own future, what then is the relationship between that individual and society?[96]

Bowie's stage was now inner space and, over the next five years, he delved deeply into the worlds of fear, envy, madness, self-loathing and isolation. It is often suggested that Bowie's interest in alienation and dystopia stems from the depressing political and economic state of Britain in the early 1970s.[97] Space Oddity', however, was written when the heady days of 1968 were only just beginning to fade.

Following the success of 'Space Oddity' in November 1969, Bowie had stardom within his reach. His complete immersion in the craft of performance in 1967–8 had complemented the understanding of audience manipulation he had already developed through his advertising experience. Over the next 20 months, Bowie acquired a new manager, a new music publisher, a new producer, a new set of musicians, new friends, new designers, new experiences,[98] a wife, a son and a new home[99]– and a new iconic identity, captured on film in September 1970 (which would eventually feature on the cover of *The Man Who Sold the World* (April 1971).[100] This cover image for his third LP, then still titled *Metrobolist*, is crucial, since it was conceived entirely by Bowie and provides a 'freeze-frame' of his ideas during a period of hectic development and creativity.[101] In the time before the music videos of the 1980s, album covers were critical in communicating identity.

The defining characteristics of the photographer Keith Macmillan's work for albums at this time were 'their rejection of Modernism, science, celebrity and professionalism – there are no glossy portraits or spaceships; no white space or fine typography … [instead] they call forth a grimness that is radically at odds with music business gloss and "rockist" self aggrandizement'.[102]

However, for *The Man Who Sold the World* Bowie would twist this approach to achieve his own ends. The cover shows a relaxed Bowie stretched out on a *chaise-longue* in a Mr Fish 'man-dress' and long brown leather boots, in a retro-Raphaelite setting (pl.27).[103] In his hand, Bowie holds the King of Diamonds (pl.28).[104] Bowie, now the complete performer, holds centre stage. He looks out coolly and slightly questioningly at Macmillan's camera and through to his audience. The shot, taken in Haddon Hall, Beckenham, projects a Universalist vision.

Firstly, Bowie is alone; there is no company of supporting actors.[105] He will be the success – but beyond that there is no obvious story. He is set among scattered fragments whose individual meaning is unclear. Together, this antique detritus evokes no specific date, but collectively it rejects the twentieth-century suburban dream. However, there is no permanence, no conclusion – the image is clearly a constructed set, outside reality. Secondly, and most remarked on, gender is subverted – through hair, clothing, gesture and pose. Interestingly, in 1970, there is no questioning of ethnicity or age. Finally, there is no exclusivity; Bowie will give up his place if you want to take it, for he is already moving on.

→**[26] OPPOSITE** • Earthrise • Photograph taken by astronaut Bill Anders during the Apollo 8 lunar mission, 24 December 1968 • NASA

In April 1971, when *The Man Who Sold the World* was finally released in the UK, the music tide had suddenly turned Bowie's way with the rise of glam rock.[106] From being an outsider Bowie now moved centre stage, eventually leaving even Marc Bolan behind, and rode the glitter wave until he jumped neatly aside as its energy dissipated.

In January 1971, Bowie went to America on a promotional tour, where he had the opportunity to try out his personal 'man-dress' character in cities as diverse as Detroit, Houston and Los Angeles.[107] He was not disappointed by the reactions, which ranged from appreciation to confusion and outright aggression – and he knew now that there were no limits to what and how he could perform.[108] Bowie landed back in London on 18 February, bringing with him a group of new songs that he registered on 1 April with Chrysalis, his new publisher – among them 'Ziggy Stardust'. Nine days later *The Man Who Sold the World* was released in Britain, but Bowie knew by then that his vision lay far beyond. There might be nothing on Mars, but there were worlds of endless possibilities inside his head, which he could explore by bringing an alien messiah down to earth – an alien capable of infiltrating any space. London was where Ziggy was launched and where he was retired – but the city's exhausted 'three-day week' existence in 1973–4 placed too great a constraint on Bowie's ambitions. He wanted a space with fewer boundaries and so he left for the world (pl.30); despite London's own distinctive reinvention over the last 30 years, there has been nothing to bring him back for a significant engagement.

For the four decades prior to the mid 1990s and the start of the PC/digital/internet age, pop music and pop culture provided a communication system for young people whose only means of sharing their likes and dislikes beyond their locality were the Royal Mail and a household hard-wired phone – or maybe a public telephone box. Pop music may have been controlled by a few corporations, been limited in its world-view, and the source of enormous amounts of rubbish, but it was the critical communication system of the era. Nobody with the access and subject opportunities of the YouTube/Facebook age would want to go back there now; not when communicating with anybody about anything is seen as a right.

Those four decades of changing social attitudes and rising personal wealth shaped a growing 'Me' culture, where people increasingly put the self before social duty. The support frameworks of increasing state intervention, organized religion, two-party politics, mass trade unions and monarchy began to be eroded and subverted. Bowie came to prominence as these changes gathered pace, and he has survived long enough to see the full effects.

The consequences, even by the late 1970s, were ambiguous and often unexpected. The statements 'every human being is equally important' and 'freedom to live your life your way' came not from Bowie, nor even from pop music, but from Margaret Thatcher's speech to the 1975 Conservative Party conference and *The Sun* newspaper's editorial on election day, 3 May 1979, which advised its readers to switch to the Conservatives and helped sweep Thatcher to victory. By the 'Thatcherite Spring' of the 1980s, anti-elitism had been mobilized to promote the market as the moral authority for public services. However, by then Bowie was far away.

↑ **[27]** ABOVE • *The Man Who Sold the World*, April 1971 • Mercury (UK)

→ **[28]** OPPOSITE • *The Man Who Sold the World* (reverse), April 1971 • Mercury (UK)

AND WHERE IS MAJOR TOM OFF TO NOW?

Neil and Edna Denny were military folk … Decent people who had successfully defended their country against Nazi invasion, endured food rationing throughout the war and for nearly ten years afterwards, and felt pride in the coronation of a glamorous young queen. They loved, nurtured and sheltered their children. But they were utterly unprepared for the bomb culture of pop.

ROB YOUNG, *Electric Eden:*
Unearthing Britain's Visionary Music, 2010

The wordless cover of Fairport Convention's album *Unhalfbricking* (1969, pl.29) speaks volumes about the gap between the generations that expanded during the 1960s – the band are inside a walled garden, separated from singer Sandy Denny's parents by a fence. As the generations parted at the end of the 1960s, was there still time for tea together?[109]

It is a truism that Britain was at its most integrated and socialist during World War II. The threat of Nazi conquest, alongside rationing, conscription for men and national service for women, created the opportunity for a modernist agenda to organize for total war. In 1945, it offered a beguiling future to the new mass society as its reward. In the 1950s, something had to fill the loss of Empire and a technocratic future offered a progressive vision for the left, and a hope of salvaging some control for the right. In the end, however, growing personal affluence and the enticing individual delights of consumer capitalism outflanked modernism's failure to provide a convincing alternative.

On 29 March 2012 a plaque(pl.31) was unveiled to Ziggy Stardust in Heddon Street, London, where photographer Brian Ward caught an image of the illusive visitor in 1972. Forty years on, the relics of Soho's rag-trade past have disappeared. The cleaned-up, pedestrianized street provides upmarket restaurants servicing the confident consuming crowds that now flow along the global mart of Regent Street. If Ziggy walked past today, there would be recognition, welcome and a positive response – probably people saying, 'I expected Ziggy would look more different'. Now, in the affluent West, Ziggy is everywhere and nowhere, a figure who has passed into general ownership. But worldwide the story continues, and beyond the 'liberated'

West there are major forces for which Ziggy is no cosy historic character, but a living threat.[110]

And here lies a dilemma. Bowie created Ziggy, but provided no guide for how to achieve such individual liberation – except through his own personal route of self-belief, iron will and complete control. There is no scripture, creed or service. The philosophy of Ziggy is utterly personal – be yourself, whatever that is.[111] It worked for Bowie, but it is not an appealing message for many today, who look for greater certainties, the reassurance of dogma and the seductive pleasure of being part of a mass. Worldwide, a counter-reformation is underway, with some now arguing that such libertarian views are WEIRD:[112]

w – estern
E – ducated
I – ndustrialized
R – ich
D – emocratic

Will Ziggy, like King Arthur, now remain sleeping forever or will he/she return to save mystic Albion from its enemies? Or will the 'Heroes' be found on other sides by then? Is Major Tom still drifting? Or has he refocused and reconnected with others to overthrow the London of global capitalism?

David Jones grew up in 1950s London dreaming of being a successful entertainer. As David Bowie he tried, tried very hard, and became a world-famous performer. In the process, he helped establish a key part of Western twenty-first century liberal belief: that anybody should be allowed to be what they want to be. Self before duty, with duty a choice. He did not invent the idea, but he did promote it to a huge audience. The marketing worked and the London of today, ethnically diverse, culturally open and relatively tolerant, is an on-going testament to this belief. In the remaining years of this century, there are plenty of groups for whom such a culture is anathema. It will be interesting to see how this journey, which started in Brixton, London SW9, continues to unfold.

When the tone of the music changes, the walls of the city shake.

PLATO, *The Republic*

←[29] **FAR LEFT** • *Unhalfbricking*, 1969 •
Fairport Convention • Island

←[30] **LEFT** • *The Rise and Fall of Ziggy*
Stardust and the Spiders from Mars, 1972 •
RCA Victor

→[31] **OPPOSITE** • Ziggy Stardust plaque on
Heddon Street, London, 2012

THIS MARKS THE LOCATION OF THE COVER PHOTOGRAPH FOR THE ICONIC DAVID BOWIE ALBUM

★

ZIGGY STARDUST

1972

Ⓡ

'THE RISE AND FALL OF ZIGGY STARDUST AND THE SPIDERS FROM MARS'

DAVID BOWIE IS LOOKING FOR INFORMATION

→[32] **OPPOSITE** ● David Bowie backstage, 1972 ●
Photograph by Masayoshi Sukita

←↑ **[33] OPPOSITE AND ABOVE** • Quilted two-piece suit, 1972 • Designed by
Freddie Burretti for the Ziggy Stardust tour • THE DAVID BOWIE ARCHIVE

→**[34] FOLLOWING PAGES** • David Bowie performing 'Star Man' with the
Spiders from Mars on 'Top of the Pops', recorded 5 July 1972 • Photographs by
Harry Goodwin • Harry Goodwin Archive

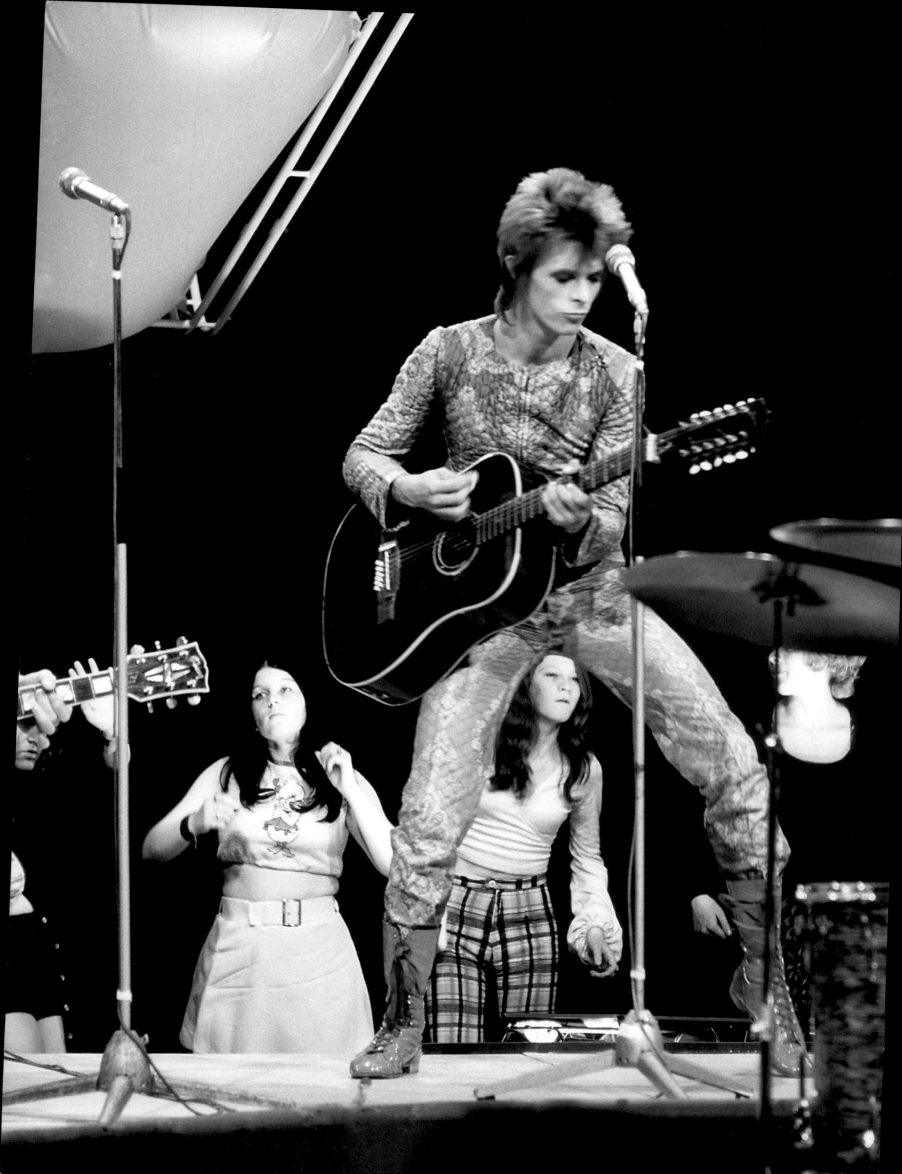

↑→[35] **ABOVE AND OPPOSITE** ◦ Quilted jumpsuit, 1972 ◦ Designed by
David Bowie and Freddie Burretti for the *Ziggy Stardust* album cover
and subsequent tour ◦ THE DAVID BOWIE ARCHIVE

DAVID BOWIE IS BLOWING OUR MINDS

→ **[36] OPPOSITE** • David Bowie, 1973 •
Photograph by Masayoshi Sukita

↑→ **[37] ABOVE AND OPPOSITE** • Asymmetric knitted
bodysuit, 1973 • Designed by Kansai Yamamoto for the
Aladdin Sane tour • THE DAVID BOWIE ARCHIVE

↑→ [38] ABOVE AND OPPOSITE ● Cloak decorated with *kanji* characters,
1973 ● Designed by Kansai Yamamoto for the Aladdin Sane tour ●
The writing translates as 'one who spits out words in a fiery manner'
and phonetically reads 'David Bowie' ● THE DAVID BOWIE ARCHIVE

↑→[39] **ABOVE AND OPPOSITE** • Metallic bodysuit, 1973 • Designed by
Kansai Yamamoto for the Aladdin Sane tour • THE DAVID BOWIE ARCHIVE

↑→ [40] ABOVE AND OPPOSITE • 'Tokyo Pop' vinyl bodysuit, 1973 • Designed by
Kansai Yamamoto for the Aladdin Sane tour • THE DAVID BOWIE ARCHIVE

DAVID BOWIE IS JUMPING FROM UNIVERSE TO UNIVERSE

→ [41] **OPPOSITE** ● David Bowie, 1973 ●
Photograph by Masayoshi Sukita

CAMILLE PAGLIA

THEATRE OF GENDER: DAVID BOWIE AT THE CLIMAX OF THE SEXUAL REVOLUTION

David Bowie burst on to the international scene at a pivotal point in modern sexual history. The heady utopian dreams of the 1960s, which saw free love as an agent of radical political change, were evaporating. Generational solidarity was proving illusory, while experimentation with psychedelic drugs had expanded identity but sometimes at a cost of disorientation and paranoia. By the early 1970s, hints of decadence and apocalypse were trailing into popular culture. Bowie's prophetic attunement to this major shift was registered in his breakthrough song, 'Space Oddity' (1969), whose wistful astronaut Major Tom secedes from Earth itself. Recorded several months before the Woodstock Music Festival, 'Space Oddity', with its haunting isolation and asexual purity and passivity, forecast the end of the carnival of the Dionysian 1960s.

In their rebellious liberalism, nature worship and celebration of sex and emotion, the 1960s can be seen as a Romantic revival. Folk and rock music, emerging from both black and white working-class traditions, were the vernacular analogue to William Wordsworth and Samuel Taylor Coleridge's epochal *Lyrical Ballads* (1798), which used rural popular forms against an ossified literary establishment. But events, mirrored and magnified by mass media, had such force and velocity in the '60s that Romanticism soon flipped over into its decadent late phase. Bowie was the herald and leading symbol of that rapid transformation – as if Oscar Wilde had appeared less than a decade after Wordsworth. Bowie has in fact described himself as an artist 'who tries to capture the rate of change' – the theme of one of his signature songs, 'Changes'.[1]

Bowie assumed the persona of a Romantic precursor, Lord Byron, in the video for 'Blue Jean' (1984), excerpted from a 20-minute narrative, 'Jazzin' for Blue Jean', directed by Julien Temple. Like Bowie, Byron was a charismatic, bisexual exile of enormous and at that time unprecedented scandalous fame. Now reduced to a footloose, effeminate nightclub entertainer, Screaming Lord Byron, he is mounting his over-the-top act at the Bosphorus Rooms ('only London appearance', blares a poster), attended by enthusiastic but depthless dating couples. His fancy Aladdin outfit of turban, Turkish trousers and gold slippers with turned-up toes recalls the 1813 portrait of Byron in the opulent crimson and gold Albanian dress of a Greek patriot. Bowie's ingeniously shadowed *trompe-l'-œil* make-up also evokes two other of his sexually ambiguous antecedents, the dancer Vaslav Nijinsky in Ballets Russes productions of *Scheherazade* and *L'après-midi d'un faune*, and Rudolph Valentino, silent-film star of *The Sheik*, who was excoriated by the press for his face powder, mascara, 'floppy pants' and platinum slave bracelet.

But Bowie is closer in spirit to the late Romantic Wilde, a provocative man of the theatre and a lover of masks. Like Wilde, who satirized Wordsworth's cult of nature, Bowie has always been urban in sensibility: the city is his wilderness and his stage. Artifice is his watchword; indeed, except for

cartoonish predators like interplanetary spiders or hybrid dog-men, nature appears in Bowie mainly as the blank void of outer space. Like Wilde, who free-lanced as a fashion journalist, Bowie is a dandy for whom costume is an art form. But his lineage descends not direct from Beau Brummell but refracted through the English dandyism imported by French decadents such as the poet Charles Baudelaire, who portrayed the dandy as an arbiter of distinction, elegance and cold apartness – exactly like the Thin White Duke persona of Bowie's 1975–6 tours (pl.42). Barbey d'Aurevilly, Baudelaire's friend and ally, called dandies 'the Androgynes of History'.

Music was not the only or even the primary mode through which Bowie first conveyed his vision to the world: he was an iconoclast who was also an image-maker. Bowie's command of the visual was displayed in his acute instinct for the still camera, honed by his attentiveness to classic Hollywood publicity photographs, contemporary fashion magazines and European art films. His flair for choreography and body language had been developed by his study of pantomime and stagecraft with the innovative Lindsay Kemp troupe in London in the late 1960s. Bowie's earliest ambition was to be a painter, and he has continued to paint throughout his life – especially, he has said, when he is having trouble writing songs.[2] The multimedia approaches that were gaining ascendance over the fine arts during the 1960s also helped foster his desire to fuse music with visuals on stage. While working at an advertising agency when he was 16, he learned story-boarding techniques that he later employed for his videos.

→[43] OPPOSITE • Annotated back cover image for *Hunky Dory* album, 1971 • Designed by David Bowie • Photograph by Brian Ward • THE DAVID BOWIE ARCHIVE

As he was searching for a voice and place in the music industry, Bowie's look steadily changed. Beatifically singing 'Let Me Sleep Beside You' for a 1969 promotional film, he appeared in standard mod dress of open-necked floral shirt and hip-huggers and projected the harmless, wiggly charm of the bashful boy next door. By his third album the following year, however, he had embarked on a challenging new course, putting his commercial acceptance at risk through unsettling cross-dressing scenarios. The cover of *The Man Who Sold the World* (pl.129) shows him sporting heavy, winsome, shoulder-length locks and wearing a luxuriously patterned pink-and-blue velvet maxi-dress over tight knee-high boots normally associated with stylish young women. (This 'man-dress' was designed by Michael Fish, who also did Mick Jagger's short white dress for the Rolling Stones' free Hyde Park concert in 1969.) Bowie's languidly seductive, serpentine reclining posture is equally cheeky – a parody of Canova's nude statue of Pauline Borghese (Napoleon's sister) as Venus. This cover was so sexually radical at the time that it was vetoed by his record company for distribution in the United States. A cartoon by Michael J. Weller showing the mental hospital to which Bowie's half-brother Terry had been committed was hastily substituted instead. It was replaced in 1972 by a mediocre black-and-white shot of a blurry Bowie kicking up his heels on stage.

In the close-up portrait on his next album cover for *Hunky Dory* (1971, pl.143), Bowie adopted a dreamy expression of sentimental, heavenward yearning drawn from the lexicon of studio-era Hollywood for women stars. Also startlingly feminine is his gesture of frank self-touching, as he smooths his long blonde hair back with both hands. The picture cleverly combines two images from Edward Steichen's great 1928 photo series of Greta Garbo draped in black (republished by *Life* magazine in 1955). The *Hunky Dory* cover was stunning at release not only for its daring gender play but for its evocation of Hollywood glamour, which was not yet taken seriously in nascent film studies. Its unnatural, metallic-yellow tinting of Bowie's hair had a Pop art edge but also recalled airbrushing conventions of 1920s fan magazines, while its soft focus replicated the flattering aura of ageless mystery produced in Hollywood by applying Vaseline to the camera lens.

On the back of *Hunky Dory* (pl.43), a long-haired Bowie sombrely stands in blousy, flowing, high-waisted trousers tailored in what was then a highly unusual retro 1930s cut (preceding Halston's contemporary variation on it). The picture resembles a canonical 1939 photo of Katharine Hepburn fiercely standing with shoulder-length hair and in similar tan slacks before a fireplace on the New York stage set of *The Philadelphia Story* (a year before it was filmed). Although Bowie cited Pre-Raphaelite precedents, the oblique inwardness and intriguingly half-concealing Veronica Lake hair were partly influenced, as was his beret photo on the back of *The Man Who Sold the World*, by Rachel Harlow (born Richard Finocchio), a Philadelphia drag queen.[3] Harlow had gained passing attention as the star of *The Queen*, a 1968 documentary chronicling a New York drag beauty pageant the prior year where the panel of judges (Andy Warhol, Edie Sedgwick and journalist George Plimpton) awarded her the crown. The film, which Bowie saw and which created a press stir at the Cannes Film Festival, showed the furious backlash by disappointed fellow contestants: Harlow's soft, feminine look was a marked departure from drag queens' traditional 'hard glamour', modelled on Hollywood stars like Marlene Dietrich. Harlow, who became a transsexual in 1972, was later linked to a rumoured scandal involving Grace Kelly's brother Jack, who dropped out of the Philadelphia mayoral race because of it.

The cover art for Bowie's fifth album, *The Rise and Fall of Ziggy Stardust and the Spiders from Mars* (1972, pl.133), enacted a brisk gender reversal from the prior two albums: a now short-haired, Nordically blonde Bowie is posted in macho mode, leg up on a rubbish bin on a London night street, his guitar slung like a rifle at his side while he warily scans the distance like a soldier on patrol. But the garish colours (superimposed afterwards) of his turquoise jumpsuit and purple wrestler's boots, inspired by the army boots of the marauding 'droogs' of Stanley Kubrick's film of *A Clockwork Orange* (1971), betray another subtext. That sexual contrary is revealed by the sensational photograph on the back of the album: Bowie piercingly meeting the viewer's eyes from within a lighted telephone box, where he loiters with the graceful hands and hip-shot stance of a woman but the bare chest and bulging crotch of a male hustler (recalling Renaissance codpieces as well as the oversized jockstraps of *A Clockwork Orange*). Bowie's eccentric posture here was his first public use of drag queen mannerisms, which have been highly stylized since the Victorian era and probably long before. The exhibitionistic brazenness of the scenario – a rent boy waiting at a telephone – markedly departed from the relaxed domestic transvestism of the cover of *The Man Who Sold the World*, where Bowie could be mistaken for a rumpled eighteenth-century lord at his glossy leisure, like Thomas Gainsborough's *Blue Boy*. There was also a disconnect in the gay persona of the telephone box: in that period, male hustlers ('rough trade') would normally affect a stereotypical masculine look, such as that of a sailor, labourer, motorcyclist or cowboy. Bowie created something entirely new in this taunting yet fey street tough, based on his own observation of the rent boys who lingered around London's hot spots and who paralleled the hunky male hustlers whom Andy Warhol filmed gambolling with the gamine Edie Sedgwick in his grainy early short films in New York.

Ziggy Stardust, Bowie's most famous invented character, did not appear on the cover of the album that bears his name but was theatrically developed on the unusually long world tour (from January 1972 to July 1973). Ziggy became so potent an entity that he virtually annihilated his creator and spun Bowie, by his own admission, into a fragile psychological state, exacerbated by cocaine, that was near 'schizophrenia'.[4] Ziggy's flamboyant make-up, rooster comb of spiky, razor-cut red hair and futuristic costumes designed by Kansai Yamamoto turned him into an alien rock 'messiah' (Bowie's term), leader of a band of space invaders come to redeem errant earthlings.[5] Bowie said Ziggy was modelled on Vince Taylor, a British-born pop singer who had lived in the US and achieved second-tier prominence in England and France until he began to suffer drug-related religious hallucinations on stage. However, there was little sexual ambiguity in Taylor's self-presentation, which surviving TV clips show to have been a straight rockabilly knock-off of Gene Vincent, a hyperactive, black-leather-clad peer of the hip-swivelling Elvis Presley.

Bowie pushed Ziggy's gender into another dimension of space-time, where sexual personae of both East and West met and melded. Then very intrigued by Asian culture, he made Ziggy a strange amalgam of samurai warrior and kabuki *onnagata* – the male actor who played female roles in traditional Japanese theatre. (On tour in Japan in April 1973, Bowie received instruction in kabuki make-up from Tamasaburo Bando, Japan's foremost living *onnagata*.) But Bowie's cynically suggestive stage manner (most overt in 'Time', with its sinister honky-tonk piano) was drawn from German cabaret. The Broadway musical *Cabaret* had had a successful London run, with Judi Dench as Sally Bowles, in 1968; a revival of Bertolt Brecht and Kurt Weill's *Threepenny Opera*, starring Hermione Baddeley and Vanessa Redgrave, opened in the West End in early 1972. Bob Fosse's movie of *Cabaret* was released the same year: Joel Gray would win one of the film's eight Academy Awards for his insinuating, repellently flirtatious performance as an epicene master of ceremonies. Bowie's very title, *The Rise and Fall of Ziggy Stardust*, alluded to Brecht and Weill's *The Rise and Fall of the City of Mahagonny*, a satire of America from which came 'Alabama Song', later performed by Bowie on his 1978 world tour.

Ziggy flashes with Weimar decadence, from the insomniac blackened hollows of his eyes to his impudent feather boa, a femme accessory that once belonged to Lindsay Kemp and that descended from Marlene Dietrich's early film roles as a cabaret singer. The love god Jimi Hendrix had often affected a pink boa, solarized to a psychedelic orange on the cover of his 1967 debut album, but it generally receded in the rainbow riot of his Portobello Road retro wear. Marc Bolan, with whom Bowie co-invented glam rock, had become known for an arch combination of lavish boa and shiny top hat that almost certainly came from Helmut Berger's drag routine as Dietrich in *The Damned*, Luchino Visconti's 1969 film about the Third Reich's war on Weimar excess. Ziggy's shoulder shimmies or bouts of hand-on-hip swish frankly signalled Weimar sleaze and *nostalgie de la boue*, which were most notoriously captured by Mick Rock's classic photo of Bowie fallen to his knees and avidly mouthing Mick Ronson's vamping guitar. Gay fellatio was shocking enough at the time, yet even more notable in that perverse ritual was that a major male star was unashamedly exhibiting himself in a sexually subordinate role. The *Ziggy* album abounds with overtly gay references, from the title song's boast about 'God-given ass' to the provocative 'Put your ray gun to my head' and 'The church of man love is such a holy place to be' ('Moonage Daydream').

But beyond his besmirched decadence, Ziggy Stardust also had a dazzling visionary beauty, above all when Bowie was wearing his short-skirted white silk kimono and high buskins, which made him resemble an Amazonian huntress like Belphoebe in Edmund Spenser's *Faerie Queene* (pl.46). With his silver lipstick and forehead astral sphere, he evoked the radiant allegorical figures of courtly masque. At key moments in the Ziggy gender mirage, Bowie would plant his feet wide and show off his rippling, muscled thighs, a blazon of his underlying masculine athleticism (pl.44). Indeed, in Ziggy Stardust's supernormal militant energy and shuffled masks, we may have come closer than we ever will again to glimpsing how Shakespeare's virtuoso boy actors performed the roles of Rosalind, Cleopatra and Lady Macbeth. With his haughty architectonic cheekbones and implacable will, Ziggy at times resembled the young Katharine Hepburn, another sexually heterodox personality who chopped off her hair and called herself 'Jimmy' in childhood and who made a spectacular Broadway entrance in 1932 as an Amazon warrior leaping down a flight of steps with a dead stag over her shoulders. Ziggy at his most lashing and relentless also recalled Mary Woronov's brilliant improvisation as Hanoi Hannah in Warhol's epic *Chelsea Girls* (1966), a flight of ferocity so breathtaking that some viewers mistook her for a rampaging drag queen. Woronov played a dominatrix doing a whip dance with the poet Gerard Malanga in a multimedia show, the 'Exploding Plastic Inevitable', staged by the Velvet Underground, a group which had a heavy influence on Bowie. Indeed, Bowie prefaced the encore to his final performance as Ziggy, as can be seen in D. A. Pennebaker's concert documentary, with a heartfelt tribute to the Velvets' Lou Reed, who was then recording in a London studio. Bowie elsewhere called Reed 'the most important writer in modern rock' and lauded 'the street-gut level' of his work.[6] The title of Bowie's song, 'Velvet Goldmine' (later borrowed by Todd Haynes for a 1998 movie), clearly riffs on Reed's band.

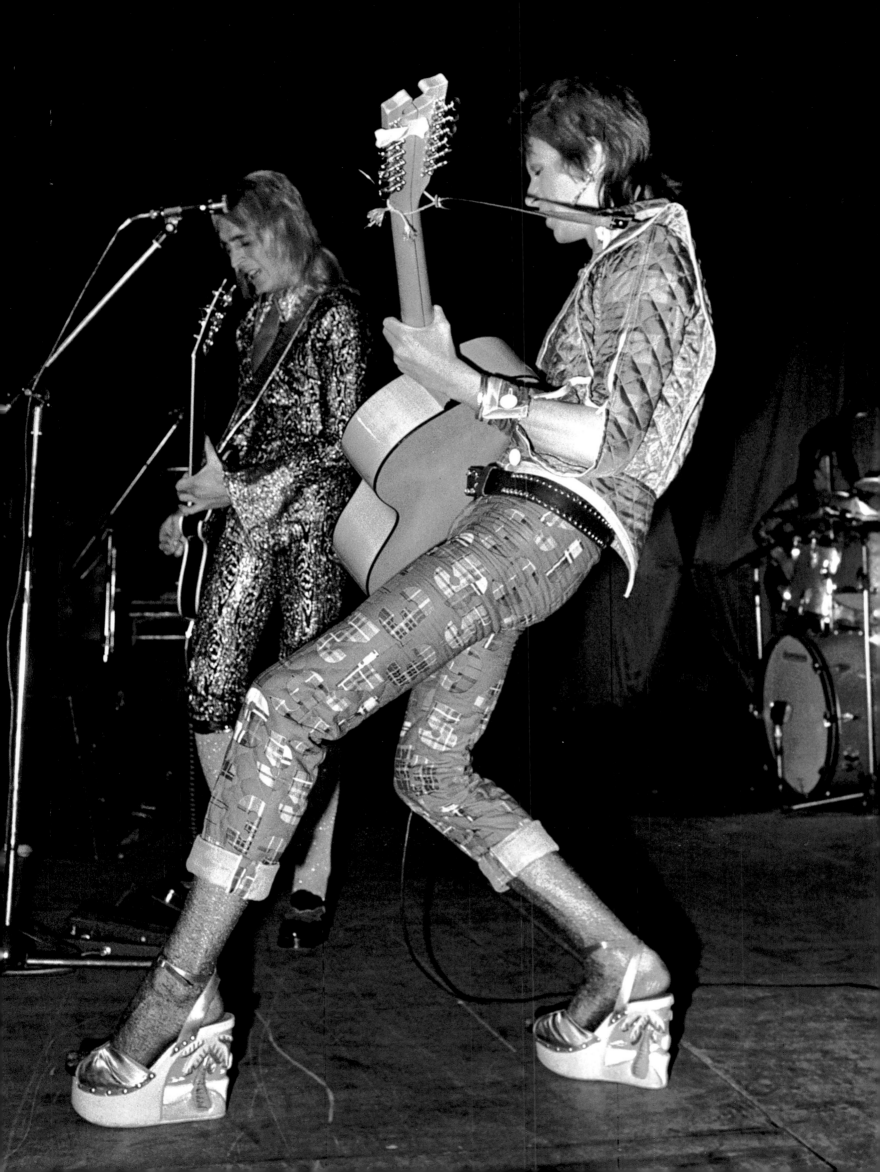

↑ [45] ABOVE ● Cover photograph for *Aladdin Sane*, 1973 ● Photograph by Brian Duffy

→ [46] OPPOSITE ● David Bowie on stage during the Aladdin Sane tour, 1973 ●
Photograph by Mick Rock

↑→ **[47] ABOVE AND OPPOSITE** ● White silk suit, 1973 ●
Designed by Kansai Yamamoto for the Aladdin Sane tour ●
THE DAVID BOWIE ARCHIVE

→ [48] OPPOSITE ● David Bowie
on stage in Scotland during
the Aladdin Sane tour, 1973 ●
Photograph by Mick Rock

By the time we saw him on the front of an album, *Aladdin Sane* (1973), Ziggy Stardust was already in eclipse. The cover photograph by Brian Duffy with its red-and-blue lightning bolt crossing Bowie's face has become one of the most emblematic and influential art images of the past half century, reproduced or parodied in advertising, media and entertainment worldwide (pl.45). It contains all of Romanticism, focused on the artist as mutilated victim of his own febrile imagination. Like Herman Melville's Captain Ahab, whose body was scarred by lightning in his quest for the white whale, Bowie as Ziggy is a voyager who has defied ordinary human limits and paid the price. Aladdin sane in the realm of art is a lad insane everywhere else. A jolt of artistic inspiration has stunned him into trance or catatonia. He is blind to the outer world and its 'social contacts' – Bowie's recurrent term for an area of experience that had proved troublesome for Major Tom as well as himself.[7]

Pierre La Roche's ingenious zigzag make-up looks at first glance like a bloody wound – an axe blow through the skull of a Viking warrior laid out on his bier. Ziggy appears to be in hibernation or suspended animation, like the doomed astronauts in their mummiform chambers in Stanley Kubrick's *2001: A Space Odyssey* (1968), which had inspired Bowie's 'Space Oddity'. The background blankness is encroaching like a freezing cryogenic wave upon the figure. It's as clinical as an autopsy, with a glob of extracted flesh lodged on the collarbone. This teardrop of phalliform jelly resembles the unidentifiable bits of protoplasm and biomorphic conglomerations that stud the sexualized landscapes of Salvador Dalí. Also Surrealist are the inflamed creases of Ziggy's armpits, which look like fresh surgical scars as well as raw female genitalia. Like Prometheus, a rebel hero to the Romantics, he has lost his liver for stealing the fire of the gods. Like the solitary space traveller in *2001*, he may be regressing to the embryonic stage to give birth to himself.

With his smooth, lithe, hairless body, *Aladdin Sane's* rouged androgyne has evolved past gender, as blatantly dramatized by the full-length picture in the inside gatefold, where Ziggy's long legs and sleek, sexless torso are turning silver robotic. His proudly aristocratic stance with its streamlined waist grip is another quotation from Katharine Hepburn's unique publicity pose for *The Philadelphia Story*, combined with a salute to Veruschka von Lehndorff, the great supermodel (seen in Michelangelo Antonioni's *Blow-Up*) who had posed nude in spectacular body paint in a 1966 photo shoot in Kenya with Peter Beard and Salvador Dalí. In a 1977 interview on American TV, Bowie compared his friend Iggy Pop's method of working to his own: Iggy's ideas, said Bowie, blocking off space with both hands, came from the viscera and crotch, while his own ideas came from the chest and head: 'I'm a cyborg', he declared.[8] The bust-like cover of *Aladdin Sane* shows the artist in creative process, having jettisoned the mundane appetites of belly and genitals. This dreaming head is lifting off into a shamanistic zone of vision purged of people and matter itself.

For the cover of his next album, *Pin Ups* (1973, pl.135), a vigorous collection of cover versions of hard-rock classics, Bowie used a photograph of himself with Twiggy taken in Paris by Justin de Villeneuve for *Vogue*. The two look lost and stricken, like Adam and Eve after the Fall (pl.48). Who are these waifs? They appear to be wearing masks – actually cleverly drawn on with make-up. The striking colour contrast on Twiggy (she was tanned from a Bermuda holiday) sparks a frisson of uncertainty about both race and gender: it might very well be a black man in a female mask leaning his head so confidently on the tensely alert Bowie. As a pop idol now bruised by fame, Bowie had arrived in the purgatorial territory of Twiggy's declining star – she who as a coltish girl-boy had been a supreme symbol of the 1960s youthquake.

Bowie returned to Weimar sensibility for the cover of *Diamond Dogs* (1974, pl.136), a lurid painting by Guy Peellaert in a German Expressionist style complementing the album's dystopian narrative. The opening howl, recitation about 'rotting corpses' and graphic bestiality – Bowie and two crouching, ghoulish women are depicted in half-dog form – was the closest he ever came to the Grand Guignol horror-movie gambits of Alice Cooper, whose 1971 European tour had been attended by both Bowie and Elton John. The setting of the *Diamond Dogs* cover is a sideshow ('The Strangest Living Curiosities') drawn from Tod Browning's disturbing 1932 film, *Freaks*, which is glossed in the title song. Bowie's canine loins (presumably alluding to Iggy Pop's breakthrough song, 'I Wanna Be Your Dog') may have been glaringly male – the genitalia were soon airbrushed away to head off rising controversy – but the rest of him is a bitch. He wears a large loop earring, a lushly enhanced silhouette of red lipstick and a lavishly teased bouffant variation of his Ziggy haircut. Despite his sinewy arms, the effect is sensuously female – an alluring prone pose propped up on elbows that was commonly used for publicity shots of bosomy studio-era stars like Lana Turner and even the mature Gloria Swanson. Peellaert worked from two sketches drawn by Bowie of his variation on an Egyptian sphinx. Precedents for the picture can be found in Symbolist paintings of *femmes fatales*, specifically Fernand Khnopff's *Sphinx* (1896), where a reclining leopard with a woman's face smugly caresses a girlish Oedipus. The songs on *Diamond Dogs* portray a decadent world of fast sex in city doorways ('Sweet Thing') and trampy boys in torn dresses and smudged make-up ('Rebel Rebel').

Young Americans (1975, pl.137) was the last album cover that Bowie used as a gender canvas. Once again he meets the viewer's eyes but no longer with the hard edge of urban prostitution seen on *Diamond Dogs*. It is another Hollywood glamour portrait, his short but flowing hair softly backlit to form a halo. The startlingly feminine silver bangle bracelets, jarringly juxtaposed with a subtly Art Deco man's plaid shirt, gleam like a starburst. The impression of wavering gender is accentuated by his discreet pink lipstick and longish mani-cured fingernails. (Russet nail polish, missing from the US album, was restored to the picture for the 1999 remastered CD release.) A ghostly spiral of cigarette smoke, airbrushed in, is another vintage Hollywood touch. This wistful, clois-tered figure might be a kept boy or a neurasthenic aesthete, like the artist Aubrey Beardsley or the poet Lord Alfred Douglas, who brought down Oscar Wilde. A similar pensive brand of guarded androgynous male beauty was captured by Peter O'Toole in his multifaceted portrayal of the cultivated, tormented Laurence of Arabia in David Lean's 1962 film.

What must be observed about Bowie's gender fanta-sia is how rarely he ever did straight drag. The significant exception was a video directed by David Mallet for 'Boys Keep Swinging', a song on *Lodger* (1979), the final album in Bowie and Brian Eno's 'Berlin Trilogy'. The song was not released in the US because of record company fears about the video's unpalatable transvestism. It begins with Bowie as a Cliff Richard-style early 1960s rock'n'roll singer clad in a generic dark suit and rollicking away with standard kinetic moves at a standing microphone. Attention then shifts to his trio of hilariously bored female back-up singers, each one played by Bowie in drag. There is a blowsy, blasé, gum-cracking Elizabeth Taylor in a tendrilous chignon wig and a big crinoline skirt topped with a violet cinch belt – Taylor's signature colour. Bowie had met John Lennon five years earlier at a party at Elizabeth Taylor's Los Angeles house. Photos of the zaftig Taylor bear-hugging the alarmingly frail Bowie – she was wearing his fedora – made it seem as if she could crush him like an eggshell.

Next in the video is an icy Valkyrie in a svelte metallic-gold sheath dress with fetishistically deformed sleeves – boxy Joan Crawford shoulder pads sprouting lateral wings like shark fins (pl.49). Her full, dark hair resembles that of the enigmatic Lauren Bacall in *To Have and Have Not* as well as the stormy Bette Davis in *All About Eve*. The dress itself recalls the clinging metallic moth costume worn by Katharine Hepburn (playing an aviatrix modelled on Amelia

Earhart) in *Christopher Strong* and also the spectacular, skin-tight 'nude dress' of beaded silk soufflé designed in 1953 by Jean Louis for Marlene Dietrich's cabaret concerts. (For the second half of those shows, which toured the world, Dietrich changed into the top hat and tails of her 1930 film, *Morocco*.) There is also a suggestion of the fashion model Jerry Hall's disruptive, sashaying entrance in a black-slashed gold tiger gown in Bryan Ferry's 1976 video for 'Let's Stick Together'. At the end of the sequence, Bowie breaks role by aggressively whipping off his wig and smearing his lipstick with the back of his hand, staring down the viewer with a frightening sneer of rage – a reversal of the usual hilarity and applause-inviting bonhomie accompanying the gender revelation at the end of drag acts. This golden androgyne is truly Bowie's 'Queen Bitch' (the tenth song on *Hunky Dory*).

The third drag impersonation is of Dietrich herself, with whom Bowie had recently starred in *Just a Gigolo* (1978), directed by David Hemmings. Bizarrely, they never met: Bowie's dialogue with Dietrich was spliced together in post-production. In 'Boys Keep Swinging', he got his revenge: the aged Dietrich, dressed in an understated knit Chanel suit, walks haltingly with a cane down the fashion catwalk, from which old women are normally banned. Pausing at the edge, she feebly yet contemptuously blows a kiss at the viewer with her cigarette, the fading superstar still hungry for dominance. In this video, Bowie penetrated to the cold masculine soul and monstrous lust for power of the great female stars, which drag queens had always sensed and turned into rambunctious comedy.

The video for 'Boys Keep Swinging' had camp wit but shabby production values. That all changed the following year with 'Ashes to Ashes', from the *Scary Monsters … and Super Creeps* album. Directed by Bowie and David Mallet (working from Bowie's own storyboards), it was at the time the most expensive music video ever made. This mini-movie, with its dreamlike collage, profoundly influenced the direc-tion of music videos, which exploded with the spread of cable TV and the introduction of a round-the-clock music channel, MTV, in 1981. Bowie called the song 'Ashes to Ashes' 'an ode to childhood', but its video became a portrait of the isolated, suffering artist, with motifs and techniques drawn from the entire history of European art films – from Carl Dreyer's *The Passion of Joan of Arc* and Luis Buñuel and Salvador Dalí's *Un Chien Andalou* to Jean Cocteu's *Orphée* and Ingmar Bergman's *The Seventh Seal*. The song's self-referential nature was signalled by the return of Bowie's debut character, Major Tom, now a notorious 'junkie' in a crisis of addiction.

In 'Ashes to Ashes' (a phrase from the Anglican funeral service), Bowie assumes the role of Pierrot, a figure of seventeenth-century *commedia dell'arte* who became promi-nent in French pantomime. Many painters, such as Watteau, saw themselves in the melancholy Pierrot, with his tender-ness and *naïveté* and his humbling enforced straddling of the line between art and entertainment. Bowie's Pierrot, wearing a tufted white clown costume and dunce cap, has a gangly

awkwardness and a timid, pre-sexual innocence. In other scenes, however, an elegantly handsome Major Tom sits caged in a padded cell and an exploding kitchen or, haggard and stony, hangs moribund in a watery grotto that is half wrecked spaceship and half nightmare womb.

Bowie has rarely spoken publicly of his mother and, in the 1970s, curtly rebuffed prominent British and American TV interviewers when they presumptuously prodded him about it.[9] The finale of 'Ashes to Ashes' addresses the matter in dramatic symbolism, like the depressed film director Guido's dream encounter with his parents in a cemetery in Federico Fellini's 8½. Hectored by a small, gesticulating older woman, whom Bowie said (when introducing this video for a 1993 MTV retrospective) resembled his mother, Pierrot strolls with abashed attentiveness and dutiful resignation along the edge of an infernal underground sea.[10] A moment before, he stands flinching and paralysed from the camera flash of a merciless paparazzo: the shooting of a picture (the video's third photo portrait) becomes a real bullet shot. Is Pierrot now dead and his mother come to reclaim his body – like Mary for a *pietà*? Bowie's ending evokes that of *The Tramp*, where another childlike, genderless clown, Charlie Chaplin in a fake moustache, rambles away down a dirt road. There are also striking visual parallels to a mordant moment in Fellini's *La Dolce Vita* where a fierce matriarch of the old Italian nobility materializes at dawn with a priest and imperiously summons her carousing adult children to Mass. The other decadent partygoers stand stupefied as they watch their recently priapic but now cowed playfellows fall in line and obediently troop away.

In the finale of 'Ashes to Ashes', Bowie was questioning his identity as an artist and a man. Despite his wandering, he evidently still felt the stubborn tug of his origins, a regulated suburban conformity from which he had escaped to a vivid universe of omnisexual fantasy that had bewitched an entire generation. In the video, his mother is both peripheral and central, a voice he can't get out of his head. The poignant refrain, echoing a traditional British children's song, identifies the mother with pressing practical reality: 'My mother said to get things done/ You'd better not mess with Major Tom'. Tom is Bowie the daydreamer who spaces out. His mother is like the poet Wallace Stevens' contrary Mrs Alfred Uruguay, who boasts, 'I have wiped away moonlight like mud.'

The video's bleak, solarized colour suggests that, at this moment, the mother is winning. Pierrot sinks slowly in the sea, while the landscape seems to be losing its fictive energy, like the anaemic, fading characters in Jaques Rivette's 1974 film, *Celine and Julie Go Boating*. Bowie's scathingly self-critical dual perspective would soon take comic form in 'Jazzin' for Blue Jean', where Screaming Lord Byron's excess and vanity are satirized by Bowie himself playing a dual role as a maladroit nerd who shouts at Byron, 'You conniving, randy, bogus Oriental old queen! Your record sleeves are

better than your songs!' In 'Ashes to Ashes', the limited personal mother is only an instrument of or proxy for larger processes of fate. The mammoth bulldozer, for example, which menacingly follows Pierrot and his troupe of female priests is a modernization of 'Time's winged chariot hurrying near' (from Andrew Marvell's 'To His Coy Mistress') – a fascist force pushing all of humanity into a mass grave.

The subterranean disturbances in Bowie's *œuvre* around the issue of women and their ungovernable power can be detected in 'Suffragette City' (from *The Rise and Fall of Ziggy Stardust*), with its heady refrain, 'Don't lean on me, man, because you can't afford the ticket back from Suffragette City!' Gender relations were changing fast after the rebirth of feminism in the late 1960s. This line shows men unprepared for the shift and running around in circles like antic squirrels. It says in effect, 'Don't ask *me* for advice, because I sure can't help!' It implies that castration, metaphorical or otherwise, is the toll exacted by women whose quest for equality may sometimes conceal a drive for dominance. The song's other blazing refrain, 'Wham, bam, thank you, ma'am!' – a common old American catchphrase probably about prostitution – tauntingly suggests that loveless hit-and-run sex is one foolproof way to avoid swampy entrapment by women.

Few if any songs in Bowie's great period contain a fully developed portrait of a woman, positive or negative, comparable to Bob Dylan's sympathetic 'Sad-Eyed Lady of the Lowlands' or the toweringly furious 'Like a Rolling Stone'. Bowie's exhilarating 'China Girl' (1983), with its wonderfully expansive video directed by David Mallet, substitutes political for psychological issues and was in any case co-written by Iggy Pop about an Asian woman he was courting in Switzerland. Bowie's most concentrated meditation on sexual identity and gender relations is contained in the staggered finale of *Aladdin Sane* – a matched set of songs, one inspired by an American man and the other by an American woman. They are pointedly introduced by a cover version of the Rolling Stones' 'Let's Spend the Night Together', which in this context posits not just sexual intercourse but dialogue and detente – which may prove impossible between the entrenched positions of the new gender wars.

The first song, 'The Jean Genie', is an anthem to boy power partly inspired by Iggy Pop, one of Bowie's closest friends in the 1970s and his flatmate during his low-profile exile in Berlin after the burn-out of Ziggy Stardust. Bowie said that in this song he wanted 'to locate Ziggy as a kind of Hollywood street rat' – in other words, one of the homeless, rootless kids who flocked to the Sunset Strip in the late 1960s and '70s, a colourful scene rife with drugs and prostitution that was also a matrix of new music and style.[11]

(A male 'trick' from Sunset and Vine forces a closeted star to his knees earlier on the album in 'Cracked Actor'.) The jean genie is a 'reptile', a 'rattlesnake', a scrappy sprite and male hustler slithering outside the system who, like Peter Pan, retains his freedom by never growing up. If there is a reference to Jean Genet in his name (as Bowie later admitted was possible), then he is Genet's ideal of the thief and outcast, representing the association of homosexuality with heroic Romantic criminality that Genet got from André Gide and that Gide got from Wilde.[12] Denim (preceding the designer jeans trend of the late '70s) still had an outlaw connotation, as shown in Warhol's snapshot of the crotch of a jeans-clad male hustler for the zippered cover of the Rolling Stones' 1971 album, *Sticky Fingers*.

Bowie's jean genie is a vagabond and derelict who savours squalor and filth as a defiance of female order and control and who even asserts the right to slash, maim and violate his own mother-made flesh. ('Ate all your razors' is a splendid Beat-style line vividly referencing the stage-diving Iggy's notorious self-cutting on broken glass.) The genie's delirious manic motion is caught by the buzz and fuzz of the aggressive guitars, which evoke the unleashed boy energy of the rave-up Yardbirds in their covers of Bo Diddley's braggart 'I'm a Man' and Howlin' Wolf's 'Smokestack Lightning', which pictures sex and its betrayals as a constantly hurtling train. (The genie 'loves chimney stacks' – belching, sparking phallic totems as well as soft entry points for home burglary.) Bowie, who daringly talks rather than sings this song, can be heard doing the legendary bluesman's eerie 'whoo-hoo' (the train's receding siren) as a chorus.

But woman gets the last word on *Aladdin Sane*. 'Lady Grinning Soul' was reportedly inspired by Claudia Lennear, an African-American soul singer who had been one of Ike and Tina Turner's back-up Ikettes. (Despite widespread claims, it remains unclear whether it was Lennear or another American, Marsha Hunt, mother of Mick Jagger's first child, who was the model for the Rolling Stones' 'Brown Sugar'.) 'Lady Grinning Soul' becomes a great archetypal sexual vision that transcends its origins – much as Percy Bysshe Shelley's 'Epipsychidion' left Emilia Viviani behind. From the first entrance of Bowie's voice, apprehensively a capella and distorted by echoes, we know we are in perilous territory.

The title alludes to Aretha Franklin's 1968 album, *Lady Soul*, but that phrase is now split by a death's head.[13] 'Grinning' almost certainly comes from 'Pirate Jenny' in *The Threepenny Opera*, a song premiered by Lotte Lenya in Berlin in 1928 and volcanically performed at New York's Carnegie Hall in 1964 by Nina Simone, who fused it with black radical politics. (Bowie deeply admired Simone and met her in Los Angeles in 1975; he recorded 'Wild is the Wind', from her 1966 album of that name, as the finale of *Station to Station*.)[14]

Jenny is a hotel chambermaid who harbours secret thoughts of class revenge and pitiless massacre: 'I'm kind of grinning while I'm scrubbing. And you say, "What's she got to grin?"' Her chilling refrain forecasts the arrival of a black freighter with a skull on its masthead as well as the privileged choice now handed to her: 'Kill them now or later?'

Bowie's chambermaid is more chatelaine or cool adventuress than brooding, vengeful servant, but 'the clothes are strewn' here too – a messy trail of sexual haste. 'Don't be afraid of the room', he confidently sings, but this is whistling in the dark (shown by his rise to vulnerable falsetto), for she rules the womb-tomb of the female body. After the brisk fresh air of the peripatetic genie, we are in a dark sensory zone of intoxicating hormonal scents – cologne and 'musky oil' from African civets. With her full breasts and impenetrable psyche, Lady Grinning Soul represents absolute sexual difference, not the misty, blurred ground of gender experiment that Bowie normally traverses. It is as if he has come face to face with Homer's Circe or Calypso, in whose realms men shrink to swine or slaves. But she is also a series of other seductive *femmes fatales* – Carmen (suggested by the Spanish guitar), Gustav Klimt's Judith (whose supercilious lolling head is mimicked by Bowie in his 1973 video of 'Life on Mars?'), and Alban Berg's heartless Lulu. The female principle is shown as mysterious, elusive, ungraspable. 'She will be your living end', croons Bowie in the hypnotic, achingly elegiac refrain: pleasure and pain, love and death (as in Wagner's *Liebestod*) are intertwined. Any man's victory in sex with a woman is transient and illusory.

The genesis of 'Lady Grinning Soul' may have been in the lyrics of a Jacques Brel song, 'My Death', a flawed translation of which Bowie had been singing on the Ziggy Stardust tour: 'Angel or devil, I don't care … My death waits there between your thighs.' Bowie turned it into a stark encounter with elemental realities, a descent to the underworld. 'Lady Grinning Soul' has hauntingly immersive atmospherics and an incisive power that standard poetry written in English was losing in the 1970s. Indeed, in its hair-raising candour yet sardonic banter, the song bears comparison to Sylvia Plath's savage Oedipal nursery rhyme, 'Daddy' (written in England in 1962). 'She comes, she goes': Bowie's restless, piratical traveller who trifles with men and has a way with cards sounds like a capricious, fortune-telling Muse, flooding the artist with ideas and then leaving him high and dry. Art-rock, a genre that showed enormous promise but failed to develop and deliver over time, produced only two enduring masterpieces: the Doors' 1967 Freudian-Jungian psychodrama, 'The End', and Bowie's 'Lady Grinning Soul' (which ends with virtually the same words as begin the Doors song). Crucially contributing to the late Romantic lyricism of 'Lady Grinning Soul' is Mike Garson's amazing piano work, a sumptuously florid improvisation that exposes the rifts, fractures, illusions and turmoil of sexual desire.

Beginning in an ominous mood of decadent Vienna and Berlin, Garson creates a compelling emotional world of anxiety and entrancement, tinged with panic and despair. With fistfuls of virtuoso runs and trills, he invokes the most flamboyant Romantic music-making from Liszt and Rachmaninoff to Liberace and Ferrante and Teicher – a style often used in classic movies such as the 1941 British film, *Dangerous Moonlight*, where Richard Addinsell's 'Warsaw Concerto' is played amidst the rubble of the Nazi invasion of Poland. Nina Simone used the same rapid, rippling piano style to accompany herself on the 1966 album version of 'Wild is the Wind'. Bowie has reportedly never performed 'Lady Grinning Soul' live – a testament perhaps to its excruciatingly sensitive material. After the infectious gaiety of 'The Jean Genie', this harrowing sojourn into the female boudoir, which is both burrow and palace, yields a Wildean revelation: men are simple, women complex.

Bowie's theatre of gender resembles the magic-lantern shows or phantasmagoria that preceded the development of motion-picture projection. The multiplicity of his gender images was partly inspired by the rapid changes in modern art, which had begun with neoclassicism sweeping away rococo in the late eighteenth century and which reached a fever pitch before, during and after World War I. Bowie told a TV interviewer in 1976, 'I was always totally bedazzled by all the art forms of the twentieth century, and my interpretation comes out *my way* of these art forms from Expressionism to Dadaism'. 'Even if the definition isn't understood', he tried to 'break it down' to convey his own 'feeling' to the audience.'[15] One of Bowie's leading achievements is his linkage of gender to the restless perpetual motion machine of modern culture. 'I have no style loyalty', he has declared.[16] His signature style is syncretism – a fusion or 'synthesising' (his word) of many styles that is characteristic of late phases such as the hybrid, polyglot Hellenistic era, when religions too seeped into one another.[17] Bowie has in fact used the word 'hybrid' to describe his approach.[18] His stylistic eclecticism in performance genres – combining music hall, vaudeville, pantomime, movies, musical comedy, cabaret, theatre of cruelty, modern dance, French chanson and American blues, folk, rock and soul – created countless new angles of perception and startling juxtapositions.

A superb example of the way Bowie brings art and gender into single focus was his adaptation of the mannequin style, a prototypical twentieth-century motif. As women were liberated in the Jazz Age, fashion sped up, promulgated by new media like high-budget movies and glossy magazines with vastly improved techniques of photographic printing. Mannequins as living models as well as department-store dummies became vivid cultural presences, as shown by the frequency of elaborate fashion show sequences in prestige Hollywood films like *The Women* (1939). The way that the self-conscious mannequin style had been instantly absorbed by the new woman can be seen in Man Ray's 1926 photograph of heiress Nancy Cunard with her arms robotically stacked with big African bangle bracelets and in August Sander's 1931 photographs of a slender secretary with boyishly cropped hair at a West German radio station in Cologne. These two women with their penetrating eyes and steely emancipation capture the intersexual look of avant-garde modernism and eerily anticipate the classic androgyny of David Bowie himself. The mannequin theme is overt when Bowie calls his diamond dogs, on the title song of that album, 'mannequins with kill appeal'. In the same lyric, the chillingly faceless 'little hussy' of his alter ego Halloween Jack wears 'a Dalí brooch', recalling the jellied teardrop fixed to the collarbone of Aladdin Sane. Mannequins became automaton-like agents of what Bowie elsewhere called a 'ritualizing of the body' in art that interested him.[19]

The Surrealists, who emerged from Dada, seized on the fashion mannequin as a symbol of modern personality – assertive and hard-contoured yet empty and paralysed. They were partly following the precedent of the Metaphysical painter, Giorgio de Chirico, who showed genderless tailors' dummies marooned in twilit deserted plazas. (Bowie explicitly voiced his admiration for de Chirico and later replicated his work, as well that of the Surrealist René Magritte, in the hallucinatory sets for the 1985 video of 'Loving the Alien'.)[20] Mannequins were major players in the 1938 International Surrealist Exhibition in Paris, where the entry courtyard was dominated by Dalí's installation, 'Rainy Taxi', with its nude mannequin seated amidst 200 live snails on a bed of lettuce. Inside the building was an avenue of mannequins stationed like streetwalkers and festooned with symbolic regalia and outright junk. In 1945, the Dadaist Marcel Duchamp, who had posed in drag as his alter ego Rrose Sélavy for Man Ray two decades before, inserted a headless, book-reading mannequin in a skimpy negligee into the window of New York's Gotham Book Mart to advertise the latest release by André Breton, the father of Surrealism. In the age of abstraction, the plaster mannequin, so easily chipped and seedy, was the derelict heir of canonical life-size Western sculpture in marble or bronze. The mannequin was so artificial that it eventually became gender-neutral. Its spectral aura was well captured in 'The After Hours' (1960) from the first season of 'The Twilight Zone', a TV series launched by America's greatest native Surrealist, Rod Serling: here department store mannequins are tracked as they roam, freeze and frighteningly come alive again.

Bowie's stunning variation on the Surrealist mannequin was that he became it: never before had a major male artist so completely submerged himself in a female *objet de culte*. Bowie's genius for using the camera as others use a paint-brush or chisel – not from behind the camera but before it – was dramatized in 'The 1980 Floor Show', his last appearance as Ziggy Stardust. This cabaret-structured programme was recorded over three nights in October 1973 at the Marquee Club in London and was broadcast on American TV the following month. (It was never aired in Britain, and the film footage is evidently lost.) In one routine, Bowie wore a see-through black fishnet body suit (designed by him and Freddie Burretti) adorned with two gold-painted mannequin's hands attached to his chest (pls 51 and 52). A third hand affixed to the crotch had been scuttled after a battle royal with the NBC film crew, who also insisted that Bowie cover up his black jockstrap with gold semi-leggings. The two cupped hands formed a bizarre brassiere that made it seem as if Bowie had sprouted breasts. Yet given women's swerve away from nail lacquer since the mid-1960s, the hands' black varnished nails (a nihilist colour not yet in the female arsenal) also suggested a man in drag: it was as if Bowie were being sexually pawed and clawed from behind by a raging queen in heat. Or was he split in gender and acrobatically embracing himself? – a trick (imitated by Bowie on tour) often employed in burlesque by strippers turning their backs to the audience (pl.53). Furthermore, it seemed as if his body were being played like a piano – not unlike the way Man Ray turned the body of Kiki de Montparnasse into a sensuous violin. The eye was titillated and confounded by an optical illusion: which of the multiple hands, including that on Bowie's glitter-sheathed right arm, were the real ones?

Bowie's mannequin masque was a tremendous *tour de force*, Dadaist in impulse and Surrealist in conception and execution. It fulfilled Baudelaire's dictum in *The Painter of Modern Life* that fashion should be 'a sublime deformation of nature'. In that one event, seen only by Americans, Bowie inserted himself permanently into the story of modern art. He instantly revived and renewed the Warhol legacy, which had been flagging since Warhol was shot and nearly killed in 1968, leaving him physically depleted and unable to advance beyond his set formulas. The Bowie broadcast on NBC's late-night variety show, 'The Midnight Special', was electrifying in its direct address to Americans who had been following the sexual radicalism of Warhol and his circle since his pioneering short films of the 1960s – notably 'Harlot' (1965), Warhol's first sound film, starring Mario Montez as a charismatic blond drag diva photographed with slow, ritualistic solemnity.

Bowie said that America had always been 'a myth land' for him.[21] The 'idol' of his youth had been Little Richard, the gender-bending, high-wattage rock'n'roller whom he had seen in person at the Brixton Odeon.[22] Andy Warhol and his coterie represented the next stage in Bowie's Anglo-American artistic journey. His contacts with Warhol figures are well documented. In August 1971, Bowie saw the London production of *Pork*, a self-satirizing farce by the Warhol coterie of Andy's obsession with gossip telephone calls. (The stage was adorned with two nude, fetchingly long-haired boys.) A slew of *Pork* personnel was immediately hired by Bowie, including Cherry Vanilla, Tony Zanetta and Leee Black Childers. Bowie and Warhol met just once the following month in New York, an awkward and mutually diffident encounter from which survives a video of the long-haired Bowie in a raffish black hat doing a strangely self-disembowelling mime. In his song, 'Andy Warhol' on *Hunky Dory* (released December 1971), Bowie hailed Warhol's perverse, voyeuristic theatricality by envisioning him as an art gallery and 'silver screen', a 'cinema' of the mind that he longed to emulate. However, the refrain 'Andy Warhol looks a scream' upset and offended Warhol. Bowie would later use the dead Warhol's own wig and eyeglasses to play him in Julian Schnabel's 1996 film, *Basquiat* (pl.204). In 1975, Bowie co-produced Lou Reed's only hit song, 'Walk on the Wild Side', with its litany of drag queens and hustlers from the Warhol Factory. Bowie gave one of them, Joe Dallesandro, a cameo role in his 1987 video, 'Never Let Me Down', directed by Jean-Baptiste Mondino.

In its brash humour and dreamlike fantasy, Pop art, as is widely accepted, was the heir of Dada and Surrealism. But by embracing commercial popular culture, Pop ended the oppositional avant-garde tradition that had been born with Romanticism. The momentum of new art styles immediately slowed after Pop and soon stopped altogether. No one style has dominated any period since. Thus Bowie, with his protean multiplicity of styles, must be acknowledged as having taken the next important step in the fine arts after Warhol. He remains Warhol's true successor. It is indisputable that Bowie, through his prolific work in the 1970s, was one of the principal creators of performance art, which would flood the cultural scene in the 1980s and '90s. Another seminal figure in that movement, Eleanor Antin, who emerged from American radical theatre and conceptual art after Fluxus, boldly declared Bowie 'one of my favorite artists' in 1973, when he was still being dismissed by many critics as a flashy fad. She explicitly paralleled his creation of volatile, autonomous cross-dressing characters to her own (such as a bearded ballerina or a melancholy vagrant king modelled on Charles I). 'Something is in the air', Antin said. 'Maybe it's in the stars'.[23]

←↑ **[52] OPPOSITE AND ABOVE** ● Cobweb bodysuit, 1973 ●
Designed by Natasha Korniloff for The 1980 Floor Show ●
THE DAVID BOWIE ARCHIVE

What Bowie and Antin were separately formulating was a theory of gender as representation or performance, antecedents for which can be found in Shakespeare's plays, where theatre becomes a master metaphor for life. Role-playing as constitutive of identity had been a basic premise of social psychology since the 1920s and had been most fully analysed in the Canadian-American sociologist Erving Goffman's highly influential 1959 book, *The Presentation of Self in Everyday Life*, which applied theatre metaphors of acting, costume, props, script, setting and stage to social behaviour. (Goffman's theory of the performative self was a primary source for Michel Foucault, to whom these ideas are often incorrectly attributed.) Gender roles were in flux from the mid-1960s well into the '70s due to a convergence of dissident energies from the reawakened women's movement in the US and from a pop culture revolution that had started even earlier in England. The unisex crusade of the 1960s was born in mod London and spread to the world – cropped haircuts, pinstriped trousers and sailors' pea coats for urchin girls; crimson satin, purple velvet and flouncy Tom Jones shirts for peacock boys.

But transsexual impersonation of the kind undertaken by David Bowie and Eleanor Antin was something new and different – or rather something as old as Teiresias, the shaman and prophet who crossed into forbidden sexual terrain. Drag was a familiar quantity in British music hall, with its rambunctiously outspoken 'pantomime dame', whose roots were in the rigidly conformist Victorian era and who begot the immensely popular entertainer Danny La Rue. From the 1920s on in Britain, Germany and the US, gay nightclubs featured drag queens doing campy parodies of glamorous Hollywood stars or lip-syncing to rousing cult classic songs. (By Bowie's formative years, the international drag anthem was Shirley Bassey's incendiary 'Goldfinger', perhaps the most terrifying manifestation of ruthless star power ever recorded.) Bowie never had a triumphalist view of sexual liberation or gender games. He told an American magazine in 2000 (in response to a question about the song 'Boys Keep Swinging'), 'I do not feel that there is anything remotely glorious about being either male or female.'[24] On the contrary, he had always systematically experimented with disorienting suspensions of gender, as in his ode to the 'Homo Superior', 'Oh! You Pretty Things' (on *Hunky Dory*), where sexually ambiguous boys and girls have shifted into an indeterminate 'thing' state, like works of art.

Bowie's shocking proclamation of his gayness to *Melody Maker* in 1972 was unprecedented for a major star at the height of his fame. It was a bold and even reckless career gamble. But the overall pattern of Bowie's life has been bisexual, something paradoxically far more difficult for many gay activists to accept, then and now. His open marriage to the equally bisexual Angie Barnett (another of his American alliances) went further toward bohemianism than did the communal '60s hippie ménage typified by the Mamas & the Papas in Charlotte Amalie and Laurel Canyon. His loquacious wife, with her brazen verve, encouraged his androgyny and helped costume it, notably apropos his 'man-dresses'.

Yet despite his pioneering stand, Bowie was on a trajectory diverging from that of both feminism and the gay liberation movement, which sprang up after the 1969 riots at New York's Stonewall Inn. Although black and Latino drag queens had been central in that first resistance to a routine police raid, the drag queen soon became persona non grata to gay men who wanted to distance themselves from the age-old imputation of effeminacy. Similarly, the women's movement was hostile to drag queens for their supposed 'mockery' of women. The flaming lipstick and rouge of glam rock flouted feminists' mass flight from make-up: cosmetics were among the accoutrements of female oppression flung into a 'Freedom Trash Can' on the boardwalk at the famous feminist protest at the Miss America pageant in Atlantic City in 1968. Bowie's orientation toward fashion, glamour and Hollywood went completely against the feminist grain in the 1970s, when identity politics made a highly ideological landfall in academe. Although 'lipstick lesbians' emerged in San Francisco in the late 1980s, the cult of beauty would not be restored to feminism until Madonna led the way in 1990 with her 'Vogue' video glamorizing high fashion and Hollywood love goddesses.

Just as Bowie was debuting Ziggy Stardust, furthermore, gay men were heading in a macho direction – first with San Francisco's Castro Street 'hippie clone' look of beards, T-shirts and tight hip-hugger jeans and later with New York's 'Christopher Street clone' uniform of thick moustaches, flannel lumberjack shirts, riveted farm jeans and work boots. The gay stereotypes were already fixed by the 1977 debut of the Village People, a comedic novelty band that won surprising mainstream acceptance. The icon-maker of that period was Tom of Finland, whose ebullient beefcake drawings of gigantically endowed, black-leather-clad orgiasts shaped the sadomasochistic urban underground documented by Robert Mapplethorpe's photographs. Bowie's first concession to this trend was the cover of "*Heroes*" (1977, pl.140), where he wears a soft, chicly continental black leather jacket, offset by the angular hand gestures of an avant-garde dancer. The pose combines Nijinsky's stylized imitation of Greek vase-painting with the stigmata scene in *Un Chien Andalou*.

After his half dozen years of uneven success on the London music scene, Bowie's artistic persona suddenly coalesced in the early 1970s at the climax of the sexual revolution. The idealism of the '60s, stoked by peaceable, communal, giddy-making marijuana, had drifted and stalled. Now dawned the cynical disillusion of the '70s, symbolized by nervous, ego-inflating, jealously secreted cocaine. Spontaneous romantic romps in the sunny or soggy meadows at Woodstock would yield to predatory stalking and anonymous pickups in murky, mobbed, deafening disco clubs or barricaded elite venues like Studio 54. Bowie's archly knowing and seductively manipulative Ziggy Stardust sprang into being at the invisible transition into this exciting but mechanically hedonistic sexual landscape.

Although himself a hyperactive athlete of the new libertinism, Bowe never viewed sex as salvation. In his classic work, identity is a series of gestures or poses. Sex is represented as a theatrical entry into another dimension, parallel to but not coexistent with social reality. Like Wilde, Bowie made sex a medium for a sharpening of self-consciousness rather than its Dionysian obliteration. The megalomania and delusionalism of Ziggy Stardust marked the start of the long and confused period of gender relations that we still inhabit. The fall of the old taboos has not enhanced eroticism but perhaps done the opposite. Women have gained widespread career status, and homophobia has receded, but divorce has soared, and the sexes still collide in bitter public recriminations. The evident progress in sexual freedom and tolerance in the secular West – given that it is hemmed in by populous conservative cultures that consider it decadent – might be just as evanescent as it was during the Roman Empire.

Bowie's darker intimations about the sexual and cultural revolution were signalled in his background vocal for Mott the Hoople's 'All the Young Dudes' (1972), which he wrote for the group when they seemed to be disbanding. The song, with its spunky androgynous misfits ('he dresses like a queen but he can kick like a mule'), was widely interpreted as a celebration of the glam rock insurgency, but Bowie warned that it was 'no hymn to the youth' but 'completely the opposite', a prelude to 'the end of the Earth'.[25] That storm clouds were already gathering over the defiant new dandies can be sensed in the song's dirge-like foreboding, nowhere clearer than in the unforgettable refrain, 'All the young dudes carry the news': the smoothly harmonizing Bowie breaks 'news' into two syllables, a rupture that sounds like a sob (boo-hoo). It was oracular prescience: the apocalypse came a decade later as the plague of AIDS, which decimated an entire generation of gifted young writers, artists, musicians and fashion stylists.

The Aeolian lyre, a harp hanging in the wind, was a cardinal metaphor for the Romantic poet, passively played upon by the forces of nature. During his supreme decade of the 1970s, David Bowie too was an Aeolian lyre, with the totality of the fine and popular arts of the time playing through him. Even when Bowie at his most alienated sings in a dissonant, jagged, splintered or wandering way (partly drawing from his early history as a saxophone player), there is always a high emotional charge to his work. Here is his salient distinction from the postmodernist artists and theorists of the 1980s with their ironic 'appropriations' and derivative pastiches. Bowie's emotional expressiveness, heard at its height in songs like 'Look Back in Anger' (whose artist's garret video adapts Wilde's *The Picture of Dorian Gray*), would help trigger the foppish New Romantic movement in British music of the late 1970s and '80s that produced Duran Duran, Boy George of Culture Club and eventually Depeche Mode.

Bowie's empathic virtuosity is on magnificent display in the gospel-inflected 'Fascination', which he wrote with Luther Vandross in Philadelphia for *Young Americans*. It is a song so passionate, powerful and grand that it can be understood as Bowie's artistic manifesto, addressed to no one but himself. 'I've got to use her': if she is a drug, then it is merely a coin of passage to his inner realm. The song describes his violent seizure by and enamoured fascination with his own aspiring, gender-conflating mind. He is his own Muse. 'Can a heartbeat / Live in the fever/ Raging inside of me?' Is there room for personal love or even life itself for the artist driven by uncontrollable flashes of inspiration? Bowie's mesmerizing theatre of costume, music and dance is animated by mercurial yet profound emotion – the universal language that transcends gender.

↑→ **[55] ABOVE AND OPPOSITE** ● 'Angel of Death' red
vinyl costume, 1973 ● Designed by Freddie Burretti
for The 1980 Floor Show ● THE DAVID BOWIE ARCHIVE

↓ **[56] OVERLEAF** ● David Bowie and Marianne Faithfull
on stage during The 1980 Floor Show, 1973 ● Photograph
by Mick Rock

JON SAVAGE

OH! YOU

PRETTY
THINGS

[BURROUGHS] The weapon of the Wild Boys is a bowie knife, an 18-inch bowie knife, did you know that?

[BOWIE] An 18-inch bowie knife ... you don't do things by halves, do you? No, I didn't know that was their weapon. The name Bowie just appealed to me when I was younger. I was into a kind of heavy philosophy thing when I was 16 years old, and I wanted a truism about cutting through the lies and all that.

[BURROUGHS] Well, it cuts both ways, you know, double-edged on the end.

[BOWIE] I didn't see it cutting both ways till now.

A. Craig Copetas, 'Beat Godfather Meets Glitter Mainman' (*Rolling Stone*, 28 February 1974)

←[57] OPPOSITE ● David Bowie with William S. Burroughs, February 1974 ● Photograph by Terry O'Neill with colour by David Bowie ● THE DAVID BOWIE ARCHIVE

On 28 February 1974, *Rolling Stone* published a remarkable encounter between David Bowie and William S. Burroughs (pl.57). Entitled 'Beat Godfather Meets Glitter Mainman', the event had been hosted in November 1973 by the American journalist A. Craig Copetas, who hoped to 'develop a new interview style'. As published it took the form of a Q & A between the writer and the musician that, in retrospect, was an inspired piece of positioning for both parties.

David Bowie was then at the zenith of his pop star cycle. Five days before the cover date, Bowie's latest single, 'Rebel Rebel', entered the British charts, where it would peak at number five. It's a powerful rocker – built around an irresistible riff – that is aimed directly at his audience: 'You've got your mother in a whirl cause she's/ Not sure if you're a boy or a girl/ Hey babe, your hair's alright/ Hey babe let's stay out tonight/ You like me and I like it all/ We like dancing and we look divine'.

With its teen address, deep androgyny and dancehall imperative, 'Rebel Rebel' was very much in a line with previous Bowie hits like 'John, I'm Only Dancing' and 'The Jean Genie'. But although nobody knew it at the time, it would be the last in that sequence. For Bowie wasn't a traditional pop star, happy to be known for one sound or one idea and then be quickly discarded by a fickle public. That was the Ziggy Stardust storyline and he was determined to avoid the fate of his fictional *alter ego*.

Late 1973 saw Bowie at a particular crossroads. Stardom had come hard and fast, after a long apprenticeship. 1972 had been his breakthrough year, with three hit singles and an extraordinarily successful album – *The Rise and Fall of Ziggy Stardust and the Spiders from Mars*. His success pulled into the charts previous albums like *Hunky Dory*, *Space Oddity* and *The Man Who Sold the World* as new fans delved into his past. He became a kind of impresario, producing hit records for Lou Reed ('Walk on the Wild Side') and Mott the Hoople ('All the Young Dudes') and promoting the most feral rock group then in existence, Iggy and the Stooges.

Ziggymania – as it was coined – had begun, but this was something more than stardom. David Bowie had become a phenomenon, the kind of performer that comes along just once in a generation, and pulls the whole culture along in his or her wake. His only contemporary competitors – Marc Bolan and Rod Stewart – did not have quite his allure or his cutting edge: during this period, Bowie was moving faster and further than the media which was trying to contain him.

1973 saw no let up: with the Spiders from Mars, Bowie toured America and Japan, travelling back by train through Russia and West Germany. A new album, *Aladdin Sane*, became Bowie's first number one. It coincided with the peak of fan mania during the group's 61-date UK tour (pl.58) through the spring and early summer – and, thanks to Pierre La Roche's red and blue 'lighting flash' make-up, served up the single most identifiable image of Bowie for fans and the general public alike.

Ziggy was on the point of saturation. The speed at which this was happening can be judged from an archetypal low-end teen product. *Aladdin Sane* was released in April 1973. Two months later, New English Library published the novel *Glam* by Richard Allen – the sixth book in the *Skinhead* series, the 1970s equivalent of penny dreadfuls. With a tag line that reads 'Johnny Holland fights to stay idol of a million fans', the cover shows a young man with a poorly executed red and blue flash right down his face.

In June 1973, Bowie decided to kill off Ziggy. It was an inspired piece of timing: the look, culture and attitude that he had fostered were in danger of being totally assimilated and superseded. Glam rock it was called, a combination of hard rock flash, often absurd silver costumes and an attempted, androgynous glamour. By the middle of 1973, the purity and power of Bowie's initial breakthrough had become dulled by imitation and repetition – the full stupidity of fashion/ trend evanescence: here today, gone tomorrow. Diluted elements of his breakthrough style were all over the pop charts: Sweet, Mud, Alvin *Stardust*.

Bowie sidestepped the issue with *Pin Ups*, an exercise in creative nostalgia in which he covered hard-edged, experimental mod singles: 'Rosalyn' by the Pretty Things, 'I Wish You Would' and 'Shapes of Things' by the Yardbirds (whose lead guitarist Jeff Beck had guested at the final Ziggy show), 'I Can't Explain' and 'Anyway, Anyhow, Anywhere' by the Who. These records were, as he wrote in the sleeve notes, 'among my favourites from the "64–67" period of London'.

That was the period when Bowie was not a leader but a follower: a young man, still in his teens, trying to make his way in the music industry and struggling to find an original voice. The mid 1960s had shaped him, by instilling an idea of experimentalism, of a true modernism. By returning to the source, Bowie hoped to buy time and gather strength. By late 1973, he was not just a pop star but a culture leader, the focus for several micro-generations of fans, ranging from teens to twenty-something urban sophisticates. And he was looking to push them, and himself, forward into uncharted territory.

So the November meeting with William Burroughs was well timed. In 1973, the author was well known, but not the cult he would later become. He was near the end of his time in London, where he had lived since 1968, and his burst of early 1960s crea- tivity – brought on by the discovery of the cut-up technique – had slowed down somewhat. However in 1971 he published *The Wild Boys: A Book of the Dead*, a nightmarish vision of a future (dated 1988) overrun by 'adolescent guerilla armies of specialized humanoids'.

Bowie later stated that he got 'the shape and the look of what Ziggy and the Spiders were going to become' from *The Wild Boys* and Stanley Kubrick's 1971 film version of Anthony Burgess' novel *A Clockwork Orange* (1962): 'They were both powerful pieces of work, especially the marauding boy gangs of Burroughs' Wild Boys with their bowie knives. I got straight on to that. I read everything into everything. Everything had to be infinitely symbolic.'

The encounter went well: as Copetas wrote, 'there was immediate liking and respect between the two'. Both parties were equally aware of what they had to offer each other. For Burroughs, who had been publishing ground-breaking books for twenty years without much appreciable financial return, it was the association with fame and the music industry, as well as the possible benefits: a wider reader- ship, possible film hook-ups and more money.

Burroughs had already had a brush with pop: he met Paul McCartney several times in late 1965 and early 1966 – having set up a tape studio with Ian Sommerville in McCartney's Montagu Square flat – and had been rewarded with a cameo portrait on the cover of *Sgt. Pepper's Lonely Hearts Club Band*. He was an under- ground press staple and a counter-cultural influence, not the least in the coinage of group names like the Insect Trust and then current hot favourites Steely Dan.

Bowie's needs were less obvious, but nonetheless urgent. Searching for an exit from conventional pop stardom, he needed another way of working and a different kind of public persona. Literary cachet offered the chance of a deeper, wider and more permanent cultural relevance, while Burroughs in particular had an impeccable avant-garde reputation and an image that was at once forbidding and forbidden, remote and culturally potent.

Most of all, Burroughs had a technique that would enable Bowie to retool his entire method of writing lyr- ics and making music (pl.65). During the early 1960s, Burroughs and his colleague, the painter and writer Brion Gysin, had developed the cut-up as a method of visual and verbal reassembly that was equally applica- ble to painting, montaged artworks, calligraphy, tape manipulation and the word. It offered, in fact, a whole new way of seeing.

The cut-up had originated when Gysin sliced through a pile of newspapers with his Stanley knife while cutting mounts for his latest pictures. He reshuffled the shredded newsprint and was fasci- nated by the way the chopped pictures and words created a new narrative. When Burroughs saw the results a few days later, he realized that this was not just a new working tool – one that was reminiscent of some Dada experiments – but a different way of processing and interpreting time.

As Burroughs observed in his essay 'The Cut-Up Method of Brion Gysin',

cut-ups are for everyone. Anybody can make cut-ups. It is experimental in the sense of being *something to do*. Right here right now ... Cutting and rearranging a page of written words introduces a new dimension into writing enabling the writer to turn images in cinematic variations. Images shift sense under the scis- sors smell images to sound sight to sound sound to kinesthetic.

↑ [58] ABOVE ● David Bowie and Mick Ronson on stage during
the Ziggy Stardust tour, 1972 ● Photograph by Mick Rock

What attracted many young people in the 1960s and '70s to the cut-up was the way in which it enabled the user to process and reprogramme the increasing volume of sheer data – the proliferation of media, newsprint and the like during those years – and the way in which it delivered a prose style that encoded this acceleration of time. The cut-up narrative was fast, asymmetrical, chopped in logic and, like a Picasso painting, it was a jump cut in the fabric of time: it made the future present.

Bowie had long been fascinated by science fiction: the central premise of 'Five Years' – the first track on *Ziggy Stardust* – was that, in his own words, 'the world will end because of lack of natural resources'. Indeed, the bulk of the interview with Burroughs hinged on this mutual interest – ranging from discussions about the speed of life, the media-sponsored 'escalating rate of change', fractured attention spans, infrasound, black noise, Andy Warhol and Wilhelm Reich's Orgone Accumulator.

This was enough to project him forward. Having read Burroughs' cut-up novel *Nova Express* to prepare for the interview, Bowie applied the technique to the words and sound of his next album, the darkly dystopian *Diamond Dogs* – a fusion of Burroughs and George Orwell. The cut-up, as he admitted later, perfectly suited his own fragmented consciousness, and it also enabled him to cut through the tangle of expectation and image that threatened to slow him down. It sped everything up.

The meeting with Burroughs was as momentous as Craig Copetas hoped it would be. As well as enhancing the author's fame and credibility, it helped to set Bowie's trajectory for the next few years – a series of dazzling physical and artistic changes that would not slow until the early 1980s. Bowie became the pop star as harbinger of the future, at the same as he injected many of Burroughs' ideas and techniques into the mainstream of popular culture.

Within five years of Ziggy, the punks were enacting *The Wild Boys* on the streets of London, Manchester, Liverpool and other cities in Britain – as if to promote and preview an inevitable collapse of society. Many accounts of punk accentuate its social realism, but it also had a very strong science fiction element, projecting into a conceivable nightmare future. The music developed further the chopped acceleration that Bowie had previewed on *Diamond Dogs* and it continued the dystopian preoccupations of that album.

Few could have foreseen in 1974 a youth culture that took many of its cues from a figure like Burroughs, but Bowie saw it and helped to bring it about. As a charismatic star, he could pull a whole section of his audience into the future – and he could do it consciously. After all, he had been in the audience himself, as a real-time teenager, and he understood the dynamic of public performance with a clarity that very few stars have had before or since.

'You see,' he admitted to Burroughs as their conversation began to come to a close, 'trying to tart the rock business up a bit is getting nearer to what the kids themselves are like, because what I find, if you want to talk in the terms of rock, a lot depends on sensationalism and the kids are a lot more sensational than the stars themselves. The rock business is usually a pale shadow of what the kids' lives are usually like. The admiration comes from the other side.'

David Bowie saw his audience raw and close-up in 1972 and 1973 (pl.59). He knew their strengths, their weaknesses, and he relished their diversity. He knew he and they were a kind of mutation, and that empowered him to push himself and his fans as far and fast as he and they would go. He felt and hoped that they would follow him, and they did, passing through their own rites of passage: glam rockers, soul boys, punk and eventually, in 1980, the New Romantics.

Those years paralleled the rapid development in subcultural theory that, in the hands of Phil Cohen, Dick Hebdige and others, sought to define and explain the extraordinary proliferation of youth types in Britain. The process had begun way back in the 1950s with the Edwardians, the Teds, who had mixed a strong sense of style with a penchant for violence and mayhem that made them front page news. The connection was made: Youth + Strange Clothes = Trouble.

The key document was Stanley Cohen's *Folk Devils and Moral Panics* (1972), which offered a sociological and criminological analysis of the infamous mod/rocker riots of Easter 1964. In his introduction, Cohen noted that one of the 'most recurrent types' of mass-media moral panics was associated with the violent and delinquent behaviour of youth types marked out by their dress and attitude: 'the Teddy Boys, the Mods and Rockers, the Hell's Angels, the Skinheads and the Hippies'.

David Bowie had encountered almost all of these groups in the mid to late 1960s and, in some cases, tried to live out their tenets in his own life. His relationship to youth subcultures is complex and fascinating, as it shadows his development as an artist and a mass-media performer. He begins as a follower, trying things out before he begins to find his individual voice; he then becomes an outsider, as he attempts to develop that voice; when he finds it, he becomes a leader – creating youth culture in his own image.

←[59] OPPOSITE ● David Bowie and Mick Ronson on stage in Japan during the Ziggy Stardust tour, 1973 ● Photograph by Masayoshi Sukita

In June 1964, Davie Jones and the King Bees released their one and only single, 'Liza Jane'. Taken from the Slim Harpo song – 'I'm A King Bee' – covered to great effect by the Rolling Stones on their first album, the group's name attempted to slot right into the first wave of British Pop R&B then making the charts. The A-side was a reasonable R&B facsimile, written by manager Leslie Conn, while the flip, 'Louie Louie Go Home' was a Paul Revere and the Raiders song later covered by the Who.

David Jones – as he was then – was 17. He had already been involved with music for two years, joining the Kon-rads – a Shadows-type instrumental group – back in June 1962. This was a transformative period in British pop culture and the few pictures of Jones tell the story: within 18 months he has changed from a plastic rocker hairdo, all quiffed up (pl.60), to a Beatle fringe and, for the promo of 'Liza Jane', a beatnik mod – scruffy with a tab collar, just like Mick Jagger (pl.61).

As a late teen, Jones was perfectly placed to track the changes, week by week, month by month. Living at home with his parents in Bromley, suburban south-east London, meant that he was close enough to visit the city centre, but far enough away to get some perspective. For a time, he worked in an advertising agency: the classic mod locus later explored in the film of the Who's nostalgic examination of the high sixties, *Quadrophenia*.

During 1964 and 1965, David Jones bounced between a variety of musical genres, a number of different groups and an almost bewildering parade of hair and clothes styles. After the failure of 'Liza Jane', there were the Manish Boys: for this incarnation, Jones assumed the long, straight, shaggy hairstyle of the then-controversial and popular Pretty Things – and attracted some media attention of his own with his fictitious Society for the Prevention of Cruelty to Long-Haired Men.

Their only single, produced by Shel Talmy (the Kinks, the Who) was a quantum leap from 'Liza Jane': 'I Pity The Fool' was a crunchy cover of a Bobby Bland song, with an assured vocal and a fiery guitar solo from session guitarist Jimmy Page. The flip, 'Take My Tip', is the singer's first-ever recorded composition, an engaging jazz shuffle in the vein of Georgie Fame – then London's hard-core mod favourite with a number one under his belt ('Yeh Yeh') and a residency in Soho's Flamingo Club.

After the Manish Boys, there was the Lower Third, whom Jones met at the Gioconda coffee bar in Denmark Street, Soho – London's Tin Pan Alley. With Talmy, they recorded one Who/Kinks sound-alike 45, 'You've Got a Habit of Leaving' – replete with two wild, atonal guitar breaks in the vein of 'Anyway, Anyhow, Anywhere'. In the summer, Jones cut off his long hair and assumed the bouffant, French mod style; in September, he adopted the stage name of Bowie.

Bowie also appeared in a fashion shoot with Jan De Souza that September. Taken by Fiona Adams and printed in *Fabulous* magazine, the photo shows the young-looking singer cradling a violin while dressed in the latest mod gear – wide whale cords, a polo-style shirt and a short fringe cut. This was the period when Bowie became, in his own words, a 'trendy mod', and the manic London youth culture began to supply him with ideas for his own songs – material that would go deeper than anything hitherto.

In 1966, Bowie released four singles that, to varying degrees, explored his relationship to the peer subculture of the day. 'Can't Help Thinking About Me' was promoted by a Cyrus Andrews photo that presents Bowie as the young mod around town, half a boy and half a man, with a perfect haircut and a slim, highly patterned, almost Op-art tie, and the song captures that confused mixture of adolescent shyness, the desire to fit in and the need to stand out.

The second single with Bowie's new group, the Buzz, 'I Dig Everything' was another jazzy shuffle, enlivened by a Hammond organ and Latin percussion. It's a song about the possibilities and drawbacks of independent, teen London life: 'Got a backstreet room in the bad part of town and I dig everything'. The lyric takes in coded drug use ('a connection named Paul'), superficial friendships and a deep, deep loneliness: 'I've made good friends with the time-check girl on the end of the phone'.

Released at the end of the year, 'The London Boys' is Bowie's first masterpiece: an unflinching dissection of Soho's mod subculture sung in a quiet, precise tone and enhanced by a sympathetic brass arrangement. The first two verses revisit the territory of 'I Dig Everything' but the third lays it all out: 'Oh, the first time that you tried a pill/ You feel a little queasy, decidedly ill/ You're gonna be sick, but you mustn't lose faith/ To let yourself down would be a big disgrace with the London boys, with the London boys'.

The song also extends the examination of the individual/ peer relationship that Bowie had begun on 'Can't Help Thinking About Me': 'You're seventeen, but you think you've grown/ In the month you've been away from your parents' home'. In the final minute, Bowie opens up his vocal chords and delivers the pay-off: 'Now you wish you'd never left your home/ You've got what you wanted but you're on your own/ With the London boys'.

'The London Boys' was powerful and heartfelt: it also marked the moment when Bowie – after three or so years of assiduously following the trends, of trying to fit in – made the break with his peer culture and began to go his own way. An avid club-goer, he had seen the Pink Floyd, fronted by the charismatic and androgynous Syd Barrett, but decided not to join them and a whole section of the mod cult in the next youth culture blowing in from the West Coast.

In 1967, Bowie released his first, self-titled album. It's almost defiant in the way that it contains almost no trace of contemporary pop modes. Despite Bowie's deep interest in Buddhism, he had no sympathy with the hippie package: the record was a strange mixture of exaggerated, cockney vocals – inspired both by Anthony Newley and Syd Barrett – intricate arrangements and songs that constantly shifted tone and mood, from horror to farce, from Edwardiana to fairy tales and back again.

→ [60] OPPOSITE • Publicity photograph for The Kon-rads, 1963 • Photograph by Roy Ainsworth • THE DAVID BOWIE ARCHIVE

One song in particular, 'Join The Gang', tackled the day's psyche-delic culture: 'Let me introduce you to the gang/ Johnny plays the sitar, he's an existentialist/ Once he had a name, now he plays our game/ You won't feel so good now that you've joined the gang'. The jaunty piano melody includes snippets of sitar, a snatch of 'Keep on Running' and hearty raspberries during the instrumental break: 'This is what to do now that you're here/ Sit around doing nothing all together very fast'.

'It's a big illusion but at least you're in', Bowie sang, but as a teen-ager he had often felt like an outsider looking in. He would remain so for the next few years: 'I was never a flower child', he told Cameron Crowe in early 1976. 'I was always a sort of throwback to the Beat period in my early thinking. So when the hippies came along with all their funny tie-dyes and things, it all seemed naive and wrong. It didn't have a backbone.'

His first chart breakthrough turned that alienation into a timely parable. Coincidental with the first moon landings, 'Space Oddity' presented space travel not as a breakthrough for mankind but merely an expensive journey to complete isolation. As an expres-sion of Bowie's tendency towards dystopia, it was also a creative extrapolation from his state of mind: if you feel out of sync with the world, then imagining that you're a space boy or a space girl is a workable fantasy.

It wasn't quite that simple. Bowie did partake of the pervading idealism when he helped to found the Beckenham Arts Lab, a local south London experiment in audience participation and engage-ment that ran from spring 1969 until the end of the year. As well as other musicians like Marc Bolan and Tucker Zimmerman, the Buddhist monk Chime Youngdung Rinpoche and Lionel Bart, the composer of *Oliver!*, were invited to give talks and performances.

In August 1969 the Arts Lab organized a free festival in a Beckenham park: the next month, "Space Oddity" re-entered the Top 40, where it would eventually peak at number five. Bowie had become a pop star, and the brief illusion of unity and inclusiveness that had sustained the Arts Lab soon shattered. 'In those days I used to be very social and idealistic,' he told Andrew Lycett in 1971. 'But the people didn't come along to take part in any of the activities. They came along to be entertained. And that became even worse when "Space Oddity" became successful. Then they came along to see David Bowie the star. There were some good things we did though: the highlight was a beautiful free festival that we put on in Beckenham with no name groups at all and 5,000 people came along to it. It was wonderful. But I realize they wanted a dictator. They didn't want a communal life. They wanted to be organized'.

Bowie's next album, also called *David Bowie*, contained two views of the Arts Lab. 'Memory of a Free Festival' was wide-eyed and gentle: 'Oh to taste just one drop of all the ecstasy that swept that afternoon'. The song ended with a 'Hey Jude'-type fade on the lyric 'the sun machine is going down, we're going to have a party'. In contrast, the nine-minute 'Cygnet Committee' unfolds with all the force of a blast from the id, as Bowie left his group and their dreams of collective action behind.

The convoluted lyric is couched as a dialogue between the voice of the crowd and their leader, the Thinker, 'growing older and so bitter', soon to be deserted like Ziggy Stardust would be two and a half years hence: 'I gave them life, I gave them all. They drained my very soul … dry'. In Bowie's voice, counter-culture slogans like 'Kick Out the Jams' and 'Love Is All We Need' rang as hollow as he felt they did in the dog days of 1969. At the time, however, there seemed to be little alternative.

In early 1970, Bowie took what were in retrospect two crucial steps. He hired guitarist Mick Ronson, whose scalpel-sharp tone would add that rock'n'roll element that fuelled his rise to super-stardom. With Ronson, producer Tony Visconti and drummer John Cambridge, he formed his first electric group since 1966: when they played the Roundhouse in Camden in March, Bowie wore silver clothes and performed a version of 'I'm Waiting for the Man' by the Velvet Underground.

These were early signs of the glitter and the glam – androgyny as the stylistic counterpoint to hippie earthiness and earnestness. For in attendance at the Roundhouse was Bowie's contemporary, friend and rival Marc Bolan, a very early mod who had gone through a similar tour through the sixties music industry as a solo artist and with the band John's Children. Bolan contributed a guitar part to Bowie's March 1970 single, 'The Prettiest Star', but the atmosphere was tense.

Bowie's success had brought jealousy, but the tables would soon be turned. In 1970, Bolan slimmed down his band name from Tyrannosaurus Rex to T. Rex and went fully electric: in October, 'Ride a White Swan' went into the charts – the first of eight top ten hits (and four number ones) within two years. Bolan became a huge teen icon – not just a pop star but a mass-media sensation, under the brand name of T. Rexstasy – as well as the leader of a new pop generation.

Bowie's feelings about his contemporary were ambivalent: hence the parody of Bolan's trademark high warble on 'Black Country Rock'. However 1970 and early 1971 saw him strangely paralysed, unable to rise to the challenge of the new generation gap. *The Man Who Sold the World* was an introspective album that explored highly personal themes – madness, the gnostic tradition, the nature of leaders and followers – in some depth. Its qualities would reveal themselves, but it was not yet pop.

In January 1971, David Bowie turned 24. Time began to accelerate: the doldrums dispersed. During that year, he released two albums in the UK and recorded the bulk of another. He visited the US twice, signing a major deal with RCA Records and meeting such touchstones as Andy Warhol, Iggy Stooge, Moondog and the Velvet Underground without Lou Reed. He recorded and wrote singles for other artists, and he began to visualize himself into becoming something more than a pop star.

In June, Peter Noone – formerly teen star Herman, lead singer of Herman's Hermits – had a top twenty hit with 'Oh! You Pretty Things', a song that reflected Bowie's fascination with the impending apocalypse at the same time as it addressed the new generation: 'Oh you pretty things/ Don't you know you're driving your mamas and papas insane'. At the same time, the parents were warned: 'Look at your children/ See their faces in golden rays/ Don't kid yourself they belong to you/ They're the start of a coming race'.

Bowie recorded the song for his new album, *Hunky Dory*, which – released right at the end of the year – laid the foundations for his impending breakthrough. It's a world away from the dense, often confused sound of *The Man Who Sold the World*: a collection of mainly light and sparsely arranged songs that sounded spontaneous, while paying homage to existing heroes – Andy Warhol, Bob Dylan, the Velvet Underground – in a way that said, 'I've assimilated the lessons: I'm next!'

'Queen Bitch' was the key: a hard rocker with lyrics and a scenario that plugged directly into the gay subculture. Mick Ronson's guitar provided the edge of instability and excitement that would mark this period of Bowie's music and a small note on the reverse sleeve gave the context: '(Some V.U, White Light Returned With Thanks)'. (For more, including a scorching version of 'White Light, White Heat', listen to the BBC Radio sessions from late 1971 and early 1972 on the *Bowie at the Beeb* album.)

1971 was the year that Andy Warhol and his world became a feature within British pop culture. The first three Velvet Underground albums were reissued, to more acclaim and sales than they had had the first time around. In August Warhol's *Pork* – a slice of his world, edited down into a play from 200 hours of his telephone conversations – opened at the Roundhouse to tabloid outrage. Several of the cast would become integral to Bowie in his pop-star phase.

In late 1971 Bowie was busy working the media, carefully positioning himself in contrast to the pop culture of the day. 'I feel we're all in a fucking dead industry that really relates to nothing anymore,' he told *Cream* magazine. 'The most important person in Europe and England today is Marc Bolan, not because of what he says but because he is the first person who has latched onto the energy of the young once again. He has got his dictatorships fixed up. He's kind of neuter and he has that star quality. That is very important. Marc Bolan is the new angry young man. Marc Bolan has that angry young life. You can quote me on that. I also like Iggy Stooge and the Flaming Groovies. Rock should tart itself up a bit more, you know. People are scared of prostitution. There should be some real unabashed prostitution in this business.'

How to cut through the half-baked products of a dead industry? In January 1972, Bowie was interviewed by Michael Watts of the *Melody Maker*, who wrote:

> David's present image is to come on like a swishy queen, a gorgeously effeminate boy. He's as camp as a row of tents, with his limp hand and trolling vocabulary. 'I'm gay,' he says, 'and always have been, even when I was David Jones.' But there's a sly jollity about how he says it, a secret smile at the corners of his mouth.

The addition of an electric hard-rock sound and a New York attitude – gay confrontation, slice-of-life lyrics and a most un-English directness – to Bowie's existing preoccupations (alienation, science fiction, the nature of crowds) pushed him further and faster than he could have imagined. As his star rose, Marc Bolan's began to falter, but Bowie's was a more complex package – one that appealed not just to the teeny-boppers, but a much wider subcultural constituency.

Bowie spoke to the weirdos, the outsiders, and those teens and post-teens up for a bit of excitement. In May 1973, Bowie reflected on how he had 'created a somewhat strange audience – but it's also full of little Noddy Holders, and little Iggy Pops. I know we used to attract a lot of "queens" at one stage but then other factions of people crept in. Now you can't tell. They're all there for some reason. And we get young people. Those lovely young people. And they have to be considered very seriously'.

On 12 May 1973, Bowie and the Spiders from Mars played at Earls Court, a cavernous Deco venue in west London, and *Cream* sent along a writer and photographer to record the event. Julie Welch described the audience as 'small scurrying groups of people, most the results of post-war copulations'. She noted 'a blue sea of denim, the beautiful young, the comic young, girls in their ballet shoes, here and there the butterfly element (men like Bowie) in gold chains and shattered dresses'.

Mick Gold's photos tell another story. There are the teens with their bipperty-bopperty hats, but there are also well-dressed and foppish young men in jackets, bow ties and white gloves; a perfectly dressed rocker with sprayed-on, studded jeans, a sleeveless T-shirt, a studded wristband and long quiffed hair reaching his shoulders (pl.63). His partner is dressed up in thirties/forties finery, with a long patterned dress, bangles, a cigarillo and a flower behind her ear. Another couple essay the French existentialist look, with belted white coats and an intense air (pl.64).

This is not just an audience, but a culture. The early 1970s were a retro time, when fashions from the twenties, thirties and forties were easily available in charity shops and market stalls and were plundered for contemporary looks. Bowie's constant reinvention – the idea that the world is a constantly revolving stage – and his powerful aura (Welch again: 'he was utilizing his most splendid gift, his sense of largeness and glory') empowered his audience to attempt the same on the streets of cities around the UK, in a living cut-up (pl.62).

After the demise of the Spiders, Bowie lost some of the closeness that he had had with his audience. Foreign tours, elaborate concepts and the deleterious effects of super-stardom meant that he would no longer see the whites of their eyes and hear the beating of their hearts in quite the same way. In this, 'Rebel Rebel' reads like the ending of the phase that had begun with 'Oh! You Pretty Things'.

Bowie's interview with William Burroughs came at the end of his intimate pop star phase. It projected him into a new set of engagements that saw him become more disengaged, more abstracted – indeed more alien: a trajectory enshrined on film by Nicolas Roeg in *The Man Who Fell to Earth*. This was deliberate: Bowie had become a leader but, as he had written in 'Cygnet Committee' and 'Ziggy Stardust', the leader always gets deserted by his followers. The trick was to withdraw before they deserted you.

↖ [62] TOP LEFT, ↑ [63] ABOVE AND ← [64] LEFT ◦
David Bowie fans outside Earls Court during
the Aladdin Sane tour, 12 May 1973 ◦
Photographs by Mick Gold

Bowie's increasingly remote persona and ever more radical image/sound changes didn't prevent the public from buying his records: although his singles sales dropped from the 1972–3 peak, his albums would all make the top five until the end of the decade. Musically, his hardcore fans would follow him wherever he directed: into science fiction dystopias, contemporary American soul music, icy motorik and the ambient instrumentals of *Low* and *"Heroes"*.

His subcultural influence would continue to be strong: in the Soul Boys of 1975 and 1976, with their Jerome Newton hairdos and plastic sandals, and the bizarre, cartoon-like punks that began to emerge from London's outer suburbs in 1976. The most visible of these were given a group name, the Bromley Contingent, and they showed the depth of Bowie's influence in their dress and demeanour.

In the mid-1970s, Siouxsie Sioux lived in Bromley: like Bowie had, she made trips up to town, in her case to the Biba building in Kensington High Street.

I was besotted with Art Deco, Art Nouveau. That was my escape from humdrum. I think Bowie and Roxy [Music] had a big part in that. Whoever latched on to them then were that way inclined. The whole thing, not just the music. It aroused something that was dormant, that was causing frustration.

Her friend Steve Severin also lived in Bromley:

Something had to happen. Mainly searching for people with shared interests. I think it was all sparked by Bowie. A lot of the people at the concerts didn't look as if they could understand what he was about. Following Bowie closely led you to all sorts of other things, to Burroughs and Lou Reed and Iggy Pop. There was a whole world behind it, rather than just someone else with a band.

In 1976, the two friends formed one of the first punk bands, Siouxsie and the Banshees. They were only among the most obvious examples of just how deep Bowie's influence had been on this generation, just old enough to be bowled over by his 1972 breakthrough. They were attracted, as were many others, by the idea that Bowie was an artist and that pop culture was a place to be experimental and confrontational, a place where outsiders could gain visibility and take their revenge.

David Bowie turned 30 in January 1977. Just as his children flooded the media with angry noises and blank poses – in an echo of *Diamond Dogs* and the Stooges' *Raw Power* – he was into his next phase with *Low*, an album of two faces: one side of short, clipped songs with cut-up music and cut-up lyrics, and another of longer, atmospheric synthesizer instrumentals. His second album of the year, *"Heroes"*, fleshed out this dichotomy to even greater effect.

In doing so, Bowie helped to set the electronic style that took over once punk was exhausted: the wave of synthesizer groups, like the Human League, that became very successful in the early 1980s. Once again, he seemed to be supernaturally in touch with future trends – just like the Beatles had been in the 1960s. But he was no longer involved intimately with youth subcultures, nor did his continued relevance depend on this closeness.

Bowie tackled this directly in a track from the 1980 album *Scary Monsters … and Super Creeps*. 'Teenage Wildlife' typifies 'one of the new wave boys/ Same old thing in brand new drag/ Comes sweeping into view, oh ho ho ho ho ho/ As ugly as a teenage millionaire/ Pretending it's a whizz kid world'. Even in his thirties, Bowie continued to cleave to his individualism, his outsider status: 'But they move in numbers and they've got me in a corner/ I feel like a group of one, no-no/ They can't do this to me/ I'm not some piece of teenage wildlife'.

The hit single from the album was 'Ashes to Ashes', a number one record that lyrically appeared to close the cycle that had begun with 'Space Oddity', 11 years before. Shot by David Mallett, the groundbreaking video featured Bowie in Pierrot costume walking along a beach with the most florid examples of the latest youth subculture that he had inspired: the New Romantics, who fused several periods of Bowie – *Aladdin Sane*, *Station to Station*, and *Low* – all at once.

In the same year, Bowie filmed a live appearance for the West German film *Christiane F. – Wir Kinder vom Bahnhof Zoo*, the lightly fictionalized story of a teenage drug addict in Berlin. Bowie was presented at the centre of German youth culture, while the city of Berlin was re-envisioned by the use of a soundtrack that included the ambient instrumentals from *Low* and *"Heroes"*. It was the most popular German film of 1981.

Bowie didn't release a new record for another couple of years, while he freed himself from his contractual obligations to RCA Records and former manager Tony Defries. He returned in April 1983 with the number one single and album *Let's Dance* – a strong mixture of blues-rock guitar and contemporary dance music promoted by the freshly ubiquitous medium of the pop promo. In the videos for the record's singles, Bowie was tanned, healthy, seemingly at peace with his demons.

Let's Dance has been retrospectively assessed in terms of its extraordinary success, but at the time there was no guarantee that it would work. It may well mark the 'normalization' of David Bowie, but there is another side to the story. One forgotten highlight of the album is a brief, melodic love song, 'Without You', sung tenderly and without irony. Like the album as a whole it contains no youth culture references, and indeed it reveals Bowie to be freed from these constraints, freed to be what he is: an individual and an adult.

→ **[65] OPPOSITE** • Cut-up lyrics by David Bowie for 'Blackout' from *"Heroes"*, 1977 • THE DAVID BOWIE ARCHIVE

me with your smile

cut hands

wine from your

walk on by

I am

I think i'll

believe but it's all you left.

cage you are

in words wh

I cannot not

to the

Me Black Out

for you

changing hearts

you left

it's only make

on my hands

life stands so still

object always out of

YOU'RE TOO OLD TO LOSE IT

TOO YOUNG TO CHOOSE IT

VICTORIA BROACKES

PUTTING OUT FIRE WITH GASOLINE: DESIGNING DAVID BOWIE

David Bowie has created not only some of the most interesting and influential music of the twentieth century, but also produced ground-breaking and iconic designs for costumes, album covers, stage sets and videos. His abilities as an artist and designer, along with his preference for directing all aspects of his image and exceptional career, make him a unique subject; and his complex and complete orchestration and involvement with the material culture of being a 'pop star' present rich opportunities for critical interpretation.

By embracing Marshall McLuhan's notion that 'the medium is the message' throughout his long career, Bowie actively participated in producing and co-producing his music, as well as playing a part in the design of his album covers, conceptualizing his music videos and designing his tours – even the merchandise to go with them. One of his great assets as an artist has been his ability to establish and develop relationships with talented collaborators – a talent that seems linked to his ability to predict and develop popular trends.

As a teenager, Bowie chose to study art at Bromley Technical High School (from September 1958 to July 1963, leaving with an A-level in art and O-levels in English and Engineering Drawing), where he was taught by Owen Frampton, Peter Frampton's father.[1] In July 1963 he left school a week before the end of term to take up a position as a trainee commercial artist at the New Bond Street offices of Nevin D. Hirst Advertising.[2] In Michael Apted's documentary film *Inspirations* (1997), Bowie recalls that the job appeared promising to a teenager with a sharp interest in style and image: 'Being very much a child and product of the early sixties, it seemed to me to be terribly exciting and maybe kind of glamorous to be a commercial artist ... At the time I thought that's Madison Avenue, you know, that's advertising. That's the place to be.'[3]

The reality was more disappointing. 'It was diabolical,' Bowie said of the job in a 1972 interview. 'I never realized being an artist meant buckling under so much.'[4] Although he found it creatively frustrating to be a commercial artist, he put many of the skills that he learned at the firm to use in promoting and developing his budding musical career. One of Bowie's first bandmates, David Hadfield, who played alongside him in the Kon-rads, said: ' [He] had thousands of [ideas], a new one every day – that we should change the spelling of our name, or our image, or our clothes, or all the songs in our repertoire. He also came up with lots of black-and-white sketches of potential advertising campaigns for the band'.[5]

In addition to his investment in all artistic aspects of his production, Bowie chooses collaborators with great care, sourcing them personally and often unconventionally. Having fully researched those with talent that he wishes to work with, he gives them creative scope to work at what he chose them to do. Adrian Belew, poached from Frank Zappa to join Bowie's band in 1978, recalls:

It was like two different worlds, Frank's music was completely created by him and the idea was for you to play it consistently and correctly. The idea was not to add something to it. The idea was to play it right, or sing it right. With Bowie, the idea was entirely different. He gave me full rein to be his guitarist and to add a lot of colours and sounds.[6]

Bowie is adept at bringing out the best in his collaborators within his chosen framework, before he decides what makes the final cut. In his book about Bowie, Nicholas Pegg highlights this composition method:

[Bowie] has systematically surrounded himself with colleagues who exert conflicting gravitational pulls on his own strongly vaudevillian instincts. Figures like Iggy Pop, Pete Townshend and Tin Machine's Sales Brothers have popped up over the years to inject into Bowie's work the kind of authentic rock'n'roll street cred he has often craved, while the likes of Eno, Fripp and Gabrels have empowered his avant-garde ambitions. Bowie is blessed with the rare ability to synthesize what he wants from two necessarily confrontational approaches; it is his particular triumph that he is neither Lou Reed nor John Cale, but a bit of both.[7]

To appropriate Bowie's lyrics for the song 'Fame' – 'what you need you have to borrow'. This atypical skill extends to Bowie's visual art collaborations, and has been key in the development of his creative work.

Bowie's unique understanding of his audience and his anticipation of future trends in a variety of media distinguish him from the artists who are either unconscious of, or unconcerned by, their audience's perception of their work. As he sings in 'Ashes to Ashes', Bowie 'never did anything out of the blue'. He is not only aware of what he intends, but also conscious of what is being received; almost certainly his early struggles to find success in the 1960s played a role in honing his abilities to understand his public. In 1974 he explained that he wanted his music to be 'three-dimensional ... a song has to take on character, shape, body and influence people to the extent that they use it for their own devices. It must affect them not just as a song, but as a lifestyle.'[8] Describing his songs as often being 'very illustrative and picturesque', Bowie continued the theme in the BBC documentary 'Cracked Actor', first shown in January 1975: 'I felt [my material] was more three-dimensional. I wanted to give it dimension.'[9] Although musical experimentation and expression is the bedrock of his career, sound is only one dimension of Bowie's complete creative vision – as the title of his 1977 song (and 1990 world tour) 'Sound and Vision' suggests.

Indeed, Bowie seems to have a rare intuition when it comes to understanding – and leading – his fans. He has consistently exhibited an uncanny ability to anticipate the next pop/cultural movement, be it glam rock, electronic music, music videos or internet distribution. Interviewed for the *New York Times* in 2002, he accurately anticipated the impact the internet would have on the music industry in the next decade:

> Music itself is going to become like running water or electricity ... You'd better be prepared for doing a lot of touring because that's really the only unique situation that's going to be left. It's terribly exciting. But on the other hand it doesn't matter if you think it's exciting or not; it's what's going to happen.[10]

This shrewdness might suggest something at odds with traditional notions of the artist (though not in the postmodern period, the values of which it seems to enshrine perfectly), but coupled with Bowie's constant quest for new inspiration and ideas, his attention to design detail, his openness to taking creative risks and his refusal to settle for a winning formula or take an easy option, this prescience has earned him his status as one of the most influential cultural figures of the late twentieth century.

Jonathan Barnbrook, the graphic designer Bowie chose to collaborate with on the cover designs of *Heathen* and *Reality* in the early 2000s, affirms that 'David Bowie understands the power of the visual'.[11] This essay will explore how Bowie chose to 'design' his career by utilizing the skills he learned and honed during his childhood and early career. Whether designing album art, staging a concert tour or making a video, Bowie's dynamic approach to the visual material associated with his music has resulted in an exceptional portfolio; investigating how he directed its creation sheds light on his wider work.

THE RISE AND FALL OF ZIGGY STARDUST AND THE SPIDERS FROM MARS

The Rise and Fall of Ziggy Stardust and the Spiders from Mars was released on 6 June 1972 (pl.70). Widely regarded as Bowie's breakthrough album, it tells the story of the otherworldly Ziggy Stardust and his rise to fame. Ziggy is the human manifestation of an alien being who unexpectedly alights upon a doomed earth some time in the not so distant future. He attempts to deliver a message of hope to the human species headed for extinction, and is inevitably destroyed by his own success and excessive lifestyle. It was this narrative-driven, theatrical and visually intriguing album that would serve to set Bowie apart from the other musicians of his day. What is more, the character of Ziggy – a persona he adopted both on and off stage – won more notoriety than any other Bowie devised throughout his career. So strong was his image that people – and even Bowie himself – came to conflate Ziggy's identity with Bowie's own (pl.116).

The Ziggy 'look' centred around an unforgettable haircut. While at the turn of the decade Bowie's hair had been long and blond, by 1972 it underwent a dramatic transformation, rendering him virtually unrecognizable. This was not a unique move, as Bill Janowitz noted in his book about the Rolling Stones: 'The English music press in particular (the weeklies, anyway) has always interpreted new hairstyles as indications of exciting new musical forms.'[12] In January 1972, Bowie's wife at the time, Angie, introduced him to Suzi Fussey, who worked as a hairdresser at the Evelyn Page salon in Beckenham. He asked her to create a new cut to his design, which was based on a striking selection of photographs from various magazines, including shots of a young female model with vivid, cropped red hair, taken by photographer Alex Chatelain for *Vogue* Paris (pl.67), and the latest designs by Japanese designer Kansai Yamamoto, as shown in British *Vogue* and *Harpers & Queen*.[13] Not only was the cut itself unusual, reminiscent of the kabuki wigs in the Yamamoto feature (pl.68), Bowie soon after also decided to dye his hair red, in keeping with the Chatelain photograph. First, Fussey used a combination of Schwarzkopf hair dye (in the shade Georgette 256/Cherry Red) and peroxide to create a red-orange colour. She then applied copious amounts of setting lotion 'to style it into a mullet'.[14] Unlike any other seen on London's streets, this hairstyle served the important function of rendering Bowie instantly recognizable (pl.71).

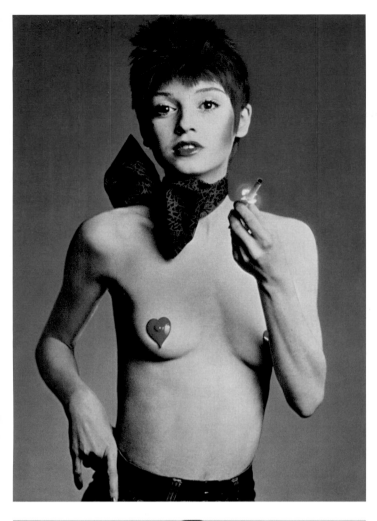

TIME: MAY 1971.
PLACE: KINGS ROAD, LONDON.
VENUE: THE FIRST LONDON COLL
OF THE BRILLIANT
YOUNG JAPANESE DESIGNER,
KANSAI YAMAMOTO.

It's an incredibly hot night.
For over an hour designers,
fashion pundits, photographers
and ladies and gentlemen of
the press have been packing the
into cramped, serried rows
of black plastic seats.
The room is almost pitchblack,
lit by a few spotlights; it's very
crowded, very hot and very late
Suddenly, at 11.23 pm precisely
the house lights go down,
and a tremendous discord of wi
upbeat Japanese music
heralds the start of
the Show of the Year.
It was a spectacular coup de thé
Kansai's models came on moving
They leapt, ran,
whirled like dervishes,
danced, flung out their arms
so that the brilliant clothes
meshed and merged into
a kaleidoscopic cartoon of color
Kansai himself, black-clothed
and masked, moved across
the stage like a Samurai warrio
tearing off layers and layers of
stripping down the beautiful,
pyramidal outer garments
right down to the vests
and body paint.
Kansai's clothes épatent les cou
stun you with their originality.
He runs his own design group in
– the Avant Garde Laboratory –
and everything, the clothes,
shoes, hair, make-up, accessori
combine to make this wildly the
totally spectacular look.
But his true originality lies deep
– Kansai is not so much a design
of clothes as an architect.
His clothes are built
round the body in layers,
wrapped round, looped and tied,
put on like a suit
of medieval armour
– sleeve-pieces, breast-pieces,
skirt waistcoat in two parts

It's a whole new concept of dres
and it's for this reason that we b
Kansai Yamamoto will have a ma
impact on the world of fashion.
All the clothes shown
are available from Boston 151,
151 Fulham Road, SW3.
Hair and make-up by
Sachiko Shibayama, Japan.

ON TOP is a quilted satin stripe
floor-length, with huge sleeves, ab
which opens to show
UNDERNEATH, a quilted cott
and wildly exaggerated jodhpur t
appliquéd with huge yellow satin
about £67. Fabric by K.K.Ogis
Matching boots, about £28,
and hat with visor, about £12.
ON TOP is a floor-length circular
appliquéd with Kabuki faces.
UNDERNEATH is an all-in-one
appliquéd to match the skirt, abo
together.
Boots with red wedges, about £28.
The 7ft long red wig, banded with

↖ **[67] ABOVE LEFT** • Christine Walton for *Vogue* Paris,
August 1971 • Photograph by Alex Chatelain

↑ **[68] ABOVE AND** ← **[69] LEFT** • *Harpers & Queen*,
London, July 1971 • Designs by Kansai Yamamoto.
Hair and makeup by Sachiko Shibayama

← [70] OPPOSITE • Cover artwork separations for *The Rise and Fall of Ziggy Stardust and the Spiders from Mars*, 1972 •
Designed by Terry Pastor and David Bowie • Photograph by Brian Ward • THE DAVID BOWIE ARCHIVE

↑ [71] ABOVE • Cover artwork for *The Rise and Fall of Ziggy Stardust and the Spiders from Mars*, June 1972 • Designed by
Terry Pastor and David Bowie • Photograph by Brian Ward • THE DAVID BOWIE ARCHIVE

Costumes were, of course, employed to similar effect. But while Bowie's hairstyle remained largely the same from 1972 to 1973, his stage costumes changed dramatically, becoming increasingly avant-garde as his popularity grew. His early stage wear was not heavily stylized – rather, his outfits were cobbled together from whatever was around. When success permitted him to wear specially designed pieces, he turned to his friends, designer and tailor Freddie Burretti and costumier Natasha Korniloff. Together, Bowie and Burretti developed Bowie's vision for concerts showcasing the album's material, creating costumes that drew inspiration from Stanley Kubrick's *2001: A Space Odyssey* (1968) and *A Clockwork Orange* (1972, in the UK). Both films were well known in the early 1970s and Bowie appreciated their themes as well as the costume designs, which he later described as being 'fab ... *2001* with its Courrèges-like leisure suits and *Clockwork's* droogs, dressed to kill'.[15] Ziggy's earliest stage costumes were two-piece suits designed by Bowie, the patterns cut and made up by Burretti and a neighbour, Sue Frost; the tour wardrobe was later augmented by one-piece jumpsuits, conceived and made by Burretti in various colours and materials (pls 33 and 35).

Increasingly, Bowie was in a position to commission original pieces from Kansai Yamamoto himself (pls 37–41 and 69). Describing these flamboyant costumes, he later said: ' [They were] everything that I wanted them to be and more ... heavily inspired by kabuki and samurai, they were outrageous, provocative, and unbelievably hot to wear under the lights'.[16]

By the time Ziggy and the Spiders finally retired in July 1973, Bowie's wardrobe had expanded considerably. His cosmetics kit, too, was overflowing. It is said that towards the end of his Ziggy period, Bowie needed to allow at least two hours before each performance to apply his stage make-up (pl.72). Although broadly self-taught, he had learned theatrical make-up techniques from mime artist and choreographer Lindsay Kemp, a close friend and mentor of Bowie's in the late 1960s. In January 1973, make-up artist Pierre La Roche applied the iconic 'lightning flash' make-up for Bowie's *Aladdin Sane* cover shoot (pl.45). The success of this look led to La Roche joining Bowie for the subsequent tour as his personal make-up artist.

In April 1973, Bowie also received instruction in kabuki-style makeup techniques from one of the stars of Japanese kabuki theatre, Tamasaburo, while visiting Japan.[17] As Jonathan Barnbrook notes of Bowie: 'He is always very actively looking for people he wants to work with – the right voice, the right tone that matches his work. [People who] express the same point of view to his or have a spirit that he requires in his work.'[18]

Bowie was Ziggy's originator, but he depended on many hair, costume and make-up collaborators to help him carry his look, and there can be no question that Bowie's fame and popularity during this period lay as much in his image as in his music. While the appearance of Ziggy and his Spiders may have evolved as they became increasingly successful, it was the album cover that firmly established Bowie's other-worldly alien credentials. 'Good record cover design connects with the music, connects the listener to the music and then enhances the understanding of that music,' Barnbrook says. 'And it's beyond logic, actually. It's about the spirit of the age, the spirit of the music and some unconscious understanding of what's going on there.'[19]

The photographs for the *Ziggy Stardust* cover were taken on a cold, wet night in January 1972 by Brian Ward, who had a studio on London's Heddon Street – the site of the shoot. Both the front and back cover photographs (which feature Bowie alone) were shot using Kodak Royal-X Pan black-and-white film and later colourized by Terry Pastor of Main Artery, the design studio set up by a childhood friend of Bowie's, George Underwood. Underwood, incidentally, was the one who accidentally damaged the pupil of Bowie's left eye in a fight at school, leaving it permanently dilated. Ward took 54 photographs in all.[20]

The album cover shows Bowie on a London backstreet, looking as if he had just been beamed down from another planet. While colourized blue on the cover, the suit was actually the green-and-cream outfit Bowie wore on the BBC2 programme 'The Old Grey Whistle Test' in early February 1972, and while his hair looks yellow (due to the light of a street lamp), contact sheets from the shoot show that it was medium-fair. Although Bowie had not yet morphed fully into a 'space samurai', the album's sleeve sets the mood for all his subsequent performances – 'a good record cover expresses the psychology of the music'. The wet, stormy weather lent the band an element of mystery, and Bowie's lone appearance under the prominent 'K. West' sign, which could be read as 'Quest', alludes to his alien 'mission', conjuring an otherworldly feeling that is reinforced by the colourization. The landscape and aesthetic of the cover image closely resemble the opening scenes of Michael Powell's groundbreaking and controversial film *Peeping Tom* (1960), and may owe something to this cult classic. Equal prominence is given, in visual terms, to the names David Bowie and Ziggy Stardust – helping to cement the idea that David Bowie *was* Ziggy Stardust. Bowie had not yet undergone the transformation into his fully-fledged performance persona, but in mid-January 1972, the seeds for this metamorphosis were already sown. 'The seventies began ... when this photograph was taken, and Ziggy Stardust presented himself in a very different guise to anything we'd seen in the sixties,' says musician Gary Kemp. 'And it did affect a generation.'[21]

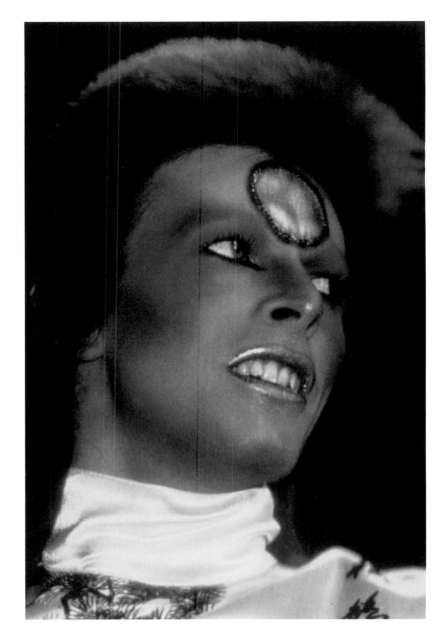

DIAMOND DOGS TOUR

Released in 1974, *Diamond Dogs* marked the end of David Bowie's glam-rock period and heralded a new phase in his career. If his 1969 single 'Space Oddity' had captured the sense of unease and wonder provoked by the first moon landing, the new album and subsequent concert tour, informed by Bowie's reading of George Orwell's *1984*, reflected a public mood of dread and foreboding. While the 1960s had been fuelled by optimism, the 1970s were tainted with misgiving and disillusionment. Bowie produced an album and concerts that simultaneously mirrored and fuelled the feelings of a generation. Rather than rebuff predictions of environmental disaster, social chaos and global annihilation, Bowie generated poignant narratives that not only confirmed his audiences' worst suspicions but also lent form to their palpable fears.[22]

In 1973, Bowie's then manager, Tony Defries, was pushing him to capitalize on the success of *Ziggy Stardust* by writing a rock musical around the character, but Bowie had moved on. He was channelling his long-standing interest in musicals, dating from the early 1960s, into the project of adapting George Orwell's *1984* for the stage. In late 1973, however, Orwell's widow, Sonia Brownell, refused Bowie the rights to use *1984* as the basis for a rock show. The planned album and corresponding tour were reconceptualized: having been denied the right to refashion Orwell's Oceania, Bowie replaced it with his own decaying and crumbling Hunger City, based on the dystopian workers' underworld in *Metropolis* (1927) and inhabited by ravaging tribes of proto-punk 'peoploids'.

Bowie settled in New York in 1974 to further develop the tour that would become *Diamond Dogs*. As Peter Doggett has observed, it brought together many of the themes that had preoccupied Bowie since 1969, 'in the service of a dark study of cultural disintegration'.[23] Bowie's enduring interest in the prophetic power of science fiction came to a head, and a number of novels and films, including Harlan Ellison's *A Boy and his Dog* and William S. Burroughs' *The Wild Boys: A Book of the Dead*, published in 1969 and 1971 respectively, as well as the 1971 film *The Omega Man* (specifically Charlton Heston's performance as Robert Neville), could be cited as key influences during this period. Bowie's personal experiences also shaped the eventual form of the tour to a large degree. After his 1973 tour of Japan, he made his way back home to England over land and sea, in order to avoid flying. This extended journey took him through Siberia, Russia, Poland and East Germany, and proffered insights into the lives of those living under totalitarian regimes.

Further personal encounters also influenced the shape of the project, particularly a meeting with Burroughs. In an encounter arranged by Craig Copetas, a writer for *Rolling Stone* magazine, the musician and the legendary Beat author exchanged views on science fiction, sexuality and the creative process.[24] Burroughs was well known for his habit of fragmenting and rearranging narrative: a collage technique termed 'cut-up' by the painter Brion Gysin, the method was traceable as an artistic approach to the Dadaists of the early twentieth century and the later Surrealist movement.[25] Bowie started to apply the technique to songwriting with the aim of subverting lyrical and musical expectations by using a familiar system and distorting it into an alarming new shape. Fragmentation and 'cut-up' lyrics would be employed to great effect in the creation of the 11 tracks on *Diamond Dogs*, which are musically highly evocative, but often lyrically opaque. As with the *Ziggy Stardust* album, the actual narrative underlying Bowie's new production remained understated. Deliberate narrative voids would, however, enable listeners to construct their own interpretations of both album and rock show.[26]

Fragmentation also heavily influenced the design of the *Diamond Dogs* project, nowhere more evident than on the album's sleeve. The work of Belgian painter Guy Peellaert, the cover image portrays Bowie as a bizarre mix of man and beast. Mick Jagger, with whom Bowie was engaged in a playful rivalry at the time, had introduced Bowie to Peellaert's work in 1973 and intimated that the Rolling Stones intended to engage him to make the art for one of their upcoming albums. Captivated by the artist's work and its grotesque Surrealist overtones (and presumably excited by the prospect of pre-empting Jagger), Bowie commissioned Peellaert to paint the *Diamond Dogs* sleeve. In January 1974 he gave Peellaert the brief to create a central sphinx-like image, combining a dog and Bowie himself. To provide Peellaert with images to use as reference material for the painting, Bowie also arranged a photo session with Terry O'Neill later that month (pls 74 and 75).

While working on the painting (pl.76), Peelleart developed a further 'circus sideshow' element, and the tagline 'The Strangest Living Curiosities' was added to the artwork.[27] Both the phrase and the image evoked Tod Browning's highly controversial 1932 film *Freaks*, in which actors with real physical deformities play circus performers who exact revenge for having been on the receiving end of acts of cruelty and discrimination. The *Diamond Dogs* cover was intended to entice and provoke its viewers to listen to a 'carnival-esque freak show' of Bowie's own creation.[28] Thematically, the album's cover art also refers back to the fictional worlds of Burroughs' novels, populated by 'desensitized mental and physical cripples ... drug addicts, criminals, and sexual "deviants"'.[29] Music writer David Buckley has suggested that with *Diamond Dogs*, Bowie succeeded in incorporating 'low-life' decadent culture into the mainstream popular aesthetic. As Siouxsie Sioux once remarked, Bowie is an unusual pop star in that he comes with a reading list.

↑ **[76] ABOVE** ● Cover artwork for *Diamond Dogs*, 1974 ●
Painting by Guy Peellaert ● THE DAVID BOWIE ARCHIVE

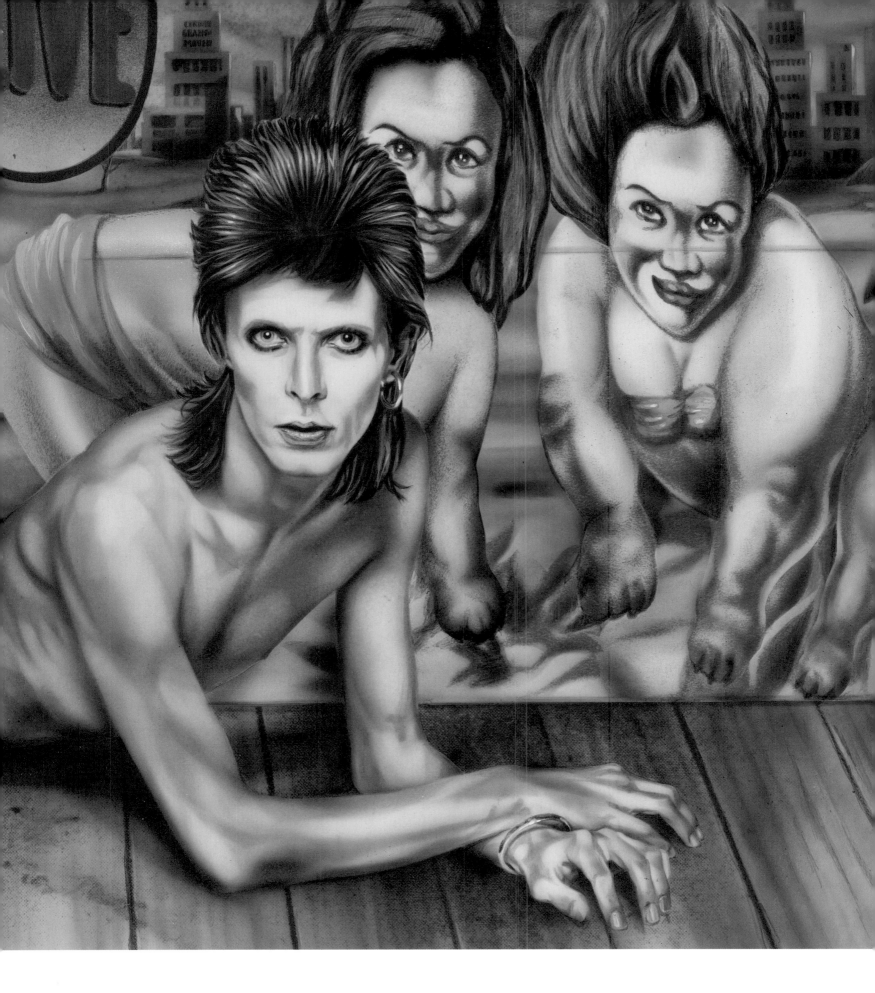

↑ **[77] TOP** • Stage set model for the Diamond Dogs tour, 1974 • Designed by Jules Fisher and Mark Ravitz • THE DAVID BOWIE ARCHIVE

↑ **[78] ABOVE** • Poster for the French release of *Metropolis*, 1927 • Directed by Fritz Lang • Designed by Boris Bilinsky

↗ **[79] ABOVE RIGHT** • Pale blue suit, 1974 • Designed by Freddie Burretti for the Diamond Dogs tour • THE DAVID BOWIE ARCHIVE

→ **[80] RIGHT AND [81] FAR RIGHT** • Set design notes by Mark Ravitz for the Diamond Dogs tour, 1974 • THE DAVID BOWIE ARCHIVE

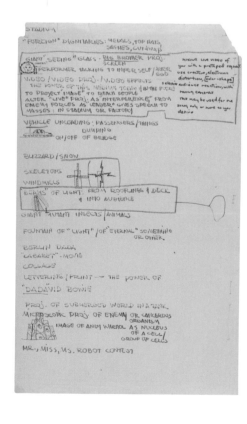

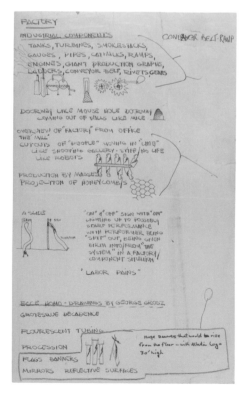

Terry O'Neill, whose photo session with Bowie provided the brief for Peellaert to work from, had come to prominence in the 1960s with the new generation of photographers – including David Bailey – who rejected the static formality of the posed photographs of the 1950s and went instead for spontaneity and unusual settings.[30] The *Diamond Dogs* photo shoot, which took place on 30 January 1974, was no exception.

The famous image depicts a seated Bowie, relaxed and dashing in a Spanish Cordoba hat, high-heeled boots, a book at his feet and looking the 'real cool cat'.[31] He seems entirely unperturbed by the enormous, rearing dog to his right. It has been claimed that the shot was an accidental stroke of good fortune – the dog reared up on its hind legs suddenly – but in fact it was carefully staged for dramatic effect. Contact sheets show that the dog was leaping towards a piece of meat dangled from above (pl.75). As O'Neill says: 'The harder you work, the more pictures you take, the more decisive moments you capture.'[32] Certainly decisive, the photograph was used to promote the *Diamond Dogs* tour, and it is now in the V&A's Photography Collection. It did not feature on the original album sleeve, but was used for subsequent RYKO/EMI releases.

The album and, later, the tour, were aggressively publicized in the United States. Defries adopted a two-pronged approach to the promotion of Bowie in America: the first stage involved the widespread circulation of the album's sensational cover art and the creation of a tremendous amount of memorabilia; the second was to be the tour itself. It was one of the most theatrical rock shows ever staged, and also reputedly the most expensive. The total cost for the set came to roughly $250,000.[33] Bowie conceived the design (pl.77) of an angular cityscape inspired by the German Expressionist cinema of the silent age: particularly Fritz Lang's *Metropolis* (1927, pl.78) and Robert Wiene's *The Cabinet of Dr Caligari* (1919). The show was designed by American lighting designer Jules Fisher[34] and set designer Mark Ravitz, with technical support from stage engineer Chris Langhart and direction from Bowie and Los-Angeles-based choreographer Toni Basil. It featured several enormous props, including street lamps, a drawbridge and a diamond-studded hand, which opened to reveal Bowie perched on it. Bowie was transported, supported by a cherry picker, over the audience while sitting on an office chair and singing 'Space Oddity' into a telephone.[35]

The choreography, the set list and – eventually – the set (pls 80 and 81) evolved during the course of the tour. The band was largely obscured behind flats for the first two shows, with the eight musicians acting like an orchestra. Dancers were on stage for many of the songs – during 'Diamond Dogs' they were attached to leashes – although Bowie remained the focal point of the performance. No film of the show was made, although a rough cut of the July performance at the Tower Theater in Philadelphia does exist.

Conceived as a narrative-driven musical or rock opera, the show materialized with only a loose storyline, but there is ample evidence that Bowie worked on a never-realized film version for some considerable time (pl.82). He produced hand-drawn storyboards for its various scenes, pages of film notes, built set models and drew character sketches of the story (pls 83–8). Set in Hunger City, the narrative revolves around Halloween Jack who, according to the film notes, was to inhabit a deserted skyscraper and travel with a gang of youths around the city on roller skates, looting furs and diamonds, subsisting on a diet of 'mealcaine'.[36] Bowie drew inspiration from accounts of Victorian London as told to him by his father, who worked for Dr Barnardo's Homes from 1945 until his death in 1969. Barnardo's patron, Lord Shaftesbury, is said to have found hundreds of children living on the streets and roofs of London during an inspection of the city's slums in the nineteenth century.[37]

The Diamond Dogs tour proved tremendously successful, but there were difficulties stemming from Bowie's worsening cocaine habit, a gruelling schedule covering enormous distances and contractual disputes with Defries' management organization, MainMan. The elaborate set had to be transported in three 45-foot trailers, and took 35 men at each venue a whole day to erect.[38] Following a road accident on the journey from Atlanta, Georgia to Tampa, Florida, much of the set ended up in a swamp. A stripped-back show had to be put on in Tampa, but the set was up and running again by 5 July and used until 17 September 1974. In October, a new set was introduced that was designed to reflect the new, more soul-influenced songs Bowie had been writing on tour, which anticipated the *Young Americans* album in style. This set was used until December 1974. Difficulties aside, this remains one of the most spectacular tours ever to have been staged, and undoubtedly paved the way for the elaborate rock concerts that followed, with the Rolling Stones commissioning Jules Fisher for their Tour of the Americas the following year.[39] Rock shows were never the same again.

19a CLOSE-UP OF TEETH, SIDEWAYS ON, PULLS BACK TO REVEAL TWO VICTIM CHILDREN FIGHTING.

21 HOLDING FRAME AT MAN-HEIGHT, WE TRACK ALONG THE QUE

22 THE MEALCAINE RATION TABLE

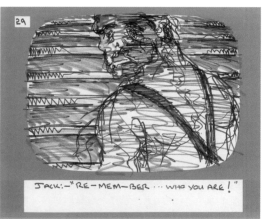

29 JACK:- "RE-MEM-BER ... WHO YOU ARE!"

33 a blindfolded woman, of mature age, is being spun around

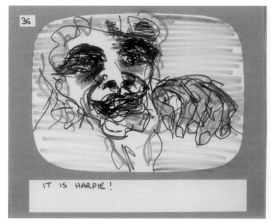

36 IT IS HARPIE!

38 CUT:- LOOSE FRONTAL ON WORKING DWELLERS CHAIR, MISS SINGLE AT CHAIR-BACK, RIGHT FRAME

40 STATIONARY, AND SLIGHTLY OVERHEAD. A SHOT OF JACK AND SURROUNDING CROWD

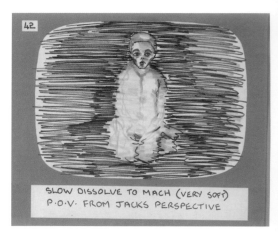

42 SLOW DISSOLVE TO MACH (VERY SOFT) P.O.V. FROM JACKS PERSPECTIVE

↑ [82] ABOVE ◦ Part of a storyboard by David Bowie for an unrealized film set in Hunger City, 1974 ◦ THE DAVID BOWIE ARCHIVE

→ [83] OPPOSITE ◦ Preparatory drawing by David Bowie for an unrealized film film set in Hunger City, 1974 ◦ THE DAVID BOWIE ARCHIVE

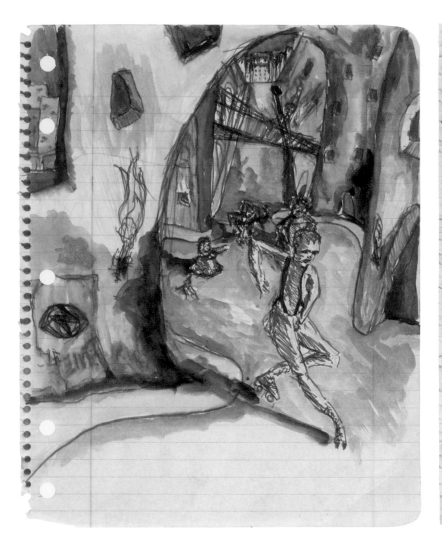

↑ → [84–8] **ABOVE AND OPPOSITE** • Preparatory drawings by David Bowie for
an unrealized film set in Hunger City, 1974 • THE DAVID BOWIE ARCHIVE

hunger city — the future

barren skyscrapers center
around the "World Assembly"
building.

ASHES TO ASHES

The song 'Ashes to Ashes' from the album *Scary Monsters … and Super Creeps*, released in September of 1980, was the single Bowie used, in his words, to 'purge' himself of the 1970s. For Bowie, that decade was marked by the rise and fall of legendary performance alter egos, excess in America (a period during which he composed the albums *Young Americans* and *Station to Station*), as well as a desperately needed recuperative escape to Berlin, which resulted in the triptych of albums *Low*, *"Heroes"* and *Lodger*. In 1979 Bowie released the final panel of the triptych – the album *Lodger* – and was eager to consolidate his musical experimentation into a new sound for a new decade. His next project marked the beginning of his 1980s creative work that, just as in the 1970s, was peppered with innovative collaboration, experimentation and creativity.

Co-produced by the familiar duo of Bowie and Tony Visconti – who had previously worked together on the albums *Young Americans*, *Low*, *"Heroes"*, *Stage* and *Lodger* – the album *Scary Monsters … and Super Creeps* was made just as the influence of visual media truly came to the forefront of pop culture.[40] Temporarily putting aside the improvisatory methods of recording he had developed while working with Brian Eno in Berlin (although at times still using the 'cut-up' technique of writing inherited from Brion Gysin and William Burroughs), Bowie carefully developed and crafted the music and lyrics of the album and made a concerted effort to translate the songs into new, visually expressive media.

As David Buckley has noted, 'In the 1980s, simply being a pop star was no longer enough. Superstars now were expected to colonize film and video.'[41] The birth of MTV on 1 August 1981 heralded a new era of the music video, with the success of a song being inextricably linked to the appeal of the accompanying video. The visual aesthetic of a pop star's 'look' became paramount for a mass audience, and the result of this heightened focus on the visual, at times, trumped the quality of the music produced. For the visually adept Bowie, it was an opportunity that played further to his strengths.

'Ashes to Ashes' was the first single from the album, and the pioneering music video was co-directed by Bowie and David Mallet. Bowie had met Mallet in April 1979 while performing 'Boys Keep Swinging' on 'The Kenny Everett Video Show', which Mallet produced for Thames Television. Impressed, Bowie hired Mallet to create videos for 'Boys Keep Swinging', 'DJ' and a pared-down, yet highly stylized, performance of 'Space Oddity' the same year. The success of 'Ashes to Ashes' in 1980 cemented their creative partnership, which continued into the 1990s.[42] 'Ashes to Ashes', like the 'Space Oddity' video, incorporated a non-linear narrative with three interconnecting characters, and features similar cinematography: intense close-ups of Bowie's face combined with stark lighting, pyrotechnics and scene fades. However, that is where the similarities end. Nicholas Pegg describes the video as an 'outstanding promo [that] redefined rock video and jump-started the New Romantic movement'.[43]

The video for the single (pl.89) was shot in May 1980 on location at Beachy Head and Hastings, on the East Sussex coast. At a cost of £25,000 it was, at that time, the most expensive music video ever made. In it, Bowie plays three distinct roles: the first is a Pierrot figure, the second an astronaut and the third an inmate of a padded cell. Bowie storyboarded the promo himself, drawing it shot-by-shot and working on the edit alongside Mallet (pls 90 and 93).

While there is no particular narrative to the video, the interconnected scenes are introduced through a series of incongruous images presented by Bowie, who holds a video postcard that displays the first shot of the following scene, as he emphasizes the words 'Oh no, don't say it's true'. Bowie at first is a sympathetic stock Pierrot character of pantomime (wearing a reproduction of a Lindsay Kemp outfit designed by Natasha Korniloff, pls 92 and 162–3), and we follow him into a Martian landscape, walking along an abandoned beach past piles of burning refuse, and promenading with pseudo-ecclesiastical companions, pursued by a bulldozer that seems to be pushing him towards the water.

This strange setting was achieved by incorporating the then new Paintbox technique to solarize the scene, turning the sky black and the ground pink to create a somewhat apocalyptic or alien landscape. Bowie's liberal direction with regard to the look he wished to achieve made an impact on Jonathan Barnbrook, who recalls seeing the video as a teenager:

> Film was as malleable as anything else. You could process film as you could process an instrument. You could cut up a piece of typography … And that kind of freedom meant that the creative source can go into anything, whether it's design, video or music, so it was quite liberating seeing this video for the first time.[44]

'I think [Bowie's] influence on early music videos was probably the greatest influence of all,' Mallet said in the 2002 documentary *David Bowie: Sound and Vision*. 'He wasn't frightened to do something that was surreal. He wasn't frightened to go back to French silent, Surrealist movies. He wasn't frightened to do anything.'[45]

The Pierrot's entourage consists of three religious figures in heavy make-up and a young woman dressed as a dancer, all serving as a chorus ready to interject in any given scene, repeating a lyric in unison: 'I'm happy/ Hope you're happy too' or 'My mother said/ To get things done/ You'd better not mess/ With Major Tom'. The chorus comprises recruits that Bowie enlisted on a visit to the Blitz nightclub in London – a haven for New Romantic musicians, including Steve Strange of Visage, as well as Marilyn and George O'Dowd (better known as Boy George), who were, to their regret, passed over for the video.[46]

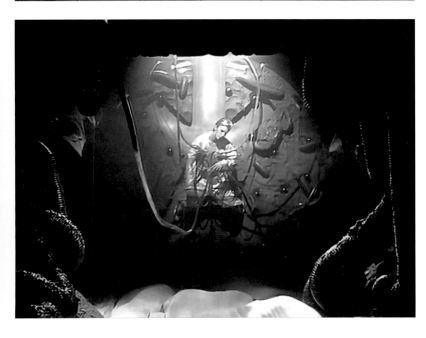

↑ **[89] ABOVE** ● Stills from the 'Ashes to Ashes' video, 1980 ● Directed by David Mallet

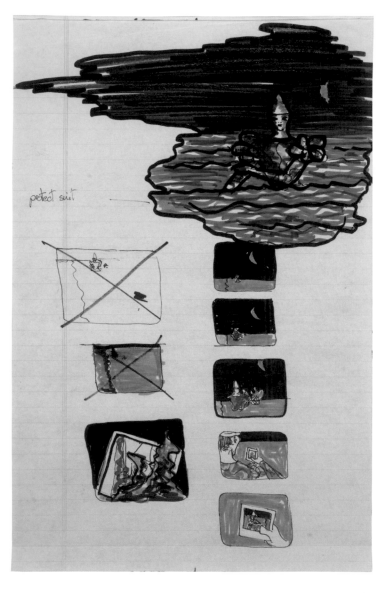

↑ [90] **ABOVE** • Original storyboards by David Bowie for the 'Ashes to Ashes' video, 1980 • THE DAVID BOWIE ARCHIVE

← [91] **LEFT** • Songbook for *Scary Monsters … and Super Creeps*, 1980 • THE DAVID BOWIE ARCHIVE

↓ [92] **BELOW** • Pierrot (or 'Blue Clown') costume, 1980 • Designed by Natasha Korniloff for the 'Ashes to Ashes' video and *Scary Monsters … and Super Creeps* album cover • THE DAVID BOWIE ARCHIVE

→ [93] **OPPOSITE** • Original storyboards by David Bowie for the 'Ashes to Ashes' video, 1980 • THE DAVID BOWIE ARCHIVE

As the character in the padded cell, Bowie is alone, without theatrical make-up and dressed in his simplest costume of the video: a white dress shirt and black trousers with studded seam, tucked into green mid-calf boots. In his cell he sits on a chair, singing directly to the camera, with backing vocals echoing over the main lyric. His gaze is glassily fixed, yet he seems subdued, broken and controlled. Next he is seen sitting on the floor in the corner of his cell, despondently singing as he gently moves his knee slowly back and forth: 'time and again I tell myself/ I'll stay clean tonight/ But the little green wheels are following me/ Oh no, not again'. Whether the desire to stay away from drugs refers to Bowie himself or the infamous Major Tom, the inmate references repeated lapses, eerily echoed by his slow movements that give a sense of 'time and again' and the spinning 'green wheels' that follow him. This most obviously Bowie-like character is last seen isolated in his corner, dramatically lit with a spotlight as he repeats the nursery rhyme-like refrain: 'My mother said/ To get things done/ You'd better not mess/ With Major Tom'.

Whereas the final scene of the inmate narrative shows Bowie trapped within the asylum, in the final scenes of the Pierrot story arc we see him releasing what appears to be a dove on the beach, before being led away along the water by an older woman, who is talking sternly to him – or possibly imploring him. The feeling of being mentally lost and physically trapped is conveyed strongly. (It is interesting to note the visual reference to Bowie's sketch for the back cover of *Space Oddity*, where a Pierrot and an old woman are shown walking away together in the bottom left corner, made 11 years earlier, pls 94–6).

The final Bowie character in 'Ashes to Ashes' is a low-tech, kitchen-sink astronaut redolent of Major Tom. He crashes on a Martian beach and is then seen hooked up to a life-support machine, amid explosions, in an environment that resembles a late 1950s/early 1960s hair salon within a domestic kitchen. Removed from this setting by an explosion, Major Tom falls to an underground lair, fastened to a wall by tubes entering his body and surrounded by some form of living, non-human growth (Ridley Scott's *Alien* was released the previous year, in 1979). There he hangs, defeated and depleted. He is attached to his organic surroundings, lifeless, with only enough energy to look up at a camera that can offer no assistance or reprieve. Major Tom remains in his prison and, as the video comes to an end, the camera zooms in one last time on the lost astronaut as he hangs in quiet desperation. The message is clear: Bowie is condemning the intrepid spaceman who has failed to bring a promise of hope, and the video, in Pegg's words, once again fuels 'the notion that "Ashes to Ashes" is a comprehensive exorcism of his [Bowie's] past'.[47]

A progression towards insanity, or a sequential mental deterioration, was a well-explored theme throughout the 1970s.[48] For Bowie, the lost idealism is manifested in the failures of Major Tom and his space exploration, or promise of modernity and cosmic hope. In reprising 'Space Oddity', the song that arguably brought Bowie his first big success, 'Ashes to Ashes' critically re-examines Major Tom and his story of space adventure gone awry. Reflecting on the album in its entirety in 1990, Bowie said:

Scary Monsters for me has always been some kind of purge. It was me eradicating the feelings within myself that I was uncomfortable with … You have to accommodate your pasts within your persona. You have to understand why you went through them. That's the major thing. You cannot just ignore them or put them out of your mind or pretend they didn't happen or just say, 'Oh I was different then'.[49]

Though Bowie had found closure for Ziggy Stardust with the character's infamous 'death' on 3 July 1973 at the Hammersmith Odeon, Major Tom had not previously been dealt with. While Bowie had identified the futility inherent in space travel in 1969 with 'Space Oddity', this same disillusionment did not become public opinion until the late 1970s. In returning to the character of Major Tom in 'Ashes to Ashes', Bowie found a means of reprising and later departing from his seventies legacy, and the outer/inner 'space' meaning it represented for him.[50]

'There was a certain degree of optimism making [*Scary Monsters*] because I'd worked through some of my problems,' Bowie said in 1999. 'I felt very positive about the future, and I think I just got down to writing a really comprehensive and well-crafted album.'[51] The album is often said, even by Bowie himself, to be a turning point in his career, providing a catharsis to the 1970s. Its release coincided with his divorce from Angie becoming absolute in 1980, as well as his gaining custody of his child, Duncan Zowie Haywood Jones. In an interview in 1980, Bowie gave his own perspective on 'Ashes to Ashes', peering forward into the new decade while simultaneously looking back at his previous work: 'It's a nursery rhyme. It's very much a 1980s nursery rhyme. I think 1980s nursery rhymes will have a lot to do with the 1880s/1890s nursery rhymes, which are all rather horrid and had little boys with their ears being cut off and stuff like that'.[52] This ties in directly to his early work, encapsulated on his debut solo album *David Bowie* (1967). That album showcases a nursery-rhyme-laden series of songs that bring out the darker side of tales for children. With the video for 'Ashes to Ashes' there is a similar perversion of child-like innocence, as we see the tale of the heroic Major Tom come to a dark, disturbing end as he hangs expressionless in his organic subterranean prison.

In 'Ashes to Ashes', Bowie created a video that heralded the New Romantic movement – which had itself been inspired by him. By referencing the copy, he popularized a cult that centred on his own heritage, relaunching his own past at the same time as putting it behind him. As Buckley notes, '"Ashes to Ashes" stands as a Bowie landmark [not simply] because it was technically brilliant, but also because it encapsulated 1980 perfectly.' In a press interview after his 1977 performance on the Dutch television programme 'TopPop', Bowie said:

> I'm a fairly good social observer and I think I encapsulate areas maybe every year or so. I try and stamp that down somewhere. What that year is all about rather than what it was all about or what it is going to be. It's very much trying to capture the quintessence of that year.[53]

In the documentary film *Inspirations* (1997), Bowie reveals not only his keenness to participate in the visual elements of all aspects of music production, but also his use of the visual arts as a creative aid in his songwriting:

> If I've found myself in some kind of cul-de-sac in the music, I'd break down a problem by actually painting it. I try and visualize what the problem was … I try and visualize those textures and paint them and then find out what was wrong, and then when I've solved that problem I'd take it back into the studio. I've never really compartmentalized things. Everything for me is just this flux of doing stuff. Some of it's music and some of it's visual, and the two have always been very entwined.[54]

At a time when the apotheosis of fame and influence is to be a pop star, and being a pop star requires a combination of the musical and the visual while embodying the spirit of the age, Bowie's musical and visual talents, which he considers as part of a continuum, have allowed him to not only embrace visual media as an organic product of his own unique visual approach to songwriting, but also to become a forerunner in production and dissemination – a sort of appropriating prophet. His exceptional breadth of interests alongside his acceptance of the mantra 'the medium is the message' have opened him to inspiration by others – but as we have seen, he takes inspiration from an exceptional breadth of subjects and creates from them something entirely new. In the words of T. S. Eliot:

> One of the surest tests [of the superiority or inferiority of a poet] is the way in which a poet borrows. Immature poets imitate; mature poets steal; bad poets deface what they take, and good poets make it into something better, or at least something different. The good poet welds his theft into a whole of feeling which is unique, utterly different than that from which it is torn; the bad poet throws it into something which has no cohesion. A good poet will usually borrow from authors remote in time, or alien in language, or diverse in interest.[55]

With these attributes Bowie has become arguably the most culturally significant and visually interesting pop musician of the twentieth century. Jonathan Barnbrook sums up his unique appeal: 'It's about the spirit of the age, the spirit of the music and some unconscious understanding of what's going on.'

put up to front

↑ [94] ABOVE • Artwork for the back cover of *Space Oddity*, 1969 •
Illustration by George Underwood • THE DAVID BOWIE ARCHIVE

→[95] OPPOSITE ABOVE • Still from the 'Ashes to Ashes' video, 1980 •
Directed by David Mallet

→[96] OPPOSITE BELOW • Sketch by David Bowie for the back cover
of *Space Oddity*, 1969 • THE DAVID BOWIE ARCHIVE

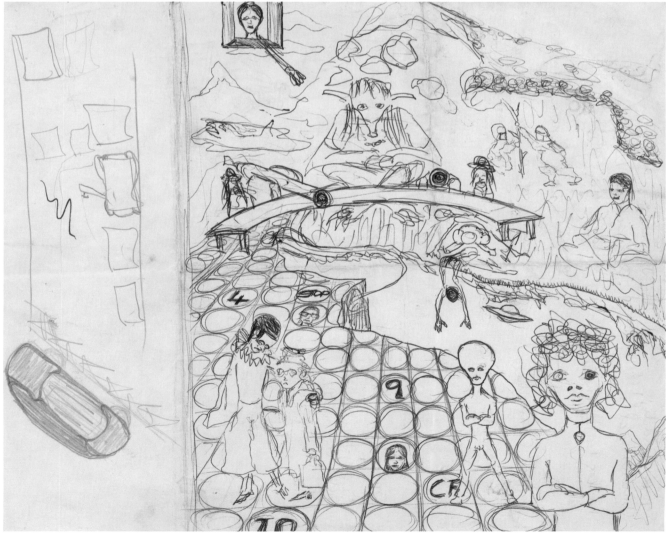

↑← **[97] OPPOSITE AND ABOVE** ● Double-breasted suit and turquoise boots, 1973 ●
THE DAVID BOWIE ARCHIVE

DAVID BOWIE IS DRESSED FROM HEAD TO TOE

→ **[98] OPPOSITE** ● David Bowie photographed for the *Pin Ups* album
artwork and promotional material, 1973 ● Photograph by Mick Rock

←↑ **[99] OPPOSITE AND ABOVE** ● Pale blue suit, 1974 ● Designed by
Freddie Burretti for the Diamond Dogs tour ● THE DAVID BOWIE ARCHIVE

↓ **[100] OVERLEAF** ● David Bowie on stage during the
Diamond Dogs tour ● Photographs by Ken Regan ● THE DAVID BOWIE ARCHIVE

↑→[101] **ABOVE AND OPPOSITE** ▢ Black suit and dress shirt, 1976
▢ Designed by Ola Hudson for the Station to Station tour ▢
THE DAVID BOWIE ARCHIVE

DAVID BOWIE IS INTENT ON PULLING EVERYTHING INTO THE PRESENT, WHERE LIFE IS ALWAYS BEGINNING

→[102] **OPPOSITE** ● David Bowie on stage during the
Stage tour, 1978 ● Photograph by Masayoshi Sukita

↑→ **[103] ABOVE AND OPPOSITE** • Nautical costume, 1978 • Designed by
Natasha Korniloff for the Stage tour • THE DAVID BOWIE ARCHIVE

DAVID BOWIE IS GAZING A GAZELY STARE

→ [104] **OPPOSITE** David Bowie, 1977 •
Photograph by Bruce Weber

I, I WILL BE KING

AND YOU, YOU WILL BE QUEEN

BOWIE MUSIC
LUCKY OLD SUN
IS IN MY SKY...

It is music's good fortune that David Bowie fell into this art form as his first medium of choice as a young man. We can now see, given the restless gallimaufry of other interests and skills revealed since, that this was by no means a certainty. What's more, his semi-formal musical training, such as it was, bore all the hallmarks of an amateur's enthusiastic but directionless exploration into the field, likely to throw up a brief entanglement with the heady, chaotic circus arena of pop, followed by an equally swift decline, talent depletion and burnout. Other pop wannabes populating the lower and middle orders of the charts in April 1967, the month that saw the release of his novelty single, 'The Laughing Gnome', had disappeared into Z-list obscurity by the end of that decade: Bowie's invasion of the world was still nearly five years in the future and would last well into the twenty-first century.

That Bowie's career did not follow the oft-trodden path taken by rock and pop artists with a touch of panache and flair, arresting looks, mastery of basic guitar technique and a knack of being at the happening party with access to happening drugs tells us that his musical instincts were of a different order altogether and that his capacity for musical growth was exceptional. His musicality reacted like a chemical with the minds of the young, first erupting in the early 1970s and reigniting time and time again in the subsequent 40 years. He may have concocted new performance personae, new costumes, new public poses, new ways of connecting with audiences, but essentially as a composer he has developed like any other, discovering fresh possibilities and collaborations as his personality has developed and matured, being open to and colliding with different cultural stimuli as time has passed. This was Beethoven's path, as it was Mahler's, McCartney's and Gershwin's.

Of course, Bowie has been a fashion icon of considerable stature and his public performances as an actor and musician have reverberated across Western culture, yet all of these colourful manifestations of his imagination we owe to the fact of his astonishing output as a composer-producer. Put starkly, even if we were to strip away the flamboyant personalities of Ziggy Stardust and the Thin White Duke, of starmen, spacemen, earth-bound falling men and video-art marionettes, Bowie's influence as the producer of Iggy Pop's *The Idiot,* as co-producer of Lou Reed's *Transformer,* as songwriter of 'Life on Mars?', 'All the Young Dudes', 'Rebel Rebel' and 'Ashes to Ashes', or as co-creator with Brian Eno and Tony Visconti of the resolutely intimate, cross-genre experiment of *Low* are reasons on their own for him to be considered one of the most significant musicians of the twentieth century.

While lovers of classical music have Leonard Bernstein conducting a multinational orchestra and choir in Beethoven's ninth symphony firmly imprinted on their memories as the musical embodiment of the fall of the Berlin Wall in November 1989, to an even greater body of millions just one song by David Bowie and Brian Eno, written in the shadow of that wall 12 years earlier, captured the essence of the moment. Even though, unlike the Beethoven, 'Heroes' was (rather surprisingly) not performed live there at that time nor broadcast via satellite to the world, its status as *the* song of the Wall, as witness to the pain it caused and its eventual vanquishing by ordinary people, has cast its spell over the historical reality of events ever since (pl.106). Add to the small list above Bowie's bewilderingly fecund catalogue of other songs and studio recordings, the scale of his creativity behind closed doors, as it were, is staggering. So his musical gift is in itself somewhat miraculous and it deserves further scrutiny: why has David Bowie's music *as music* made such a profound impact on other artists in all fields, as well as on the public at large, over so extended a period?

↑ [106] ABOVE • EMS Synthi AKS synthesizer
purchased in 1974 by Brian Eno and used for the
recording of *"Heroes"*, 1977 • THE DAVID BOWIE ARCHIVE

The first consideration is Bowie's knack of capturing and reprocessing the musical trends of the moment. Broadly speaking, composers of all periods in history can be divided into three groups: genuine innovators, 'second-wave' absorbers who synthesize pioneer developments and adept, polished sweepers who satisfy the public's delayed appetite for what *was* new five or ten years previously. It is a common misconception that the 'famous', landmark composers like Bach, Mozart, Beethoven, Brahms, Wagner or Gershwin were cutting-edge innovators of the first group, whereas in fact all of the above fall into the second category, as does Bowie.

Very few of the true pioneers of musical change come down to us, decades or centuries later, as the leading names of their age. Mozart considered J. S. Bach's son Carl Philip Emmanuel the modern vanguard of his youth and never thought of himself as a challenger of older traditions (far from it, Mozart was an avid admirer of Bach and Handel, definitely yesterday's almost-forgotten men during his lifetime). Joseph Haydn, often credited with the invention of the orchestral symphony, would have been surprised to have been awarded such an epithet, knowing that if it belonged to anyone, such a claim belonged to Mannheim-based Czech composer Johann Stamitz (or Stamic). The young Beethoven's apparently novel dramatic piano style, alarming and titillating to audiences in staid early nineteenth-century Vienna, was gleaned in part from his insider's familiarity with another Czech composer, London-based Jan Dussek, unknown to all but the ultra-musically-informed of the day. Wagner would be nowhere without the visionary advances in musical style and technique made by the man who would eventually become his father-in-law, Franz Liszt.

What all these 'second-wave' composers have in common is a highly developed sense of what else is in the ether, what styles are emerging and where to find such ingenuity. They are then able to blend new, exploratory ideas with their own well-developed skills, packaging the ensuing mix for the general audience in such a way as to intrigue and delight without leaving them utterly bewildered. These are rare gifts, sometimes – perhaps always – intuitive rather than studied, which is why the number of composers whose work results in a universal change in stylistic direction remains small. Bowie's name is among them.

Nor is the sleight of hand involved – digesting and transforming the experimental, the contemporary, the not-yet-modish into something personal and fresh – in any way secretive. Bowie himself has never been coy about the process. Why should an artist as honest and courageous as he has been have been anything other than open about it? All musical invention is built on the source material of others and the world of pop/rock and lately hip-hop is mostly beguilingly free from the deathly taint that has hung around the notion of 'borrowing' in newly composed classical music since the deaths of Bach and Handel in the mid-eighteenth century. Some aspects of this taboo (which these two composers would not have recognized, accustomed as they were to regular and widespread borrowings from their own and others' works) were carried into twentieth-century popular music. Fear of the accusation of plagiarism inhibited many a budding writer long before the internet made 'copy and paste' an idlers' charter. Fear of nothing, on the other hand, has been a hallmark of Bowie's career, and his devouring and reshaping of the cultural department store of the late twentieth century is one of its most stimulating features. It also explains his ability to renew his musical output over a 40-year stretch.

With his first recordings in the 1960s, Bowie was mining the whimsical seam of English music hall novelty songs (in 'Uncle Arthur', 'The Little Bombardier' and 'Ching-A-Ling', as well as in 'The Laughing Gnome', the song that causes the subsequent hardcore Bowie faithful to wince, pl.107), though, to be fair, so were many others in the swinging London of the Beatles, the Kinks, Herman's Hermits and (the name says it all) the New Vaudeville Band. By November 1969 and the release of his album *Space Oddity*, a new set of influences was evident: psychedelic hippie folk-rock, Bob Dylan, Paul Simon, the Beatles' *Sgt. Pepper* and *Magical Mystery Tour* and the fledgling glam-rock style soon to be the calling card of his friend Marc Bolan. For the next four decades, similar amalgams of sometimes incongruously combined ingredients would be stirred into Bowie melting pot after melting pot, each stew, however delicious, abandoned after each extended recording project and accompanying tour(s), to the chagrin of waves of newly converted fans. Bowie has made a habit of thwarting any likelihood of his sound settling into any chosen groove. It is quite possible to love one Bowie album and hate another, simply because very few of them (there are more than 20 in total) are alike.

Early Bowie (prior to 'Space Oddity'), while trawling the attic of cockney music hall, had a weirdness to it that set it apart from much of the whimsy skirting the charts in the mid-1960s. 'The London Boys' (released in December 1966) is an unsettling example. Apart from an opening nod to the sound of brass bands, practically obligatory on English pop songs after the Beatles' landmark *Revolver* had introduced them into 'Yellow Submarine' (the single of which installed itself at number one for the summer of 1966), and a similarly disjointed, brassy playout, the core of 'The London Boys' is altogether more sinister, with an R&B-style Hammond organ, bass and drums mixed starkly to the front, making no concession to the easy-going catchiness of pop whatsoever. Bowie's lyric, part-autobiographical, part-prophetic, traces a teenage wannabe's initiation to Soho's club, drug and celebrity scene of the time (and, as it has turned out, any time since): 'Oh, the first time that you tried a pill/ You feel a little queasy, decidedly ill/ You're gonna be sick, but you mustn't lose face/ To let yourself down would be a big disgrace/ With the London boys'.

Though the lyric caused Bowie's record companies on both sides of the Atlantic enough anxiety to attempt to bury the song, in fact it is the song's musical component that is most unexpected – after all, Paul McCartney's admitting that his Motown-inspired 'Got to Get You Into My Life' on *Revolver* was a tribute to marijuana didn't stop it being enormously popular. Bowie's disorientated, meandering melody with its uneven phrase lengths, drifting listlessly across an accompaniment that seems oblivious to it, defies cosy accessibility. Unlike McCartney, a social commentator who stood impartially aside from his fictitious characters, from Mr Nowhere Man and the meticulous barber of Penny Lane to the melancholic Eleanor Rigby and Lovely Rita, meter-maid, Bowie *became* his characters, and despite 'The London Boys' being written in the third person, he appears to have taken his victim's voice for his own vocal performance. This impulse has reoccurred countless times in his work.

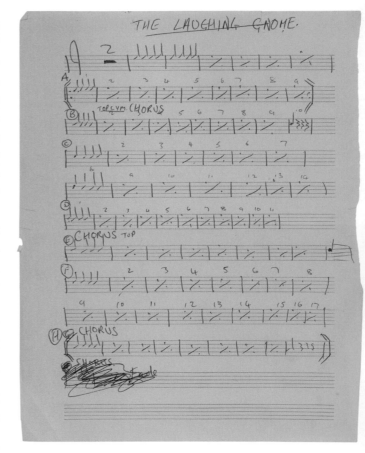

↑ [107] **ABOVE** • Original lead sheet (drum) for 'The Laughing Gnome', arranged by Dek Fearnley and David Bowie, 1967 • THE DAVID BOWIE ARCHIVE

→ [108] **OPPOSITE** • Original lead sheet (guitar) for 'Space Oddity' by David Bowie, 1969 • Handwritten by Paul Buckmaster • THE DAVID BOWIE ARCHIVE

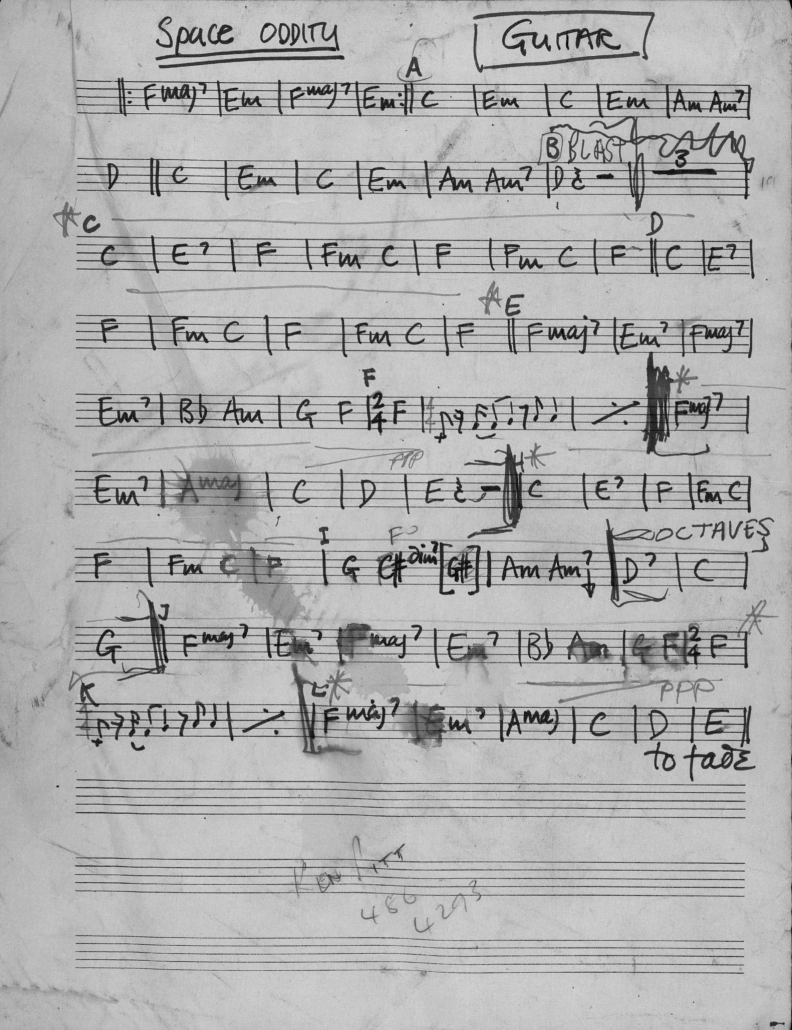

← [109] **OPPOSITE** • Original lead sheet (electric guitar) for 'Space Oddity' by David Bowie, 1969 • Handwritten by Paul Buckmaster • THE DAVID BOWIE ARCHIVE

↑ [110] **ABOVE** • Original lead sheet (violin) for 'Space Oddity' by David Bowie, 1969 • Handwritten by Paul Buckmaster • THE DAVID BOWIE ARCHIVE

The unpredictable harmonies of 'The London Boys', underlining the sense of alienation in the voice, are out of place in late 1960s pop, defiantly so, but they are wholly appropriate to the mood of the song. Shifting uneasily from chord to chord, the Hammond B3's vibrato further undermining the stability of the tuning, the overall musical effect of the accompaniment of this song feels more at home next to Blur's *Parklife* of 1994, particularly the track 'London Loves', than it does nestled up to the other hits of late 1966 – the Beach Boys' 'Good Vibrations', Donovan's 'Mellow Yellow' and Frank Sinatra's 'That's Life'. Bowie's messed-up runaway was also characterized by his uncompromisingly south London accent, a sound that is heard across Bowie's output until he began touring the United States in earnest and the reedier, more cosmopolitan voice of Aladdin Sane took over in the mid 1970s.

'Space Oddity' (July 1969) was Bowie's breakthrough from quirky also-ran to front runner, helped in no small part to its capturing the *Zeitgeist* with impeccable timing. Stanley Kubrick's *2001: A Space Odyssey* had been released the previous summer and the single started receiving heavy radio play as Apollo 11 made its historic manned landing on the moon. But typically for Bowie, this was no sing-along celebration of technological endeavour, nor was 'Space Oddity' a feast of metaphor like Bart Howard's 'Fly Me to the Moon', the carefree anthem to the 1960s high life as epitomized in Sinatra's swing cover of 1964. No, Bowie placed his astronaut in isolated jeopardy and, in contrast to the cynicism of 'The London Boys' or the clownishly ironic, rum-ti-tum 'Love You till Tuesday', the single that immediately preceded 'Space Oddity', responded to the man-on-the-moon moment with a hymn to humanity, the doomed astronaut's last words being 'Tell my wife I love her very much'.

Musically rich, with one of Bowie's best-ever narrative melodies, 'Space Oddity' mixes the open-stringed warmth and rhythmic precision of strummed acoustic guitars – very 1969 – with a pseudo-orchestra provided by Rick Wakeman on a string mellotron, the staple sound wash of the Moody Blues – also very 1969 (pls 108–10). Again, Bowie's vocal identifies equally with the Ground Control and Major Tom characters, but instead of delivering both with tongue firmly in cheek, as he might have done two or three years earlier, he invests them with a sincerity that makes the song far more than a comic-book novelty single, of which there were a great number in the 1960s. It was as if Bowie had found in the song a new recipe that combined his natural theatricality with a musically broadened palette, bringing together, if you like, the imaginative observation and symphonic ambition of McCartney with the grainy, urbane realism of Lennon.

Bowie rarely returned to the lush, benevolent, film-score-style soundscape of 'Space Oddity' in his later career, with the distinguished exception of the magisterial 'Life on Mars?' Even when he revisited the character of Major Tom in the 1980 hit 'Ashes to Ashes', the sweeping, wide-screen panorama of 'Space Oddity' was replaced with a distorted, quivering piano, jerkily syncopated internal rhythms and backing vocals that obscured and surrounded the lead voice like a cloaking fog. Musically, it was as if the first encounter with Major Tom had the infinity of space as its backdrop, while the second took place in the claustrophobic metal box where he met his nemesis.

Ziggy played guitar
Jamming good with Wierd and Gilly
A known as Spiders from Mars
And our as "Spiders from Mars"
He played it left hand
But he made it too far
Became the Special Man
Then we were Ziggy's band

Ziggy really sang
Screwed up eyes and screw down hairdo
Like some cat from Japan
He could lick 'em by smiling
He could leave em to hang
Came on so loaded, man
Well hung and snow white tan

So where was the Spiders
While the Fly tried to break our balls
Just beer-light to guide us
So we bitched about his fans
And should we crush both his hands

Ziggy played for time
Jiving us that we was Voodoo
The kids was just crass
He was the Nazz
With God-given Arse
He took it all too far
But boy could he play guitar

Bowie was working hard enough in the three years between the UK hits 'Space Oddity' and 'Starman', but the general public would have been forgiven for forgetting about his existence. His re-emergence in spectacular fashion with the second of these space-travel ballads on 'Top of the Pops' on 6 July 1972 recalibrated where he stood in the public eye and his own image of himself. Yet the pot-pourri of sources for 'Starman' were characteristically numerous and varied. His unassuming opening chordal dissonances, on the instrument whose light, jangling, chordal presence on a track was virtually compulsory in the 1970s, the 12-string guitar, betrayed the unravelling of musical surprises about to take place. Marc Bolan's period of wizards, witches and fairies (as exemplified in songs like 'Ride a White Swan', 'By the Light of a Magical Moon' and 'Cosmic Dancer') was giving way to his harder, more electric, T-Rex glam-rock style in songs like 'Hot Love' and those with frequent calls to 'boogie', and elements of both phases are found in 'Starman' (particularly in its exhortation to 'let all the children boogie', a refrain that also references John Lee Hooker's 'Boogie Chillen').

The most obvious debt, though, was a melodic one, to Harold Arlen, composer of 'Over the Rainbow' from *The Wizard of Oz*, the 1939 musical film starring Judy Garland. By happy accident or design – and I strongly suspect the former – the identification of Bowie's new extra-terrestrial loner, complete with technicolor jumpsuit, almost vertical crimson-orange hair, eyeliner and mascara, and lasciviously bisexual body language directed at his fellow (male) guitarist, with Dorothy and all she represents to the gay community was a stroke of tongue-in-cheek, up-yours genius that royally relaunched Bowie. It also announced to the world the metaphorical centre-stage-entrance of Ziggy Stardust (pl.III), a moment worthy of Marilyn in *Diamonds Are a Girl's Best Friend* or Streisand in *Hello, Dolly!*, in front of 15 million open-mouthed Britons. It was a moment of theatre, for sure, but acted out in an arena, pop, of such contemporary power and resonance that it had the urgency and impact of a news report. What was original was the gesture, the culture shock, the artifice, even if the individual musical components had been heard before in their separate guises.

It is important to stress that Bowie's flirtations with the musical idiosyncrasies of others around him have never been simple imitations or lazy reproductions in the hope of commercial popularity-surfing. For one thing, actively seeking popularity has never been his principal driving force, not since 'Starman', at any rate. His interest in other people's music, from whatever source or genre, is first and foremost a personal passion such as he might have developed if visual art had been his chosen path instead of music. His musical education, rather than being concentrated into his childhood and student days, as it is with many professional musicians, has been virtually uninterrupted since boyhood. His discovery of the catalogue of German-American composer Kurt Weill (1900–50), for example, was made not as part of a university syllabus (as was mine) but as an intrigued, self-motivated adult.

Weill-like chords and melodic corners seep into Bowie's style and – most noticeably – into his vocal delivery throughout his career. In his 1978 world tour, he programmed Kurt Weill's 'Alabama Song' (from the musical play-turned-opera Weill wrote with Bertolt Brecht, *The Rise and Fall of the City of Mahagonny*, first performed in 1930), which he subsequently recorded and released as a single in February 1980. The way the lyric of this song is constructed, with its series of disjointed, theatrical declamations and exclamations in the verse followed by a chorus that paints a seemingly unrelated picture, shares many similarities with a classic Bowie lyric shape. While the rest of the musical play/opera of *Mahagonny* is in Brecht and Weill's native German, these words were written in English for Brecht by Elisabeth Hauptmann (who had previously contributed significantly to the text of another Brecht-Weill music theatre work, *The Threepenny Opera*, which is set in London's Soho, while *Mahagonny* is set in a fictional dystopian wasteland representing America). Hauptmann's verse snaps:

> *Oh, show me the way*
> *To the next whiskey bar*
> *Oh, don't ask why*
> *Oh, don't ask why*
>
> *(repeated)*
>
> *For if we don't find*
> *The next whiskey bar*
> *I tell you we must die*
> *I tell you we must die*
> *I tell you, I tell you*
> *I tell you we must die*

The music, hitherto staccato and unfriendly, abruptly changes gear, broadening and warming into a sweepingly memorable tune for the chorus:

> *Oh, moon of Alabama*
> *We now must say goodbye*
> *We've lost our good old mama*
> *And must have whiskey, oh, you know why*

Compare this with Bowie's lyrical architecture for 'Ashes to Ashes' (pl.112) from his album of the same year, 1980, *Scary Monsters … and Super Creeps*. The verse throws out unanswered questions, random memories and disconnected utterances:

> *Do you remember a guy that's been*
> *In such an early song?*
> *I heard a rumour from Ground Control*
> *Oh no, don't say it's true*
> *They got a message from the Action Man*
> *'I'm happy, hope you're happy too*
> *I've loved all I've needed love*
> *Sordid details following.'*
>
> *The shrieking of nothing is killing*
> *Just pictures of Jap girls in synthesis*
> *And I ain't got no money and and I ain't got no hair*
> *But I'm hoping to kick but the planet is glowing aglow*

→ [112] OPPOSITE ● Original lyrics for 'Ashes to Ashes' by David Bowie, 1980 ● THE DAVID BOWIE ARCHIVE

Do you remember a guy that's bin
In such an early song
I've heard a rumour from Ground Control
Oh no — dont say it's true

They~~'ll~~ ⁿᵒᵗ message from the Action Man

I'm happy ~~~~ hope you're happy too

I've loved all ive needed love
Sordid details following

he needs help from me and you

You The shrieking of nothing is Killing —
just pictures of jap girl in synthesis
and I aint got money aint got no hair
and I hear the clash and I don't react
all this music's so strange
but im hoping to Kick ~~~~
~~but the planets~~ ~~~~ is glowing glowing
✗ and I can't clean ~~~~
~~~~ up my act.

Major Tom ~~don't like~~ hit the ashes To ad front to
~~passed~~ ~~face to~~ funky
~~Time has sone~~
We know Major Toms a junkie
~~strung out~~ in heavens High
hitting ~~~~ an all time low

time and again i tell myself
I'll stay clean tonight
But the little green ~~doctor~~ wheels ~~are~~ rolling me
Oh no not again

I'm stuck with a valuable friend
One ~~~~ Flash of light, but no smoking pistol *im happy hope you're happy too*
~~Every day my reason is ebbing~~
I've never done good things,
ive never done bad things
I never did anything out of the blue. wo o w
I want an axe to break the ice
I wanna come down right now

Then, as we slip into the refrain, the tune fills and simplifies, replacing the haiku-like parade of haphazard thoughts with an image of Bowie's earlier alter ego, the lost, confused astronaut Major Tom, abandoned in space:

Ashes to ashes, funk to funky,
We know Major Tom's a junkie
Strung out in heaven's high
Hitting an all-time low

Undoubtedly highly effective live on stage, dominated as it was by Bowie's superlative, characterized singing, the recording of 'Alabama Song' featured an attempt, ingenious in conception, to disrupt the expected drum beats of the Weill accompaniment (which has the feel of a tiny, ragged street band) by overdubbing the deliberately non-rhythmic drum pattern after all the other parts had been recorded. The result is chaotic (not in a good way), sounding as if a passer-by has been let loose with a cheap toy drum machine somewhere within earshot of a real band of musicians. No one said experimentation always worked.

On the EP (extended-play single) released in February 1982 of five songs from Bowie's performance in the TV dramatization of Brecht's play-with-songs *Baal*, he covered a song from Weill's *Berlin Requiem* of 1928 (the texts of which were also written by Brecht). His rendition of 'The Drowned Girl', as well as four other songs with music by Brecht himself (arranged beautifully on this occasion by composer Dominic Muldowney, a Weill expert) reveals both how suited Bowie's voice was to the sardonic, gritty delivery usually associated with Brecht-Weill stage works and also how Weill's edgy *Singspiel* style had surreptitiously crept into Bowie's own compositional armoury by the 1980s, since the five-song *Baal* EP does not sit awkwardly outside the rest of his recorded output, but seems to fit neatly within it. The EP was recorded at the Hansa Studios in Berlin – the 'studio by the Wall' – where Bowie had made parts of *Low* and all of *"Heroes"*, and which was within walking distance of the cabaret clubs and low-rent theatres that had inspired Weill and Brecht's music theatre collaborations in 1920s and '30s Weimar Germany. Intentionally or subconsciously, Bowie's haunting 'I Can't Read' (first released in September 1989, with a revised version prepared for Ang Lee's 1997 film *The Ice Storm*), with its melancholic fatalism and its angular harmonies supporting a semi-dissonant tune, looks on the page remarkably like the kind of song Weill would have been proud to have written had he lived beyond his meagre 50 years.

Bowie's unorthodox relationship with the music that has inspired him – not to imitate but to use as a launching pad for his own creations – can be seen at work in his interplay with the signature riff-oriented rock and roll or, more accurately, the Chicago-derived urban rhythm and blues of the Rolling Stones. The Stones' first three British hits were Chuck Berry's 'Come On', Lennon-McCartney's 'I Wanna Be Your Man' and Buddy Holly's 'Not Fade Away', but by late 1965 their international status was confirmed with a worldwide hit composed by Keith Richards and Mick Jagger themselves, '(I Can't Get No) Satisfaction'. Whatever smorgasbord of tastes had gone into their formative years, from 1965 on the Stones had a distinctive sound of their own, one that a skilled guitarist could pastiche without much difficulty.

→ [113] OPPOSITE • Original lyrics for 'Rebel Rebel' by David Bowie, 1974 • THE DAVID BOWIE ARCHIVE

REBEL
~~Rebel~~

You got ya mother in a whirl
Not sure if you're a boy or a girl
Hey babe, your hair's ~~ok~~ ~~fine~~ alright
Hey babe, let's out tonight.
You're like me and ~~me~~ ~~like~~ I like it ~~all~~
We like dancin and we ~~like~~ ~~to bed~~ look divine
You love bands when they play it hard
You want more and you want it fast

They put ~~me~~ you down
They say I'm wrong
You tacky thing
You put them on

Rebel, Rebel ~~✗~~
You've torn your dress
Rebel, Rebel
Your face is a mess
Rebel Rebel
How could they know
~~✗✗✗~~ Hot Tramp
I love you so

REPEAT!

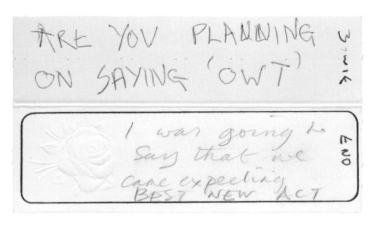

ARE YOU PLANNING ON SAYING 'OWT'

BRIAN

I was going to say that we came expecting BEST NEW ACT

ENO

So Bowie's inclusion of a song penned by Jagger and Richards in 1966, 'Let's Spend the Night Together', on his 1973 album *Aladdin Sane* might have been a straightforward cover tribute: after all, the Stones were the biggest band in the world that year, particularly successful in America. *Aladdin Sane*, despite its title name-checking a Chinese character from a Middle Eastern compendium of stories popular in English Christmas pantomime, was primarily Bowie's response to his impressions of the grimy, unstable underbelly of American culture, as he had experienced – or imagined – it from the windows of his tour bus. Elsewhere on the album, Mick Ronson's in-your-face electric guitar is unashamedly Stones-like, Bowie's vocal mannerisms owe more than a little to Jagger's swagger and the opening track, 'Watch That Man', seems like a re-run of the 1971 Jagger-Richards soon-to-be standard, 'Brown Sugar'. The bizarre, brittle, at times avant-jazz, at times high camp overarching atmosphere of *Aladdin Sane*, though, nodding in the direction of the prog-rock band King Crimson as well as 1950s Americana, is largely inhospitable territory for the unambiguous R&B of the Rolling Stones, and Bowie's treatment of 'Let's Spend the Night Together' is as unexpected as it is thrilling.

Bowie speeds the song up and adds in some fabulously demented, discordant, high-energy piano from Mike Garson and some equally crazed gyrating synthesizer and Hendrix-like lead-guitar figures, taking the song, which had courted controversy enough when first released by the Rolling Stones in 1967 thanks to its 'suggestive' lyrics, to a new level of sexual abandon. In Bowie's version, the night in question promises to be not merely wild but illegally so. Drugs and under-age sex may well have been meat and drink to touring rock groups of the 1970s, no less so for Bowie and his entourage by all accounts, but the manic energy with which they are celebrated in this recording is unusual. Most of the excesses described in the rebellious, psychedelic music of the 1960s and '70s now seem tame, even rather quaint, but Bowie's radical makeover of 'Let's Spend the Night Together' remains uncompromising, brutal and electrically charged in the twenty-first century, in a manner that is not dissimilar to the continuing challenge of Stanley Kubrick's *A Clockwork Orange*, which scandalized audiences across the free world in the year before the recording of *Aladdin Sane*.

Aladdin Sane was not Bowie's final brush with a Rolling Stones sound. One of his most enduringly popular songs, 'Rebel Rebel' (pl.113), first worked on in the studio in London over Christmas 1973, bears the unmistakable imprint of a Keith Richards-type riff (though rumours that Richards himself played on the sessions are groundless: on the record the player of the famous riff was Alan Parker). Again, despite the stated aim of mimicking a Stones intro, what Bowie and his musicians create is typically decoupled from its given starting point, veering off into a glam-rock anthem to transsexualism/transvestism (it is worth noting that 'Rebel Rebel' was released in 1974, two years before *Come Back to the Five and Dime, Jimmy Dean, Jimmy Dean* opened in Columbus, Ohio, eight years before its film adaptation and four years before the release of the French-Italian film version of *La Cage aux Folles*). The song's now iconic phrase, 'not sure if you're a boy or a girl', derives from the ubiquitous street shout of 1960s navvies in London: 'Are you a boy or a girl?'

It is a measure of Bowie's highly idiosyncratic performance in the song that in the nearly 40 years since the release of 'Rebel Rebel' it hasn't occurred to most listeners that it was originally prompted by another band's style. In both 'Let's Spend the Night Together' and 'Rebel Rebel' the process Bowie engages in is a form of distortion of the template provided by another band, rather than a homage. This is a crucial distinction, since it is the process he adopts time and time again, colliding, for example, with Philadelphia soul in *Young Americans* (1975), with Nile Rodgers' New York dance scene in *Scary Monsters* (1980) and with Trent Reznor's industrial metal soundscapes and early drum'n'bass grooves in *I. Outside* (1995). He does it most drastically in his three 'Berlin' albums, which deserve and receive discussion of their own below.

The urge to experiment has extended well beyond the multitude of musical and non-musical influences that have fed into each Bowie recording project (for the intelligently uncomplacent *Heathen*, made in his fifty-fifth year, Bowie cited Richard Strauss' 'Four Last Songs' of 1948 as musical preparation and Nietzsche's 1882 philosophical tract *Die Fröhliche Wissenschaft*, not to mention defaced medieval and Renaissance Christian art as non-musical elements: not a combination of influences likely to be found in any other popular artist of the early twenty-first century, I suspect). Long-term, on-off working relationships with a small group of key musical partners notwithstanding – Tony Visconti, Brian Eno, Carlos Alomar, Mike Garson, Gail Ann Dorsey, Reeves Gabrels, Mark Plati and Mick Ronson chief among them – Bowie has sought out a diverse range of musicians in his career, often (one imagines deliberately) placing himself or the musician in question out of their comfort zone, challenging him or her to avoid the expected, the easy reliance on muscle memory or deeply ingrained training.

Sometimes musicians were asked to exchange instruments in sessions, to provoke the potential novelties arising from a beginner's inexperience or technical innocence. Brian Eno introduced Bowie to games played by classical avant-garde composers in the 1950s, whereby chance – the throwing of a dice, the dealing of numbered cards and so on – would determine how or what players might play, a technique known formally as 'aleatory' composition. Eno's favourite method of encouraging unpredictable musical behaviour was the use of a set of cards he had devised with artist Peter Schmidt called 'Oblique Strategies', which involved musicians picking up cards (pl.114) with instructions on them, such as 'What would your closest friend do?' The commands on the cards could also be more specific to music: 'You are a disgruntled ex-member of a South African rock band. Play the notes you were not allowed to play.' Pretentious though some of these theories of musician-manipulation may now appear, on the whole the players themselves, perhaps dulled by years of sessions where they did indeed rely on familiar tricks, seemed open to them. For all the artificiality of the process, the aural results, in albums such as *I. Outside* and *Low,* are certainly original and unpredictable. Whether they would have been anyway, given Bowie's strange state of mind for the latter and the unusual circumstances of the recording sessions – in a converted French château, in a studio adjacent to the Berlin Wall during the Cold War and, in the case of *I. Outside*, up a mountain in the Alps – we will never know.

Low (1977) did not set the musical world on fire at the time of its release and many Bowie admirers found the switch of direction from *Station to Station* (1976) too drastic for comfort, but with the benefit of a longer period of reflection it has rightly been judged one of the seminal musical recordings of the late twentieth century. *Low* is traditionally grouped with *"Heroes"* (pl.122) and *Lodger* into a trilogy of 'Berlin' albums, though of the three only *"Heroes"* was recorded in its entirety at the Hansa Studios. The triptych is distinguished not so much by the Berlin studio premises as by the creative chemistry of Bowie, Eno and producer Tony Visconti working in a milieu of electronic-acoustic experimentation, in a closed, creatively claustrophobic, often inescapably tense atmosphere. Despite the fact that Bowie was submitting himself to the painful process of trying to shake off his addiction to cocaine at the time and that a dark mood would often descend on proceedings, these unpropitious conditions nevertheless bred a surprising degree of artistic freedom and the creative outcome successfully defied the commercial imperatives of the record industry – no mean feat in itself for an asset as valuable as Bowie.

Underpinning this pressure-cooker working environment was the inspiration of German synthesizer-based groups Kraftwerk, Neu! and Tangerine Dream. These so-called Krautrock bands, as well as Eno and others in the vanguard of electronica, were able to develop and thrive in the late 1970s thanks to advances in synthesizer technology, led by Moog and ARP. Bowie met the members of Kraftwerk – Ralf Hütter, Florian Schneider, Wolfgang Flür and Karl Bartos – at their purpose-built, state-of-the-art Kling-Klang studio in Düsseldorf, West Germany, in 1977, not long after the release of the group's groundbreaking album *Radio-Activity*. One critical difference between Kraftwerk's approach and Bowie's was the emphasis placed by the Germans on finding electronic means for all departments of the sound: processing vocals in keyboard-operated vocoders, usurping acoustic drums with machines and so on. By contrast, to the newly synthesized, 'ambient' washes of sound made available by machine technology, Bowie and Eno added human players on guitar, drums, bass, acoustic piano and cello, with Bowie providing emotionally taut vocals on some tracks, alongside occasional male and female backing vocals.

Put bluntly, *Low* redefined what a pop album might be. While underground and niche-market artists and technicians had been playing with the concept of long, slowly shifting rivers of synthesized and modulating wave forms for some time before Bowie, Eno and Visconti joined the party, Bowie's engagement with the movement ensured its transition to the mainstream, where it reacted with a huge number of musicians and listeners across the globe. In its way it was as much a redrawing of the musical map as the Beatles' *Revolver* had been ten years earlier. What's more, Bowie's entanglement with German electronica released it from the limitations it had placed upon itself. *Low*, unlike the mechanistic ramblings of Kraftwerk's *Autobahn* (1974) and *Radio-Activity* (1975), or Neu!'s *Neu 1* (1971), was filled with human emotion, even if it was invariably confined to melancholia or ennui.

Low's genesis lay in Bowie's too-late-for-inclusion soundtrack ideas for Nicolas Roeg's darkly futuristic 1976 film *The Man Who Fell to Earth,* in which Bowie played the leading role of the humanoid alien Thomas Jerome Newton. Much of the pessimistic tone of the album reflects the film's themes of isolation and the consequences of greed. The most startling feature of the record's overall musical impression for listeners at the time (I can still recall vividly the shock at my first playing of it, as a Bowie-idolizing music student) was not its black mood, common enough in rock, but its apparent rhythmic, harmonic and melodic inactivity. It was like frozen music. What mainstream music lovers were mostly unaware of in the mid-1970s was that this bare, musical stasis was in fact part of a growing, soon-to-be all-conquering movement across modern culture.

The term 'mimimalism' was coined by English composer Michael Nyman in 1968 to refer to a trend in classical music that began in the 1960s on the fringes of musical activity with experimental composers Terry Riley, La Monte Young and John Cage, before gradually occupying the centre ground with composers Steve Reich, Philip Glass and John Adams in the 1970s and '80s. In essence this trend was a reaction to the frantic complexity and theoretical overload of so much modernist music in the first half of the twentieth century, though minimalism's apparent 'simplicity' is deceptive. The undisputed master of the genre is American composer Steve Reich, who in studying the drumming and mallet-based musics of Africa and Indonesia came to the realization that what seemed to be endless, hypnotic repetition in this music was in fact continuously, subtly changing. He sought to adapt this theory of incremental transformation to Western music in a series of landmark works, which also extended its scope to include voice sampling and the derivation of rhythmic patterns from looped tapes of speech. David Bowie is the conduit through which this relatively private, art-music idea made the leap across genres into modern pop: *Low* was the project in which he brought about this cross-fertilization. Brian Eno was his pilot into the new territory.

Eno's 1975 album *Discreet Music*, an obsessively favourite vinyl record of Bowie's at the time, had taken many of the same precepts Steve Reich was exploring – the looping of musical phrases back on to themselves, the repetition of units of melody or harmony so that their timbre gradually morphs into new sounds, almost imperceptibly (the album's title track is over half an hour long, the length of a Haydn symphony). *Discreet Music* is reserved, gentle and unobtrusive (this is no criticism, it is intentionally so), investigating the possibilities of French composer Erik Satie's theories on *musique d'ameublement*. Satie's 'furniture music' was meant to form part of the background of a room or scene or moment, rather than be its primary focus. He introduced the concept with five short pieces in 1917, whose subtitles carried various descriptors such as 'to be played in a vestibule' or 'for a drawing room'. Eno applied this logic to what has since been termed his 'ambient' music. It is no fault of Eno's, whose ideas were fresh and searching, that his ambient music was to become the template for myriad listless wallpaper-like soundtracks to dentists' surgeries.

Eno's urge to withdraw ego from music, to allow chance and accident to play a viable part in the creative process, was, in the context of the mid-1970s, courageous, radical and renewing. The subdued, almost pastoral calm of *Discreet Music*, though, stands in stark contrast to the menacing, suppressed energy of *Low* and even more so to the muscular, industrial intensity of *"Heroes"*. What Bowie and his rock players brought to the 'ambient' ethos was a raw forcefulness. The combination of rich synthetic textures (totally new aural sensations for the majority of listeners), Bowie's languorously emotive vocals – as if always teetering on the precipice of some unspecified calamity – and the grinding, often disorientatingly slow rock pulse of the three-album set was thoroughly dynamic. It proved liberating to musicians the world over.

Within months, if not weeks, of the release of *Low*, the landscape in which other composers stood shifted in its direction. For myself, I borrowed a stupendously unattainable ARP 2600 synthesizer from a kindly producer and immediately put it to work accompanying the stage antics of my fellow student, the then barely known comic Rowan Atkinson. And soon, with the revolutionary Yamaha CS-80 polyphonic synth in my Kilburn bedsit, I was creating endless cassettes of *Low*-inspired songs and meandering instrumental expositions. My experience was multiplied a thousandfold among young musicians. A whole pop movement, the so-called New Romantics, was to be spawned from Bowie's subsequent 1980 song and video, 'Ashes to Ashes' (a craze I confess I mischievously lampooned in 'Nice Video, Shame About the Song', a song I wrote for 'Not the Nine O'Clock News', the first line of which reads, 'Let's spend our honeymoon in East Berlin'), but the musical impact of *Low* and its sequel *"Heroes"* was far deeper and longer lasting, stretching out beyond pop into the culture at large, embracing film music, performance art, dance and classical concert works.

As we have seen, the American composers John Cage, Terry Riley, Steve Reich and Philip Glass were a significant influence on the minimalist style of the Berlin albums. In the wake of *Low*, *"Heroes"* and *Lodger*, the flow of influence reversed on itself and Glass composed two symphonies based on source material from two of the set – the *Low* symphony in 1992, followed in 1996 by *Heroes*, which was also adapted into a contemporary dance work choreographed by Twyla Tharp. The interaction of these two worlds, contemporary classical and pop, in the to and fro of Bowie, Eno and Glass, represents a milestone in the convergence of musical genres that has been the story of recent musical history. It must also be immensely gratifying to Bowie, a man whose artistic appetite has been unusually eclectic since his teens, to witness the gloriously fruitful interplay of art forms that is the reality of modern creativity: not many who dream of these *rapprochements* can also claim hefty responsibility for their coming into being. David Bowie, composer, is one such catalyst.

→ [116] **OPPOSITE** ◦ Character notes for Ziggy Stardust by David Bowie, 1972 ◦ THE DAVID BOWIE ARCHIVE

↓ [117–122] **FOLLOWING PAGES**
[117] ◦ Original lyrics for 'Oh! You Pretty Things' by David Bowie, 1971 ◦ THE DAVID BOWIE ARCHIVE
[118] ◦ Original lyrics for 'Lady Stardust' by David Bowie, 1972 ◦ THE DAVID BOWIE ARCHIVE

[119] ◦ Original lyrics for 'Fascination' by David Bowie, 1975 ◦ THE DAVID BOWIE ARCHIVE
[120] ◦ Original lyrics for 'Fashion' by David Bowie, 1980 ◦ THE DAVID BOWIE ARCHIVE

[121] ◦Original lyrics for 'Battle for Britain (The Letter)' by David Bowie, 1997 (signed 2007) ◦ THE DAVID BOWIE ARCHIVE
[122] ◦ Original lyrics for "Heroes" by David Bowie, 1977 ◦ THE DAVID BOWIE ARCHIVE

① How he was a bum and the boy with him and knowing he was against the system.

② How he shined and the adulation and money and respect came.

④ How he knew he had to out-hip those queens and gets into the role oh so well.

⑦ How his attitude to Joe Public changes and how fucked-up he comes as to the audience

⑧ the new Sensation comes

Wake up you sleepy head, Put on some clothes ~~got~~.
                                    Shake up your bed
Put another log on the fire for me
I made some breakfast and coffee
I look out the window and what do I see
A crack in the sky and a hand
reaching down to me
All ~~you~~ nightmares came today
~~And~~ Would you tell them to stay away

What are we coming to
There's no room for me no fun for you
I think about a world to come
Where our books are found by the
                                  Golden Ones
They're written in pain, written in awe
By a ~~puzzled~~ man who question'd what
                              we were here for
All ~~the~~ strangers come today
And it looks as though they're here
                              To stay

People would stare at the make-up
on his face,
Laughin' at his long black ~~blond~~ hair
his animal grace

Lady Stardust sang his songs
of rebels, Kings & Queens

The ~~femme~~ fatales immerged from
shadows to ~~watch~~ ~~this~~ this creature fine
While boys ~~stood~~ up on chairs
To make their point of view
And I smiled sadly
for a love I could not obey

Lady Stardust sang his songs
darkness & dismay

And ~~always~~ Oh how I lied
when they asked me if I knew his name
For he was "So Right"

Every time I see fascination
I just can't stand still   gotta use 'ker
Every time I think   ~~you dear~~ of what you put me thru dear
Fascination moves °°° ~~somewhere~~ ~~near~~ sweeping near me
Still I take you

Fascination -- sho nuff - takes apart of me
Can a heartbeat — ~~drive a man~~ — ~~upon knees~~
~~be the~~ ~~candy~~ fever — raging inside me
live in the fever
Fascination — Oh yea - takes apart of me
I can't help it — I gotta use her — everytime
Fascination ~~lays me down~~ , comes around

If your soul is calling me — when I'm walking
seems like everywhere I turn — I know ya ~~talking to me~~
          waiting for
I know People think — I'm a little crazy
~~Gotta get my fill~~   like this
Gotta hunt ~~that thing~~ — like fascination
Still I take you

Stand by your station/boys
/or.

There's a brand new dance
but I don't know its name
that people from bad homes
do it again and again
it's ~~big~~ and bland
full of ~~horror~~ tension and fear
They do it over there
But we don't do it here

They go ~~stop stop~~ Fashion
~~rock rock~~ turn to the left
   "   "   Fashion   "   " right

~~Hell up ahead   burn a flag~~
~~Shake a fist   start a fight~~
~~If you're covered in blood~~
~~You're doing it right~~

we midgets and fools
should learn not to dance
on concrete poured for
GIANTS

land stamping
dance sounds
take out same
instruments.

Fashion

We are the ~~goon~~ squad
and we're coming to town
We'll ~~break every bone~~
We'll turn ~~into~~ upside down

Beep Beep
Beep Beep.

There's a brand new talk
but it's not very clear
~~throw it in the path~~
~~shout it at the ph~~
that people from good homes
will be talking this year
Its loud and it's tasteless
I've ^not heard it before
Shout while your dancing
On the – er dance floor

Marison

Fashion   Fashion
~~listen to me~~   ~~talk to me~~
don't listen to me   don't " " "
~~see it~~

beep-beep   beep-beep   Fashion
instead of beep-beep

Battle for Britain (The Letter)

My my, but time do fly
When it's in another pair of hand
And a loser I will be
For I've never been a winner
In my life
I used the sucker pills
And pity for the self
Though it's the animal in me
But I'd rather be a begger man
On the shelf

Don't be so forlorn
It's just the payoff
It's the rain before the storm
On a better day
I'll take you by the hand
And lead you thru the doors
~~Don't be so forlorn~~
Don't be so forlorn
It's just the payoff
It's the rain before the storm

Don't you let my letter
Get you down

My my, but time do fly
When it's in another pair of pants
And illusion #1 I will be
For I've never been a sinner
La-de-dah.

I will be King
You will be Queen
~~they~~ ~~and~~ nothing will drive them away
We can beat us/them We can be heroes
Just far ~~&~~ one day

mean
drink
We're rovers and that is a fact
  "   "   "   " is that
~~they~~ nothing will keep us together

We can steal time

swim
dolfin can swim

can
I remember ~~when we hit~~ standing by the wall
~~I remember~~
       ~~when we~~
And the guns   shot above our heads
~~And the~~ ~~mirror~~ ~~covered~~ lest we fall
And we ~~kissed and~~ you ~~felt~~ ~~nothing~~
       as though nothing could fall
And shame was on the other side

38/500

Bo 78

↑ **[124] ABOVE** ⬥ David Bowie during the *"Heroes"* album
sessions, 1977 ⬥ Photograph by Masayoshi Sukita

DAVID BOWIE IS FOREVER AND EVER

↑ **[125]** **ABOVE** ◦ *"Heroes"* album cover mock-up, 1977 ◦
THE DAVID BOWIE ARCHIVE

CHRISTOPHER BREWARD

FOR 'WE ARE THE GOON SQUAD': BOWIE, STYLE AND THE POWER OF THE LP COVER, 1967–1983

David Bowie's special place in an iconography of extremist British style was spotted quickly by Peter York, one of the sharpest of Britain's pop-culture pundits. In his influential essay 'Them', published in the October 1976 issue of *Harpers & Queen*, he isolates Bryan Ferry, the Roeg/Bowie film *The Man Who Fell to Earth* and Andrew Logan's Miss World competition as quintessential examples of 'Themness', and describes subscribers to the 'Them' cult:

> [They are] examples of a new breed, the creators of the dominant high-style of the seventies. These new aesthetes have in common a visual sensibility so demanding that they are prepared to sacrifice almost anything for the look … Thems are the word made flesh. Thems put the idea into their living; they wear their rooms, eat their art.[1]

Such intensity pervades Bowie's metamorphic career and responses to it. As a high priest of 'Themness', his music, lyrics, public utterances, body and wardrobe continue to be scrutinized for prescient meaning, for clues about the last or the next big thing. If the dominant quality of 'Them' style could be described as the capturing of the 'soon' rather than the 'now', then Bowie's co-option of it, particularly during the 1970s, operated like a compass, pointing magnetically towards its future (or sometimes confusingly to its past) material manifestations. Successive framings of his compelling form seemed to combine the qualities of nostalgia and futurism in tandem, ensuring that his image resided not in the present, but tantalizingly elsewhere. As captured on the cover of an LP, Bowie's style retained a talismanic power with wide-reaching influence. Certainly my own experience, growing up far from London in the 1970s, was, like that of many other sensitive, isolated boys of my generation and after, ineffably marked by Bowie's spectral presence – glowing through the television screen, emblazoned across a record sleeve.

In the digital age we perhaps forget how important album covers were in the promotion of stars, as vehicles for artistic collaboration and as signifiers of allegiance and aspiration among fans. Their vivid visual appeal and haptic immediacy offered a tangible connection between performer and listener: albums were chosen and purchased with devout intention, and their covers opened up decorative possibilities that turned teenage bedrooms into holy shrines. For those (and I counted myself among them) whose provincial location kept them distant from, and subservient to, the pulse of metropolitan fashionability, from 'Them', an LP cover propped against a skirting board could stand in for all sorts of imagined and hoped-for affiliations.[2] Bowie's were always among the most effective, yet disorientating, productions in this regard, perhaps because he had such a direct creative influence on their format. In focusing on their construction and content, this essay explores how key covers, from 1967's *David Bowie* onwards, distilled both the elusive fashion moment and the character of the artist in extraordinary ways.

LONDON

Gerald Fearnley's June 1967 head-and-shoulders shot for Bowie's eponymous debut set the bar in offering a format that was both seemingly generic and yet slightly unsettling of the status quo (pl.126). Photographed in Fearnley's basement studio in Bryanston Street, near Marble Arch, the young artist carries all the trappings of 'Swinging London', then in its Indian summer, on his narrow shoulders. The modish (as in 'mod' and mode) Robert James page-boy haircut and the quasi-military coat (designed by Bowie himself) suggest the laddish dandyism of Carnaby Street (glinting gold button reflecting burnished blond hair), while the Disney-like, West-Coast graphics and wistful gaze betray a sense of other-worldliness that almost undermines Bowie's emerging notoriety as a recognizable 'face', sharp and streetwise. Such willful contrarianism placed him in the same milieu as the more whimsical and experimental of his music contemporaries, including his elfin friend Marc Bolan and Ray Davies of the Kinks. Yet as Peter Doggett notes in his account of Bowie's career in the 1970s, true fame remained elusive. Following the release of the album Bowie was forced to take up part-time work in a West End reprographics store and seemed to disappear for two years.[3] In some ways then the visuals of *David Bowie* perfectly capture the universal longing of the star-struck suburban shop-boy: hungry for success, 'in fashion' though not yet 'of' it.

By the summer of 1969, however, following the release of 'Space Oddity' (pl.127), Bowie had both escaped from his rut and established a more convincing and suggestive creative grounding. In July 1967 he had met the mercurial avant-garde mime artist and dancer Lindsay Kemp, who would become a mentor and regular collaborator throughout the following decade, and from there on life had changed. The Keith McMillan image chosen for the cover of the first UK version of Bowie's next LP, *The Man Who Sold the World* (pl.129), already shows Kemp's interstitial sexuality wielding its influence. Here Bowie reclines across a day-bed draped in shimmering blue silk, sporting a Mr Fish 'man-dress' of cream velvet with a Beardsley-esque print of indigo fruits and flowers, which strains open across his pale chest, accentuates the curve of his hip and flares out to the calves, where black leather boots emerge and cross. Long, lightly curled hair falls to his shoulders while he raises a bejewelled arm to adjust the brim of a fedora. In his other hand he elegantly holds a single playing card above the pack of cards that has been strewn across the floor of a studio whose red curtains and exotic accessories mimic the fittings of a Victorian opium den, a bordello or one of the many bohemian squats that peppered Notting Hill, Kensington and Camden Town in the period.

By 1971 Bowie is the ultimate odalisque, resplendent in his provocation. In some ways his chameleonic persona was again simply soaking up the influences already surrounding him. Mr Fish and his generation of tailors on Savile Row and Jermyn Street had been selling kaftans and tightly cut unisex suits to wayward aristocrats, fashion photographers, interior designers and pop stars since 1968. Mick Jagger had long since laid claim to that turf, but Bowie is flirting more determinedly with the dangerous territory of sexual ambiguity. In his survey of the wider music industry's relationship with homosexuality, John Gill notes the prescience of Bowie's interview with *Jeremy*, the UK's first mainstream gay magazine, in 1970. 'Though an unremarkable and wholly anodyne piece', the interview was in the nervous context of the times 'a radical act, and could only have started pushing buttons with a gay audience starved of contemporary queer culture'.[4]

If talking to *Jeremy* was one thing, Bowie's infamous interview with Michael Watts of *Melody Maker* in January 1972 was quite another, and explosive in its suggestions. Many of the signifiers already displayed across the first UK cover of *The Man Who Sold the World* are reprised in the piece, ballast to Bowie's mischievous assertion, halfway through the interview: 'I'm gay ... and always have been.' Watts opens with an album-referencing tongue-in-cheek complaint that 'even though he wasn't wearing silken gowns right out of Liberty's, and his long blond hair no longer fell wavily past his shoulders, David Bowie was looking yummy'. He goes on to make the following assertion:

> David's present image is to come on like a swishy queen, a gorgeously effeminate boy. He's as camp as a row of tents, with his limp hand and trolling vocabulary ... He knows that in these times it's permissible to act like a male tart, and that to shock and outrage, which pop has always striven to do ... is a balls-breaking process ... The expression of his sexual ambivalence establishes a fascinating game ... In a period of conflicting sexual identity he shrewdly exploits the confusion surrounding the male and female roles. 'Why aren't you wearing your girl's dress today?' I said to him ... 'Oh dear,' he replied, 'you must understand that it's not a woman's. It's a man's dress.'[5]

Though at the time the interview went relatively unremarked, in later years its message caused the predictable flurries of manufactured controversy that Bowie continued to manipulate and encourage. But as Gill cautions, 'you didn't need to be Roland Barthes to decode the public persona that David Bowie was projecting. Although maybe you did: Barthes might have picked up on the subtext of artifice and performance that everyone else seemed to overlook at the time.'[6] Indeed subsequent alternative covers for *The Man Who Sold the World* (pls 128–31) indicate a much more fluid approach to intentionality, meaning and audience, revealing Bowie's willingness to test and exploit possibilities at this formative stage of his career. They included a US version that featured a cartoon by Mike Weller of a deranged cowboy, stetson shot to pieces, blanket-wrapped Winchester shotgun under his arm, passing the south London mental asylum in which Bowie's brother was receiving treatment and emitting a speech-bubble, the words of which ('Roll up your

[126] *David Bowie* • 1967

[127] *David Bowie* (re-released as *Space Oddity* in 1972) • 1969

[128] *The Man Who Sold the World* (original US release), 1970

[129] *The Man Who Sold the World* (original UK release) • 1971

[130] *The Man Who Sold the World* (original German release) • 1971

[131] *The Man Who Sold the World* (worldwide re-release) • 1972

sleeves and show us your arms') Mercury Records had excised. This riff on madness was perhaps closer to the themes of the record within, but its power to shock paled beside that of a preening Bowie in a man-dress.

The second UK version of *The Man Who Sold the World*, released in 1972 with a monochrome image by photographer Brian Ward of a guitar-wielding Bowie kicking his leg in the air, could not have been more different to the effete Pre-Raphaelite ennui of its predecessor, or to the intervening retro-camp glamour distilled into the cover for *Hunky Dory* in 1971 (pl.132), where Ward's tinted portrait transforms the star into a latter-day Greta Garbo. In many ways, while referencing the grittier queer machismo of New York contemporaries such as Lou Reed (a close friend, whose album *Transformer* Bowie produced in 1972), the second version of *The Man Who Sold the World* also echoed the explosive and simultaneous debut of Bowie's most successful persona, Ziggy Stardust. Here was a look infused with a strange, superhuman, sexual energy, captured by Watts' description of Bowie's wardrobe in the 1972 *Melody Maker* interview:

> He'd slipped into an elegant-patterned type of combat suit, very tight around the legs, with the shirt unbuttoned to reveal a full expanse of white torso. The trousers were turned up at the calves to allow a better glimpse of a huge pair of red plastic boots with at least three-inch rubber soles; and the hair was Vidal Sassooned into such impeccable shape that one held one's breath in case the slight breeze from the open window dared ruffle it. I wish you could have been there to varda [see] him; he was so super.[7]

Ziggy's heart-stopping image bestrode four album covers. Released in June 1972, *The Rise and Fall of Ziggy Stardust and the Spiders from Mars* was the first (pl.133). Brian Ward captured the alien star outside his studio in London's Heddon Street, clad in a Bowie-designed costume, cut and sewn by Freddie Burretti, who would go on to design subsequent Ziggy outfits. The costume was inspired by the get-up of the Droogs in Stanley Kubrick's notorious film of the Anthony Burgess novel *A Clockwork Orange*, released in the UK earlier that year. The colourized photograph exudes mystery,

menace and the anticipation of perverse sex and violence among the rain-soaked, litter-strewn backstreets of depressed early 1970s London. A fan recalls having intense feelings about Bowie at this time, as described in a volume of pop-star fantasies collated by Fred and Judy Vermorel in 1985:

> Bowie was magic and he was supreme. He had the qualities of a type of ruler. He was science fiction personified. To me he represented the most bizarre things which were evil and not of this world and completely beyond the imagination. I really believed he was an alien of some kind. I didn't think he was normal, human ... I would look at him in his posters and try to understand the sexuality in his records. I'd analyse them to death. I'd think that means this and this means that ... I think he should be made aware of how he's influenced people's dress, their manners, their behaviour ... It's a terrible thing he did really. He's got a lot to answer for.[8]

The next two album covers exploited the propagandist potential of the poster format in their stark presentation of Ziggy's spiky, painted, naked narcissism, all overlaid with the sheen of a peculiarly 1973 version of elegance (a look that Bowie would later characterize as 'a cross between Nijinsky and Woolworths' in a 1976 *Daily Express* interview[9]). Released in April 1973, *Aladdin Sane* (pl.134) featured a cover shot by fashion photographer Brian Duffy that was so innovative in its use of seven-colour printing that the album sleeve could only be printed in Zurich. The effect was hyper-real: Ziggy's trademark copper hair and Flash Gordon lightning bolt make-up (applied by Bowie's new personal stage make-up artist, Pierre La Roche of the House of Arden, who would go on to be in charge of make-up for the Ziggy Stardust/ Aladdin Sane tour of 1973 and later worked on the *Rocky Horror Picture Show*) searing against the pure white background. The strong fashion references continued in *Pin Ups* (pl.135), released six months later. The cover was photographed by Justin de Villeneuve and features his protégée Twiggy, who leans her polished frame into Ziggy's neck, the blank expressions of both as fragile as china Pierrot dolls. These are

[132] *Hunky Dory* • 1971

[133] *The Rise and Fall of Ziggy Stardust and the Spiders from Mars* • 1972

[134] *Aladdin Sane* • 1973

[135] *Pin Ups* • 1973

[136] *Diamond Dogs* • 1974

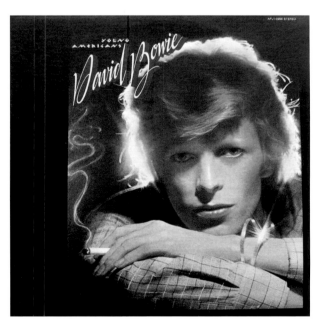

[137] *Young Americans* • 1975

images of such attenuated artificiality that they chime perfectly with the sensibility of a contemporary international fashion world that through the work of Yves Saint Laurent, Halston, Ossie Clark and Walter Albini valorized a vague elision of camp Art Deco revivalism, a sensual attention to surfaces and the glittery brilliance of Futurism.[10]

NEW YORK AND LOS ANGELES

The prettiness of *Pin Ups* did not survive for long, and Ziggy was famously abandoned by his progenitor, like Frankenstein's hapless monster, at a dramatic concert at the Hammersmith Odeon in July 1973. His final appearance, as a mutant canine/human in a painting by Guy Peellaert (a Belgian artist purloined from the stable of Mick Jagger) on the cover of the May 1974 album *Diamond Dogs* (pl.136), anticipated the coming shift to darkness in Bowie's repertoire. The fashion photographer Terry O'Neill had previously produced a striking monochrome portrait of a louche Bowie in pseudo-gaucho dress, a huge and angry snarling hound leaping up next to him (pl.175). Peellaert's version was no less disturbing, with its sphinx-like star sprawled across the gatefold as if in an American-Gothic freak show, the prominent genitals painted out to pacify conservative US mores. As a reflection of the dystopian vision revealed by the LP's music and the deteriorating state of Bowie's mental equilibrium the cover worked perfectly. And though Bowie later disavowed that punk held any sway over him, its visual codes and nihilistic nastiness did seem to herald the coming of the end of glam aesthetics for something far more disturbing.

Diamond Dogs coincided with Bowie's self-enforced exile, first to New York and Los Angeles and then, from 1976, to Lake Geneva and Berlin. The cover of his 1975 release *Young Americans* (pl.137) briefly reprised the nostalgic haziness of *Hunky Dory* in its use of a backlit and heavily airbrushed portrait by Stephen Jacobs (an image that owes a debt to the cover of Toni Basil's 1974 album *After Dark* – Basil was the choreographer for the Diamond Dogs concert tour). With his checked shirt, glinting bangle and sinuously smouldering cigarette, Bowie comes across like a young and androgynous Katharine Hepburn. But the soft-focus effects were not to last. The move to America marked

Bowie's increasing reliance on cocaine, just as the shift towards a colder, harder-edged creative impulse was transforming cultural production in the worlds of art, theatre, fashion, film and music. Hugo Wilcken puts it succinctly:

> There's a part of his drug addiction that falls into cliché. After all, Bowie was hardly the only rock star in mid-seventies LA burning himself out on cocaine. Each era has its drug, which translates its myth – in the mid sixties LSD reflected a naïve optimism about the possibility of change; and in the mid seventies, cocaine echoed the grandiose nihilism of post-Manson LA. And Bowie fell into that trap.[11]

The covers of the four albums produced between 1976 and 1979 betray both the vicissitudes of Bowie's personal inner tumult and this lurch towards the paranoid, introspective, post-industrial, dehumanized character of late Cold-War pop culture. Their harsh visual bleakness was irresistible to a generation of NME-reading sad young men (and they generally were young men) whose imaginative parameters were sketched out by the novels of J. G. Ballard, the music of Kraftwerk and the films of Nicolas Roeg. *Station to Station* (pl.138), released in January 1976, used a photograph taken by Steve Schapiro on the set of Roeg's film *The Man Who Fell to Earth* on the cover. Bowie, who starred as the alien Thomas Jerome Newton, is walking through the doorway of his spaceship (represented in the film by an anechoic recording chamber). Writing about the way the image was used on the album, Wilcken notes:

> On the original release it was cropped and black and white, giving it an austere, Expressionist flavour redolent of the European Modernism of the 1920s and the photography of Man Ray. The stark, red sans serif typography – the album title and artist are run together – adds to the retro-Modernist feel. Bowie himself hovers somewhere between America and Europe, his hair in a James Dean quiff, his tieless white shirt severely buttoned to the neck.[12]

[138] *Station to Station* • 1976

[139] *Low* • 1977

[140] *"Heroes"* • 1977

[141] *Lodger* • 1979

[142] *Scary Monsters … and Super Creeps* • 1980

[143] *Let's Dance* • 1983

BERLIN

By the release of *Low* (pl.139) and *"Heroes"* (pl.140) the following year, the transition to Europe was complete, musically in terms of *Low* and aesthetically in so far as the visual references of the *"Heroes"* cover went. The cover of *Low* fell back once more on the imagery of *The Man Who Fell to Earth*, featuring a manipulated still from the film, one 'already used for a paperback reissue of the original Walter Tevis novel, and designed by Bowie's old school friend George Underwood ... The dominant colour is an autumnal orange. Bowie's hair is exactly the same shade as the swirling, Turner-esque background, underlining the solipsistic notion of place reflecting person, object and subject melding into one.'[13] With its Neo-Expressionist photographic portrait by Masayoshi Sukita, *"Heroes"* of October 1977 is more clearly revealing of Bowie's obsession with German culture of the first half of the twentieth century, which appeared to encompass everything from the cabaret scene of the 1930s evoked in Christopher Isherwood's *Goodbye to Berlin* through the rise of Fascism (the trappings of which Bowie seemed to flirt with) to the bleak psycho-pathology of the divided city. In common with the cover chosen for Iggy Pop's *The Idiot* (produced by Bowie during this period), the *"Heroes"* cover seemingly makes reference to the angular, attenuated gestures of those paintings by members of *Die Brücke* that fascinated Bowie as he sought refuge in Berlin's art galleries, and quotes directly from a scene in Luis Buñuel and Salvador Dalí's Surrealist masterpiece *Un Chien Andalou* (1929), in which ants pour out of the stigmata in the centre of the artist's palm.

While unpopular with the music critics, 1979's *Lodger* (pl.141), the final album of the 'Berlin triptych', marked a watershed in terms of the design concept, as Peter Doggett records:

> Its rather alarming cover art, photographed by Brian Duffy, outstripped any of the music for boldness ... *Lodger* represented a deliberate step into a world in which Egon Schiele became the art director for a futuristic horror movie, directed perhaps by David Cronenberg. Bowie's body was depicted across the gatefold sleeve, prone

like Schiele's portrait of Friederike Maria Beer, distorted like the same artist's lacerating self-portraits. It was as if the turmoil of the previous records had been focused on to the artwork of *Lodger*, leaving the music itself unsettlingly free of emotion.[14]

Deliberately shot in low resolution with a Polaroid SX-70 camera, a black-suited Bowie, in full victim make-up with an apparently broken nose, starred, masochistically, in a 'crime scene' scenario. Strikingly reminiscent of Weegee's shockingly violent Lower East Side social documentary photographs of the 1940s, the image would also prove eerily close in spirit to New York artist Robert Longo's stark *Men in the Cities* drawings of 1981 (Longo would himself go on to direct New Order's 'Bizarre Love Triangle' video in 1986 using similar motifs).[15] Inside the gatefold sleeve, a collage of found images arranged by artist Derek Boshier included a picture of Che Guevara's corpse, Mantegna's *Lamentation over the Dead Christ* and studio shots of Bowie being prepared for his death scene.

NEW YORK

If *Lodger* marked a bereavement, then the first album of the following decade indicated, in the words of its author, a 'purging'.[16] Released in September 1980, *Scary Monsters ... and Super Creeps* washed away the disturbing memories of Los Angeles and Berlin with the help of fashion illustrator Edward Bell's delicate drawing of a tousled Bowie in Pierrot costume, superimposed against ethereal photographs by Brian Duffy (pl.142). This cover image returned its protagonist back to his shape-shifting of the early 1970s, but also seemed to reveal the mechanics that lay behind his former incarnations as simple acts of performance. By choosing Bell, Bowie seemed to be signalling an understanding of the superficialities and contingency of fashion and its importance in his own work – an arena he had explored in the recent single 'Boys Keep Swinging', with its attendant 'drag' video, and in the mildly cynical track 'Fashion' on *Scary Monsters*. On the album's cover, Bowie seems caught in the act of robing or disrobing as he adjusts the frills on his shoulder, and the graphic facility with which Bell indicates stage make-up and scrawls the title in expressive calligraphy around the edge of the LP suggests nothing more than a spread in *Vogue* or an advert for lipstick. It is all too theatrical to be true.

LONDON

Peter York included a short piece entitled 'Bowie Night' in *Style Wars*, a collection of his essays launched in 1980 – the same year as *Scary Monsters*. He describes the aftermath of a party in fashion designer Thea Porter's Greek Street shop that must have taken place a few years previously, around 1976, just as punk hit London and at around the same time that *Harpers & Queen* ran his feature on 'Them':

> In the corner is the *biggest Bowie casualty I've ever seen*, and I've seen a few … She's done up completely as late '72 Bowie, i.e. the ginger Joe Brown crop … a wasp striped leotard, all in one job … and the little ballet shoes and the one chandelier earring, which is actually a silver leaf hanging from a red star. But the main thing is, *she's got the full tilt mime face on*, red circles on the cheeks, red lips and red around the eyes on a white base – the full clown job. Her teeth, like David's, are a bit … weaselish.[17]

York goes on to describe how the company moves on to the lesbian bar Louise's next door, a venue where 'the evolved Bowie freaks, and the original punks' feel at home, but where tensions are emerging: 'Down Louise's that night are Malcolm McLaren – with Sid and Nancy – and Steve Strange, who had a different name then and is done up like a miniature Vivienne Westwood with black candy floss spikes and a camouflage bondage suit.' Frankie, the Bowie casualty, introduces York to her lesbian punk friend Caroline and the evening ends messily in a squat in Kensington Gardens Square, in a space that seems to telescope the previous ten years of subcultural history: 'I meet her pals, which is to say a cross-cut of sci-fi, alternative rock 'n' roll, art hippie life, right across from 1966/7.'[18] York could almost see the conceit of *Scary Monsters* coming: 'We see the morning in, listening to *Diamond Dogs*. Through the window you can see the twinkling sci-fi red on the Post Office Tower. We talk about apocalyptic nonsense and Bowie and the end of everything.'

York finished the essay with a postscript, written at some point in the present:

> Louise's closed soon after. Just couldn't handle the punk invasion. Steve Strange went off to do the Moors Murderers. Caroline went to DJ at Billy's, another little gay *boîte* on Meard Street … Steve Strange was on the door, and a lot of the freaks went … Most of Billy's people were into Bowie … In November 1978, a Tuesday, they got up a Bowie night. Frankie did her act, which was taking on some secondary Bowie characters … *developing them in mime*. Out of that, of course, came Neon Night at the Blitz, the ascent of Steve Strange, Studio 21 and the whole new old world.[19]

In their moment of fame, Steve Strange and the habitués of the Blitz club unsurprisingly took starring roles in the video for 'Ashes to Ashes', the lead single on *Scary Monsters*. This marked a paradigm shift in British pop music, where the promotional film and the world of the visual perhaps began to take prominence, eclipsing the importance of the album cover and even, arguably, the music.

Meanwhile, in 1980 I still resided in a teenage bedroom in provincial England. For me the video for 'Ashes to Ashes' represented a perverse world of impossible glamour that I feared but desperately needed to join; and the old Bowie LPs, propped against the skirting board like trophies, would soon start to take second place to a mournful singer from Manchester called Morrissey, with his vaguely dangerous and arousing album covers featuring grainy shots from Warhol's *Flesh*, and rough boys in vests with Jean Cocteau-inspired tattoos on their shoulders. By the autumn of 1984 I had left home and arrived in London. Bowie's hugely successful (in commercial terms) album *Let's Dance*, with its glossy cover art by Greg Gorman and Derek Boshier (pl.143), had supplied the soundtrack to the previous valedictory summer, but our old Bowie records had been packed away, never to be displayed in that way again.

[144] *Tonight* • 1984

[145] *Never Let Me Down* • 1987

[146] *Tin Machine* • 1989

[147] *Tin Machine II* • 1991

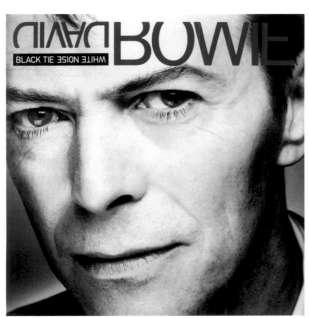

[148] *Black Tie White Noise* • 1993

[149] *The Buddha of Suburbia* • 1993

[150] *I. Outside* ∘ 1995

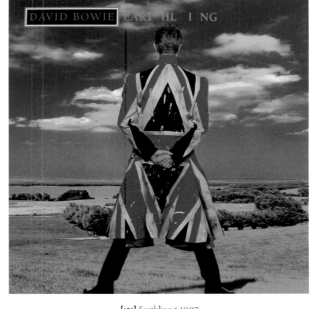

[151] *Earthling* ∘ 1997

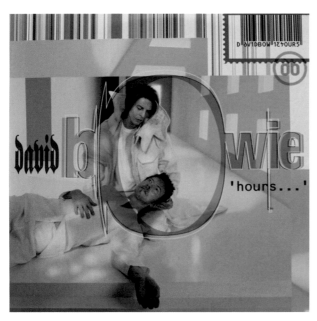

[152] *'Hours…'* ∘ 1999

[153] *Heathen* ∘ 2002

[154] *Reality* ∘ 2003

The Next Day ∘ 2013

DAVID BOWIE IS A HUMAN BEING

→ **[155] OPPOSITE** • David Bowie at the time of his performance
in *The Elephant Man*, 1980 • Photograph by Anton Corbijn

↑→ [156] **ABOVE AND OPPOSITE** ● Jumpsuit with a graphic pattern inspired by
Le Corbusier, 1979 ● Designed by Willie Brown and worn for Dick Clark's
'Salute to the Seventies' ● THE DAVID BOWIE ARCHIVE

↑→ [157] **ABOVE AND OPPOSITE** ◦ Skirt suit, 1979 ◦ Designed by
Brooks Van Horn costume house, New York, for a performance on
'Saturday Night Live' ◦ THE DAVID BOWIE ARCHIVE

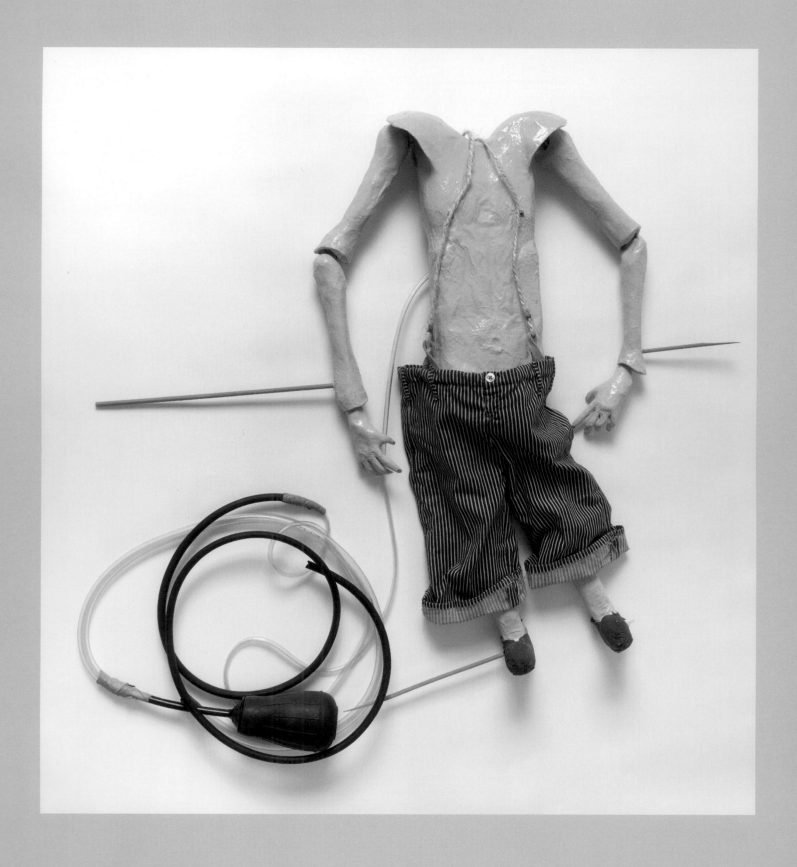

↑→[158] **ABOVE AND OPPOSITE** • Puppet and poodle props, 1979 • The television in the poodle's mouth screened the performance on 'Saturday Night Live' as it happened • Designed by Mark Ravitz • THE DAVID BOWIE ARCHIVE

→[159] **FOLLOWING PAGES** • Costume inspired by Sonia Delaunay's designs for Tristan Tzara's play *Le Cœur à Gaz* (1923), 1979 • Designed by Mark Ravitz and David Bowie • THE DAVID BOWIE ARCHIVE

→[160] **PAGES 214–15** • David Bowie performing 'The Man Who Sold The World' with Klaus Nomi and Joey Arias on 'Saturday Night Live', 1979 • Photograph by Edie Baskin • THE DAVID BOWIE ARCHIVE

↑→ [161] **ABOVE AND OPPOSITE** ◦ Jumpsuit with vintage trenchcoat, 1979 ◦
Designed by Willie Brown and worn for the 'DJ' video ◦ THE DAVID BOWIE ARCHIVE

←↑ [162] **OPPOSITE AND ABOVE** • Pierrot (or 'Blue Clown') costume, 1980 •
Designed by Natasha Korniloff for the 'Ashes to Ashes' video and
Scary Monsters … and Super Creeps album cover • THE DAVID BOWIE ARCHIVE

DAVID BOWIE IS TURNING US ALL INTO VOYEURS

←↑ **[164] OPPOSITE AND ABOVE** ● Military-style suit, 1983 ● Designed by
Peter Hall for the Serious Moonlight tour ● THE DAVID BOWIE ARCHIVE

←→ **[165] OPPOSITE AND RIGHT** •
Lime-green suit, 1983 • Designed by
Peter Hall for the Serious Moonlight
tour • THE DAVID BOWIE ARCHIVE

↑→ [166] **ABOVE AND OPPOSITE** • Red suit, 1987 • Designed by
Diana Moseley for the Glass Spider tour • THE DAVID BOWIE ARCHIVE

←↑ **[167] OPPOSITE AND ABOVE** ● Black silk suit, 1990 ● Designed by
Giorgio Armani for the Sound + Vision tour ● THE DAVID BOWIE ARCHIVE

DAVID BOWIE IS AT ANY GIVEN MOMENT IN TIME A GIVEN MOMENT IN TIME

ONE MORE WEEKEND OF LIGHTS AND EVENING FACES

FAST FOOD LIVING NOSTALGIA

ORIOLE CULLEN

CHANGES
BOWIE'S LIFE
STORY

'*Changes* is Bowie's life story. All he ever does is change. That's why there's never an identifiable direction. He's everything all at once. Every song is a different side of Bowie and the world he sees.'

(*New Musical Express*, 'Albums: Bowie at his brilliant best', 29 January 1972)

On 23 September 2011, the *Financial Times* reported on the latest incarnation of the David Bowie fashion phenomenon, currently sweeping the nation. In a piece entitled 'Men's wear ch ch changes', Mark C. O'Flaherty noted that 'fashion has had a four-decade love affair with Bowie that's only getting stronger. Indeed, Bowie may be the most referenced musician in fashion history'.[1] Designers such as Phoebe Philo at Celine, Lucas Ossendrijver at Lanvin and Dries Van Noten had all included references to Bowie in their Autumn/Winter 2011 collections. *Vogue* Paris produced a Bowie-inspired cover in December 2011, and the following month German *Vogue* published a fashion shoot starring Daphne Guinness, styled in a tribute to Bowie's career. The previous season, London-based designer Richard Nicoll had shown a collection inspired by Bowie's manifestation as the Thin White Duke, with Bowie's *Station to Station* album playing throughout the presentation. On the subject of Bowie, Nicoll said: 'I've always loved the decadence and fearlessness of his style and music.'[2]

In the capricious world of fashion, it's extraordinary that Bowie has continued to be a source of inspiration for so many years. But it is specifically the characters that Bowie created in the decade from the early 1970s to the early 1980s, and the images in which they are recorded, that have become such important points of reference: he has built an unparalleled bank of different looks and characters that have been captured not only through music but also in photographs, documentaries and feature films. Bowie's collaborations with highly regarded photographers and film-makers have been key to his style legacy, with Mick Rock, Masayoshi Sukita, Brian Duffy, Terry O'Neill, D. A. Pennebaker and Nicolas Roeg all contributing to the visual archive available to today's designers. It is interesting to note that as Bowie's public appearances and musical output have become more intermittent, the appetite for his image and influences has soared.

Cultural historian Janice Miller has written about the symbiotic relationship between the worlds of fashion and rock music, suggesting that the fashion world is drawn to the music industry because of rock's authenticity, its 'underground credentials and, in particular, the notion of rock as something powerful and dangerous'.[3] She notes that 'truthfulness and authenticity in music performance have a pervasiveness that, in turn, adds value when placed in association with fashion'.[4] The fashion industry also relies on the visceral quality and impact of music for the seasonal show presentations: according to journalist Tim Blanks, 'the role of music in a show is to amplify – or clarify – the designer's vision'.[5] And year after year, Bowie's music is played at fashion shows – it is rare not to hear 'Fashion', his ironic homage to the industry, at some point over a season.

Emmanuelle Alt, editor-in-chief of *Vogue* Paris since 2011, has always acknowledged the importance of rock music to her work as a fashion stylist. She was responsible for styling and propagating the incredibly popular rock-inspired collections designed by Christophe Decarnin at Balmain from 2008 to 2011 (Autumn/Winter 2008 featured garments with crystal-embroidered lightning bolts, à la *Aladdin Sane*). Her tenure as editor of *Vogue* has seen an emphasis on images inspired by rock music, including a music-themed issue that featured Kate Moss on the cover in a Ziggy Stardust pose (pl.169).[6] Photographed by Mert Alas and Marcus Piggott, Moss is shown wearing a spiked red wig and a metallic Balmain jumpsuit open to the navel. She is lit from the side, holding up her wrist to reveal a tiny ship's anchor tattoo. The composition and lighting recall Mick Rock's 1973 promotional film for 'John, I'm Only Dancing', which featured Bowie with spiked red hair, jacket open to the navel and a tiny ship's anchor on his left cheek. (Bowie later claimed this tattoo was inspired by Samantha from the 1960s television series *Bewitched*, who often wore little shapes painted on her face.)[7]

Bowie has always used artifice as part of his act. In a 1974 interview, asked if he regretted that much of his publicity was about his image, his response was a frank acknowledgement of how the star system and publicity worked:

> People must write about me as they feel. I like to think my most important contribution is the music but I've got no right to insist that others feel the same way. If someone thinks of me as an important fashion trend-setter, good luck. Just as long as they write about me.[8]

This attitude was recognized by his fans, as Simon Frith noted in 1983: 'To appreciate Bowie was not just to like his music or his shows or his looks, but also to enjoy the way he set himself up as a commercial image. How he was packaged was as much an aspect of his art as what the package contained.'[9] Bowie's stage personae may have been artfully constructed, but the passion and energy he put into these characters, his performances and his music were completely authentic:

> When I go out onto a stage I try to make the performance as good and as interesting as possible, and I don't just mean by singing my songs and moving off. I think if you're really going to entertain an audience then you have to look the part too. I feel very comfortable in the clothes I wear and they're part of me, and part of my act.[10]

Bowie has never claimed to be an inventor of fashion – rather, he has always declared his magpie tendencies for picking up disparate elements and melding them together to present something that uniquely channels the *Zeitgeist*. He has drawn from high fashion and channelled it to the street via his fans, but he has also channelled elements of street and subcultural fashion into the mainstream. His early 1970s collaboration with Kansai Yamamoto brought the work of the Japanese designer to a worldwide audience, while his 1980 video for 'Ashes to Ashes' did the same for the underground London style of the Blitz Kids. Bowie consistently acknowledges the designers whose clothes he has worn and those he has collaborated with, from Freddie Burretti and Kansai Yamamoto to Thierry Mugler and Alexander McQueen, recognizing their contributions to some of his most important looks.

From his earliest teenage years, Bowie seems to have been an avid consumer of fashionable style: a photograph shows him as a neatly coiffed 13-year-old in a three-button jacket, tapered trousers and a pair of sharply pointed winkle-pickers. He had already begun to experiment with dying his hair and modifying his school trousers.[11] As someone who understood first-hand the thrill and excitement of consuming fashion, Bowie was able to comprehend and appeal to the passions of his fan base. Fearlessly experimenting with changes in style and look in his early career, Bowie morphed from a sharp-suited mod to a shaggy-haired hippie, taking in fringed suede boots, leather jerkins and numerous hairstyles along the way. Displaying an attitude perfectly in tune with the constant renewal and shifts that structure the fashion world, he rapidly assimilated and projected the look of the moment, then moved swiftly on. In 1972, Bowie said:

> I've never had any direction. I'm very faddy; I always have been ever since I was 13 or 14. It just keeps my interest. I find if I do one type of thing too long, I'm a little bored. It is out of necessity really to keep my functions alive.[12]

Bowie's image really began to stand out as his projected androgyny developed. The cover of the 1970 album *The Man Who Sold the World* shows him in a dress (see pl.129), one of a range of menswear pieces by the flamboyant London designer Mr Fish, whose clothes were labelled with the legend 'Peculiar to Mr Fish'. Michael Fish had opened his shop in 1967 at the height of London's 'Dandy Revolution', supplying a more exclusive and radical version of the cheap disposable fashion of the Carnaby Street boutiques to a young and moneyed elite who dabbled in the hippie aesthetic – 'see-through voiles, brocades and spangles, and miniskirts for men, blinding silks, flower-printed hats'.[13] Bowie was not the first figure in the public eye to wear a Mr Fish dress: in 1969 Mick Jagger had chosen to wear a short white man-dress by the designer to the infamous Brian Jones memorial concert in London's Hyde Park. Echoing the pleated tunic or *foustanélla* of traditional Greek menswear, Jagger's outfit at least had some, if vague, menswear credentials. Bowie's dress, however, was a flowing silk velvet garment decorated with a floral print. An ankle-length skirt with inverted pleats fell from a tightly fitted bodice fastened with two decorative frogged closures, exposing the chest. While Fish's clothing was not cheap, Bowie was fortunate to find two of his dresses on sale for £50. The other dress, in a slubbed blue raw silk, had a more modest zipper fastening down the centre front, but was cut with the same tight bodice and pleated skirt. A head shot of Bowie in this garment appeared on the back cover of the album.

Writing about Bowie in *Melody Maker* at the time, Michael Watts noted that 'the expression of his sexual ambivalence establishes a fascinating game: is he or isn't he? In a period of conflicting sexual identity he shrewdly exploits the confusion surrounding the male and female roles.' 'The important fact is that I don't have to drag up,' Bowie says in the article, 'I want to go on like this long after the fashion has finished.'[14] Bowie's American record label, Mercury, felt the dress image was too provocative for their audiences and chose to release *The Man Who Sold the World* with a different cover (see pl.131). Asked about the dress in 1972, while he was on the American leg of the Ziggy Stardust tour, Bowie said: 'It was a velvet handprint by Michael Fish. I like clothes design; I'm interested in his clothes … That was a dress designed for a man: there were a lot of those things going around in London three years ago.'[15] The contrast between the 1970 commitment to wearing dresses 'long after' the fashion moment was over, and the knowing acceptance a couple of years later that the moment had passed – and the style partially dismissed – is intriguing. Bowie would later say of the controversial image:

> It was a parody of Gabriel Rosetti. Slightly askew, obviously. So when they told me that a drag-queen cult was forming behind me, I said, 'Fine, don't try to explain it; nobody is going to bother to try to understand it. I'll play along, absolutely anything to break me through.[16]

Bowie also wore the Mr Fish dress to promote the single released by his experimental band the Arnold Corns Project. He and frontman Freddie Burretti, a.k.a. 'Rudi Valentino', appeared on the cover of the May/June 1971 issue of *Curious* magazine in similarly styled dresses: Burretti, seated, is wearing a deep purple satin version, while Bowie is standing by his side in the floral-print velvet, clutching Burretti's arm, with his long hair blowing across his face. Bowie had met Freddie Burrett, a young tailor and fashion student who went by the name Burretti, in the Sombrero, a gay bar in London's Kensington. Trevor Bolder, who played bass with Bowie in the early 1970s, remembers that Burretti 'was girly and skinny, but always wore suits'.[17] Burretti and Bowie began to collaborate on both musical and fashion projects, but while the Arnold Corns Project quickly faded away, the sartorial relationship between the two men grew to become a key component of Bowie's style in the following years, with Burretti designing the early look for Ziggy Stardust as well as the signature suits that Bowie wore off-stage.

In 1967, *Sgt. Pepper's Lonely Hearts Club Band* had introduced mass audiences to the concept album, with the Beatles donning their bright satin band uniforms for the sleeve. When Bowie extended the idea in January 1972 by bringing his own concept of Ziggy Stardust and the Spiders from Mars to life, he depended on the album's music to introduce Ziggy's story to the fans, but the visual image was key to marking out this new identity (pl.170). Bowie later acknowledged the influence of Stanley Kubrick's film *A Clockwork Orange*, released in 1971: 'The initial clothes I designed for the Spiders from Mars were very much based on the Clockwork Orange jumpsuits. I had them made out of very flowery material, very feminine material, very colourful.'[18] Describing the outfits he and the other members of Bowie's backing band were given to wear, Trevor Bolder said:

> We were supposed to look like Droogs out of *A Clockwork Orange*. He took us to see the movie, and our costumes were kind of the same: boots, boilersuits, but more colourful. But then we went on to these black and silvery, sparkly suits, and Mick [Ronson, lead guitarist] had his pants tucked into his socks, with little bows on. That was a bit weird.[19]

Bolder also recalled the influence of Bowie's wife Angela at this time: a driving force behind the new look, she urged the band – and Bowie – to go further with their outrageous identities. She was constantly on the lookout for new clothing and styles for her husband and, as they wore the same size, they often shared garments. Images of David and Angie Bowie from this period have been endlessly referenced and re-created by the fashion world, with stylists and designers finding inspiration in shots of the Bowies at home in their flat at Haddon Hall, a Victorian Gothic villa in suburban south-east London, with styled hair and glam-rock fashions, often accompanied by their young son. As fashion images go, these photographs epitomize the bohemian rock-star world of the 1970s. In a 2001 American *Vogue* shoot by Stephen Meisel, models Hannelore Knuts and Diana Meszaros were dressed as David and Angie Bowie respectively, in a riot of snakeskin and multicoloured glam-rock-inspired suits. The March 2011 edition of *i-D* magazine – the 'Exhibitionist' issue – featured a story by photographer Benjamin A. Huseby (pl.171) based on the Bowies: styled by Jacob Kjeldgaard, a flame-haired James Jeannette Main in the character of David lounges decadently with peroxide-blonde model Britt Maren in the role of Angie. While David and Angie Bowie's relationship had come to an end by the mid-1970s (they divorced in 1980), the strength of the couple's image from this period remains an inspiration that perfectly encapsulates the early seventies for the fashion world.

← [170] LEFT • Quilted jumpsuit, 1972 • Designed by David Bowie and Freddie Burretti for the *Ziggy Stardust* album cover and subsequent tour • THE DAVID BOWIE ARCHIVE

→ [171] OPPOSITE • Photograph for the 'Exhibitionist' issue, *i-D magazine*, March 2011 • Photograph by Benjamin A. Huseby, styling by Jacob Kjeldgaard

Bowie designed the suit he wore on the cover of *The Rise and Fall of Ziggy Stardust*, Freddie Burretti cut the pattern for the blouson-style jacket and trousers, and the clothes were sewn by Burretti and Sue Frost (the Bowies' neighbour at Haddon Hall). Bowie had found the material for the suit at a stall run by Takis Andriou in a street market the year before: a quilted fabric printed with a geometric dark-green pattern on a white ground (which was later tinted turquoise by the album's graphic designer), with a green-dot print on the same white ground for the lining.[20] It is interesting to reflect on the low-key production of what became one of the twentieth-century's most referenced garments, as described by Bowie himself:

> The very first series of outfits for Ziggy and company were made by Freddie and anyone else in Haddon Hall who could reasonably handle a needle. This would usually be our babysitter Sue who lived downstairs … Although full of good intentions no-one else would last more than about 20 minutes before the pure hard graft of threading and stitching wore down all enthusiasm for the job.[21]

Freddie Burretti also worked closely with his friend Daniella Parmar, who sourced much of the fabric for the Ziggy costumes at Indian markets in south London. Burretti and Frost made a number of identical suits, three of which survived the rigours of touring, which took its toll on many of Bowie's stage costumes. Rock journalist Lenny Kaye attended a Ziggy Stardust concert at Friars Aylesbury in Buckinghamshire in 1972:

> At the end of the show he took off his satin blouse and threw it into the audience. And I, a fan/writer, grabbed the sleeve. The next day when I interviewed him, I tied it around my upper arm. At one point he said, 'What's that on your arm?' and I said, 'Oh, it's just a rag I picked up somewhere.' I still have it.[22]

Bowie's clothing was now taking on the form of reliquary for fervent fans, but these were not Beatles-chasing teenagers. Through Ziggy, Bowie appealed directly to a new young audience, addressing them in his songs and inspiring them to mimic his style, but to do so individually. His influence spread way beyond the realms of the suburban British teenager described artfully by Michael Watts in *Melody Maker* in July 1972:

[He was] clutching his copy of the new David Bowie album, *The Rise and Fall of Ziggy Stardust*, which he hoped David would autograph after the show. He was wearing his red scarf, flung nonchalantly over his shoulder, and his red platform boots. His hair was long down the back but cropped fairly short on top so that it stuck up when he brushed his fingers through it. He hated that it was dark brown. He'd promised himself that when he eventually split to London he'd have it done bright blond.[23]

For American guitarist Reeves Gabrels, who has worked with Bowie on many occasions, including as a member of Tin Machine in the late 1980s and early 1990s, 'it was a great period – 1970 to 1973 – because you could go to school with a green streak in your hair and say, "Fuck you, I look like David Bowie."'[24]

In the early 1970s the world of international high fashion was a rarefied place. Readers of the more exclusive fashion titles, such as *Harpers & Queen* and *Vogue*, could see a carefully edited selection of garments for that season, but they were only able to access fashions that had been shown to buyers six months previously, and these would gradually filter down to the high street some six months later. Newspaper reports from international fashion shows were illustrated with the occasional line drawing, while television programmes might report on youth trends and the work of local designers. New collections from Paris and Italy, let alone Japan, could have little or no immediate impact on the general public – they were not available.

In July 1971 *Harpers & Queen* eagerly reported a fashion moment – the 'first London show of the brilliant young Japanese designer Kansai Yamamoto'. Under fashion editor Jennifer Hocking (the magazine's masthead also listed Anna Wintour, then a young assistant), the magazine devoted the cover and a six-page editorial to the clothes of the first Japanese designer to show in London. Photographed by Hiroshi, the images featured model Marie Helvin, eyebrows shaved and wearing bright pink make-up, in fantastically sculptural multi-coloured garments: giant padded coats, dramatically curved trousers, floor-length circular skirts and PVC platform boots (pl.69). The accompanying text proclaimed: 'It's a whole new concept of dressing, and it's for this reason that we believe Kansai Yamamoto will have a massive impact on the world of fashion.'[25] The final part of this statement proved to be prophetic, but – the positive reception of London's fashion crowd notwithstanding – it is unlikely that the writer could have envisioned that the audience who would be inspired by Yamamoto's clothes would find them via an alien from outer space: Ziggy Stardust.

The conduit for this fashion breakthrough, David Bowie, was at that time living in the London suburb of Beckenham, where a copy of the July 1971 edition of *Harpers* would find its way. The PVC boots by Kansai Yamamoto caught Bowie's eye but, at £28, they were out of his price range, so he had them copied by south London bootmaker Stan 'Dusty' Miller.[26] When he did eventually purchase his first piece of Yamamoto clothing from the exclusive stockists of the designer's collection in London, the Boston 151 boutique on the Fulham Road, Bowie chose a leather leotard with 11 red poppers down the front. It was decorated with hand-drawn winged rabbits and hand-painted black swirls along the edges (pls 172 and 173). Once again, as with the Mr Fish dresses a few years previously, he acquired the garment at a reduced price: 'I did get my hands on my first Kansai Yamamoto costume quite cheaply as nobody wanted to buy it, let alone wear it. It was the impossibly silly "bunny" costume'.[27] Bowie and Yamamoto met on Valentine's Day 1973, when the designer flew to New York to present the musician with five specially created garments (Yamamoto had been informed of Bowie's admiration for his work by stylist Yusuko Takahashi). Yamamoto designed a further nine tour costumes for Bowie, and presented them to him in April of that year when the tour arrived in Japan.[28] At the time, Yamamoto said: 'He has an unusual face ... He's neither man nor woman ... which suited me as a designer because most of my clothes are for either sex.'[29]

→ [172] OPPOSITE • David Bowie on stage at the Hammersmith Odeon, 1973 • Photograph by Debi Doss • Getty Images

↑→ **[173] ABOVE AND OPPOSITE** • 'Woodland Creatures' leather leotard, 1972 •
Designed by Kansai Yamamoto and worn for the Ziggy Stardust and
Aladdin Sane tours • THE DAVID BOWIE ARCHIVE

'There were elements of kabuki theatre thrown in,' Bowie later said of the Ziggy look. 'It was a real hodgepodge, there was no kind of direct through-line with Ziggy at all. It just kind of evolved. I very much had the idea of Japanese culture as the alien culture because I couldn't conceive a Martian culture.'[30] Key to Ziggy's 'alien look' was his signature spiked, bright-red hair. Hairdresser Suzi Fussey (later the wife of Mick Ronson) put the final coloured touch to the Ziggy hairstyle in February 1972, having cut it into shape the previous month. The style echoed that of a female model in an Alex Chatelain photograph, which appeared in *Vogue* Paris in 1971 (pl.67), but in 2005 Bowie set the record straight:

Daniella Parmar's dye-job convinced me of the importance of a synthetic hair colour for Ziggy. This turned into reality when I spied the Kansai Yamamoto model on a fashion magazine cover. It was a slightly 'girlie' magazine like *Honey*, definitely not *Vogue*.

In 1972, I duplicated not only the colour from this cover but the cut as well. A complete lift. I've read in different accounts that the Ziggy cut came from a number of different sources, or was designed by a local hairdresser in Bromley or Beckenham. Absolute tosh![31]

Style journalist Dylan Jones observed that 'clothes, though vital to the success of Ziggy, were nothing compared to the influence of the haircut ... [it] epitomized the androgyny of glam rock and, copied by both boys and girls ... became the hit of 1973.'[32] Make-up was also a key part of the image. Bowie had learned the importance of the effect it created while working with mime Lindsay Kemp: 'From make-up to costume, his ideas of an elevated reality stuck and his commitment to breaking down the parameters between on-stage and off-stage life remained firmly in my soul.'[33] Bowie applied his own make-up, but later worked with make-up artist Pierre La Roche on tour and, while in Japan, he received make-up lessons from

Tomasaburo, a star of kabuki theatre. A 1973 article in *Music Scene* offered tips: 'David tells us that mostly all of his make-up comes from a little shop in Rome, Italy, that imports fantastic coloured powders and creams from India ... Basic essentials also include a white rice powder from Tokyo's Woolworth's equivalent – Indian kohl usually in black – for his eyes'.[34] However, while make-up was key, it wasn't always straightforward. Bowie recalls his first appearance at Radio City Music Hall in New York: 'I'd had some make-up done by Pierre La Roche ... and he did some brilliant things, but he used glitter on me for the first time, and it ran in my eyes. I did the whole show almost blind.'[35]

Off-stage, Bowie continued to wear sharply tailored suits by Freddie Burretti, one of which can be seen in a 1973 promotional film for 'Life on Mars?', directed by Mick Rock (pls 177–9). In the opening scene the camera pans down past Bowie's thatch of spiked orange hair, focusing on the metallic blue orbs painted around his eyes before revealing a shiny light-blue suit designed by Burretti. With its tight, streamlined fit – long jacket with wide lapels and wide-legged trousers with large turn-ups – the suit was of the moment. In fact, this was a fashionable silhouette for women's trouser suits from Yves Saint Laurent and Barbara Hulanicki's Biba store in London. However, Bowie's otherworldly appearance, the hair, make-up and the choice of metallic blue fabric combined to create an unmistakable 'Bowie' look. The Autumn/Winter 2006 Gucci collections, designed by Frida Giannini, featured long, narrow, sharply tailored suits paired with platform shoes to echo the silhouette of the 'Life on Mars?' outfit. Giannini told journalist Suzy Menkes where she found her inspiration: 'My most important images are from David Bowie and that period, because he was an icon in terms of influence and edge.'[36]

↗ **[174] ABOVE** • Chloë Sevigny in Miu Miu • Autumn/Winter 2012 • Photograph by Mert Alas & Marcus Piggott, styling by Katie Grand

↗ **[175] OPPOSITE, ABOVE** • Black and white jacket by Givenchy • Spring/Summer 2012 •

↘ **[176] OPPOSITE, BELOW** • David Bowie during the Ziggy Stardust tour, 1973 • Jacket designed by Freddie Burretti • Getty Images

While the light-blue suit followed the fashionable lines of the time, Burretti was experimental with his cut and patterns, using different seam arrangements, curved lapels without notches and an integrated waistband to give the suit a unique finish. Seams running diagonally from each shoulder towards the centre create an unusual V-shaped insert on both the back and front of the jacket. The strong, sharp, slightly exaggerated shoulder line was a signature of Burretti's tailoring that remained a constant throughout the different cuts he created for Bowie. (The suits were an inspiration for the Autumn/Winter 2012 Miu Miu campaign, photographed by Mert and Marcus, and styled by Katie Grand, pl.174. Draped languidly in a chair with orange hair, turquoise eyeshadow and a hyper-patterned suit with high-collared shirt and tie, Sevigny recalled Mick Rock's images of Bowie in Burretti suits, pl.178.)

Bowie wore an almost identical version of the blue suit at the 'retirement party' thrown at the Café Royal on 4 July 1973 to celebrate the demise of Ziggy Stardust (the only difference was a waistcoat made from a purple and green satin hound's-tooth fabric, to match the shirt Bowie wore with the suit). Bowie had announced the end of Ziggy and the Spiders at a concert at the Hammersmith Odeon on 3 July, and a star-studded 'wake' was held in central London the next day. Bowie described the event in a letter to fans, published ten days later in *Mirabelle* magazine:

Oh, what a night it turned out to be! Mick Jagger, Lou Reed, Jeff Beck, Lulu, Spike Milligan, Dana Gillespie, Ryan O'Neal, Elliott Gould, Ringo Starr and Barbra Streisand ... all there at my last concert party at the luxurious Café Royal – everyone looking so lovely in their sparkling evening clothes and colourful make-up ... me in my ice-blue iridescent Freddy [sic] suit.[37]

The article was ghost-written by Bowie's American publicist Cherry Vanilla. Kevin Cann reports that in 2002 Bowie said, 'I remember nothing of this party, absolutely nothing.'[38]

The Burretti suit was reprised in 2003 for a music-themed edition of British *Vogue*, which featured photographs of Kate Moss by Nick Knight. Knight has often referenced Bowie in his work, with images that seem to capture and channel the energy, lighting and glamour of a rock performance. He has also collaborated directly with Bowie: in 1993 he shot the cover photograph for the *Black Tie White Noise* album. Moss appeared on the cover of this special issue of *Vogue* in the guise of Bowie's *Aladdin Sane* album sleeve, interpreted as a black-and-white head shot with an overlaid graphic of a lightning bolt. In a reference to the back cover of Bowie's album, an outline version of the same image of Moss appeared inside the magazine. In her editor's letter, Alexandra Shulman said that Bowie's 'seventies performance of Ziggy Stardust at Earls Court was one of life's seminal moments'.[39]

Knight also shot Moss for an editorial story in the same issue. The clothes for this shoot were supplied by Bowie's archive, and Moss is pictured in original pieces by Kansai Yamamoto and Freddie Burretti. Wearing the ice-blue Burretti suit (pl.179), she moves across the starkly lit studio space, reminiscent of the setting of Mick Rock's original video of 1973, a twist in her hips, elbows drawn up and back as though performing on stage. The suit is still sharp.

Another garment from this period highlights Burretti's stylish, yet slightly whimsical, approach to tailoring – a jacket made from black-and-white horizontally striped fabric with a metallic silver thread, cut so that the stripes follow the shape of the wide lapels (pl.176). Worn by Bowie on a journey from London to Aberdeen in May 1973, it was captured by Mick Rock in a series of intriguing photographs. These images later inspired designer Riccardo Tisci at Givenchy to open his Spring/Summer 2010 show with a black-and-white striped blazer with identically striped lapels (pl.175). In January 2010, the piece was photographed by Stephen Meisel for American *Vogue*: the Givenchy jacket was worn by model Sasha Pivovarova in a story entitled 'Rock the House', which featured young rock musicians.

↑→ [177] **ABOVE AND OPPOSITE** • Ice-blue suit, 1972 •
Designed by Freddie Burretti for the 'Life on Mars?' video •
THE DAVID BOWIE ARCHIVE

← [178] OPPOSITE • Still from the 'Life on Mars?' video, 1973 • Photograph by Mick Rock

↑ [179] ABOVE • Kate Moss wearing the 'Life on Mars?' suit in a photo shoot for British *Vogue*, 2003 • Photograph by Nick Knight • Courtesy of Trunk Archive © Nick Knight

Bowie's use of suits was summed up by Marc C. O'Flaherty in his piece for the *Financial Times*: 'Bowie demonstrated that the suit could be outrageous and expressive as much as it was smart or a slightly dandy uniform.'[40] At the Autumn/Winter 2011 Celine show, a booklet of pictorial references left on seats for members of the audience included a picture of a mustard-yellow Burretti suit. The 1974 Terry O'Neill photograph shows Bowie in this suit, wearing a shirt with yellow-and-white horizontal stripes, with a cigarette in his mouth and a pair of tailor's shears dangling from his fingers (pls 181–3). Fashion historian Cally Blackman noted that 'although he is obviously posing, he isn't in costume. And it's a great outfit … He's very beautiful, very ambivalent so appeals to both genders, very elegant and has always shown considered taste in everything he does, despite appearances to the contrary, as some might see it.'[41] In 1974, Bowie said:

> I'm turned on by people who have taste, especially my kind of taste. One of my great loves is clothes. I'm really mad about them. I go through so many different phases, at the moment I'm into short-jacketed double-breasted suits, but next week I might be into something completely different. With all my changes of mood Freddie is extremely patient. He just listens to my ideas and has this sort of telepathy. Because whatever I think of in my mind he produces for real. I suppose I've come to admire Freddie as a person through his work, because people's personalities really come through when they are working, as much as any other time. Freddie comes across as a really tolerant and talented guy. I just hope he'll continue to design incredible clothes for me.[42]

London-based hat designer Craig West remembers the Bowie Mania that accompanied the musician's 'plastic soul' phase, around the time of *Young Americans* in the mid 1970s (pl.180). Advertisements in the back of the *NME* promised the Bowie look: readers could send off for short jackets 'as seen' on the *David Live* LP released in 1974, as well as eight- and 20-pleat trousers, all supplied by Christopher Robin of Carnaby Street. West ordered the 20-pleat version, priced at £16.95. He and his friends would saunter around with long bleached fringes and the requisite pleated trousers, the whole look finished with a copy of Kafka peeking out from an overcoat pocket.[43] Noting a new 'trend for elegance' in the Autumn/Winter 2011 menswear shows, journalist Godfrey Deeny singled out the collection of Dries Van Noten, 'whose choice of inspiration was David Bowie – though not space-age Major Tom, more *David Live* Bowie, in outsized pants and double-breasted jackets' – a world away from the synthetic creations advertised in the back of the NME.[44]

↑ [180] **ABOVE** • Nautical costume, 1978 • Designed by Natasha Korniloff for the Stage tour • THE DAVID BOWIE ARCHIVE

→ [181] **OPPOSITE** • David Bowie at the time of the Diamond Dogs tour, 1974 • Photograph by Terry O'Neill

↑→ [182] **ABOVE AND OPPOSITE** • Mustard-yellow suit, 1974 •
Designed by Freddie Burretti • THE DAVID BOWIE ARCHIVE

←↑[183] **OPPOSITE AND ABOVE** ● David Bowie at the time of the
Diamond Dogs tour, 1974 ● Photographs by Terry O'Neill

In 1975 Bowie began working with director Nicolas Roeg on the film *The Man Who Fell to Earth*, based on a novel by Walter Tevis. Bowie starred as Thomas Jerome Newton, an alien who lands on earth on a quest to bring water back to his drought-stricken planet. The costumes for the film (pl.199) were designed by Ola Hudson, who had previously worked closely with performers such as John Lennon, Ringo Starr and Diana Ross. The image Hudson created for Newton owed much to Bowie himself: the white-blonde hair of the character in the original book was changed to Bowie's orange; the trilby he wears is similar to one that Bowie wore to the 1975 Grammy Awards several months before filming commenced (pl.184). Bowie was so taken with Hudson's tailored pieces that he wore them, along with white shirts supplied by recently established designer Paul Smith, on his 1976 Isolar tour, appearing as his latest incarnation, the Thin White Duke. This new character owed much to Berlin cabaret of the Weimar era (with a touch of Marlene Dietrich), and the tour featured an almost bare stage with dramatic white lighting (pl.42). A reviewer noted that 'Bowie appeared in a simple outfit consisting of a white shirt with French cuffs, and matching black vest and pants ... His hair was the same severely slicked-back red with frontal highlights that he sported in *The Man Who Fell to Earth*'.[45] In 2008 the *New York Times* reported on a video presentation of Stefano Pilati's menswear for Yves Saint Laurent, which included 'shiny David-Bowie-in-*The-Man-Who-Fell-to-Earth* blousons ... and '70s-inspired suits with cuffed wide-legged trousers' – making it one of many collections that have referenced this period in Bowie's style evolution. In August 2011, celebrated actress Tilda Swinton appeared on the cover of *W* magazine in the guise of Bowie's Thin White Duke, as shot by Tim Walker and styled by Jacob Kjeldgaard (pl.185). The magazine contained an editorial featuring Swinton in various looks inspired by Roeg's film. Asked to name her style icons, Swinton replied: 'David Bowie – whom I've been orbiting ever since I saw *The Man Who Fell to Earth* in 1976.'[46] She went on to say that she and Bowie 'share the same planetary DNA'.[47]

While Britain was witnessing the birth of the punk movement in the mid to late 1970s, Bowie was touring the world and living in Berlin. But Tim Blanks notes that while Bowie was not physically present, his music and image had a presence within that movement: 'The dystopian vision Bowie conveyed in his music, acting and style in 1976 was a huge influence on the punk scene that was coalescing in London – Bowie was one old-waver who was cool to the new.'[48] Bowie later said of the early punk era:

> I didn't get the full brunt of all that, because it was just when I was settling in Berlin, so it came from a different direction there and it didn't have the full wrath and anger of what happened in England. For me it's all just footage and I can't feel the same thing. I really regret missing out on that. I'd love to have seen the dialogue on television ... and the feel of the clubs at that time.[49]

As the 1970s turned into the '80s, another London scene – centred around the Blitz club in Soho – paid a more direct debt to Bowie's influence. Defined by outrageous costumes and dramatic make-up for both sexes, proponents of the style were christened Blitz Kids and later New Romantics by the press. Steve Strange, the club's host, was only too happy to be asked to round up some friends to appear in Bowie's video for 'Ashes to Ashes'. In one of the most expensive music videos of the time, the club kids wore long gothic robes by Judith Frankland and dark imposing headwear designed by the newly established milliner Stephen Jones. Jones later recalled how everyone was in awe of Bowie's appearance at the Blitz, but also felt it was a little weird that someone so *old* would come to the club (Bowie was 32 at the time).[50] Bowie's own costume was a Pierrot suit by Natasha Korniloff (see pl.162), a close friend from his days with Lindsay Kemp, and with whom he had collaborated several times for his stage costumes.

After 'Ashes to Ashes', Bowie's stage wear became less obviously outlandish.

The outfits I use on stage now are far more functional … I think the major difference, of course, is that I was designing for characters, which I've kind of stopped. I wrapped that up in the early 1980s and I didn't do characters after that. Those first years, the Thin White Duke and all those guys, I really was dressing in character.[51]

Bowie did, however, toy with more dramatic looks for the Outside and Earthling tours of 1996–7, reprising a spiked crop of bright-orange hair. He had become interested in the work of an irreverent young London designer called Alexander McQueen, and began to collaborate with him in 1995 on stage wear for the Outside tour (McQueen also dressed Bowie's bassist Gail Ann Dorsey). McQueen was a Bowie fan, and had based his Spring/Summer 1996 collection, which included garments that appeared to have been slashed open and a shirt stained with bloody handprints, on the film *The Hunger* (1983), which starred Bowie and Catherine Deneuve.

In a conversation between the two men published in *Dazed & Confused* magazine, Bowie invited McQueen to come to the 1996 VH1 Fashion Awards in New York: 'Cos you know I'm wearing the Union Jack on that. Because millions of people deserve to see it'. McQueen's comeback was 'You've got to say "This is by McQueen!"'[52] The Union Jack in question was a frock coat McQueen had made at Bowie's request from a British flag. Bowie had actually asked for a distressed garment based on the 1960s jacket worn by the Who's Pete Townsend, but in the style of McQueen's signature frock coat. The designer obliged with a beautifully constructed coat, which he had then artfully burnt and aged (pl.186). Bowie opened each show of the Earthling tour in the McQueen coat, standing with his back to the audience, and wore it on the cover of the *Earthling* album, in a similar pose. The coat was included in the Anglomania exhibition at the Metropolitan Museum in New York in 2006 – 'ruined yet precisely tailored, the coat is a pastiche of patriotism',[53] a perfectly considered symbol for the subversive collaboration between Bowie and McQueen.

Discussing his approach to fashion in 2005, Bowie inadvertently highlighted how his influence on fashion had come full circle. Explaining that he was currently wearing clothes by one particular designer, he said: 'I just rely on Hedi Slimane … I've always been extremely lucky that there's always been some designer or other who wants to give me clothes. For the last little while Hedi Slimane has wardrobed me.'[54] Slimane, who is currently head designer at the house of Saint Laurent Paris, received global acclaim for the slim, tailored menswear he created for Christian Dior Homme in the early 2000s. Bowie was sent some early designs by Slimane: 'The stuff was apparently influenced by the film *The Man Who Fell to Earth*, and it was all that very slim-line black, and it's very much become his signature look.'[55] Slimane acknowledges the debt: 'I was … born with a David Bowie album in my hand … He was Adam and Angie Bowie was Eve.'[56]

The unparalleled impact that Bowie in his various incarnations has had on several generations of adolescents is directly responsible for his persistent importance to the fashion world. As Tim Blanks has pointed out, Bowie 'elevated sensibilities to a degree acute enough that those so changed were able to exert similar influence when they became editors, designers, musicians and artists in their later lives'.[57] It is abundantly clear that throughout his collaborations with designers, Bowie has always retained a laser-sharp view of the image he wishes to project. He has always been in control, and while he appropriates and appreciates the work of fashion designers, he considers fashion a tool to enhance his overall performance: 'I'm far more interested in the theatrical implications of clothes than I am in everyday fashion.'[58] It is precisely his theatrical, often androgynous interpretations of clothing, alongside his music, that have kept the fashion world intrigued for so long. As designer Dries Van Noten says: 'Bowie has proven to be timeless and relevant in a moment when many musicians fade into oblivion … his playing with androgyny was so powerful. I think that what was avant-garde back in the 1970s is consistent with today's psyche.'[59] As each new generation rediscovers each incarnation and character, the fashion world repeatedly finds in Bowie and his personae the point where style, metamorphosis, performance and presentation converge.

DAVID BOWIE IS STARING AT YOU SO WHAT DO YOU DO?

← ↑ **[188] OPPOSITE AND ABOVE** ⬩ Gold brocade jacket, 1997 ⬩ Designed by
Alexander McQueen for the Earthling tour ⬩ DAVID BOWIE ARCHIVE

DAVID BOWIE IS SHOWING YOU HE'S REAL

→ [189] **OPPOSITE** ● Gold brocade jacket, 1997 ●
Designed by Alexander McQueen for the Earthling tour ●
DAVID BOWIE ARCHIVE

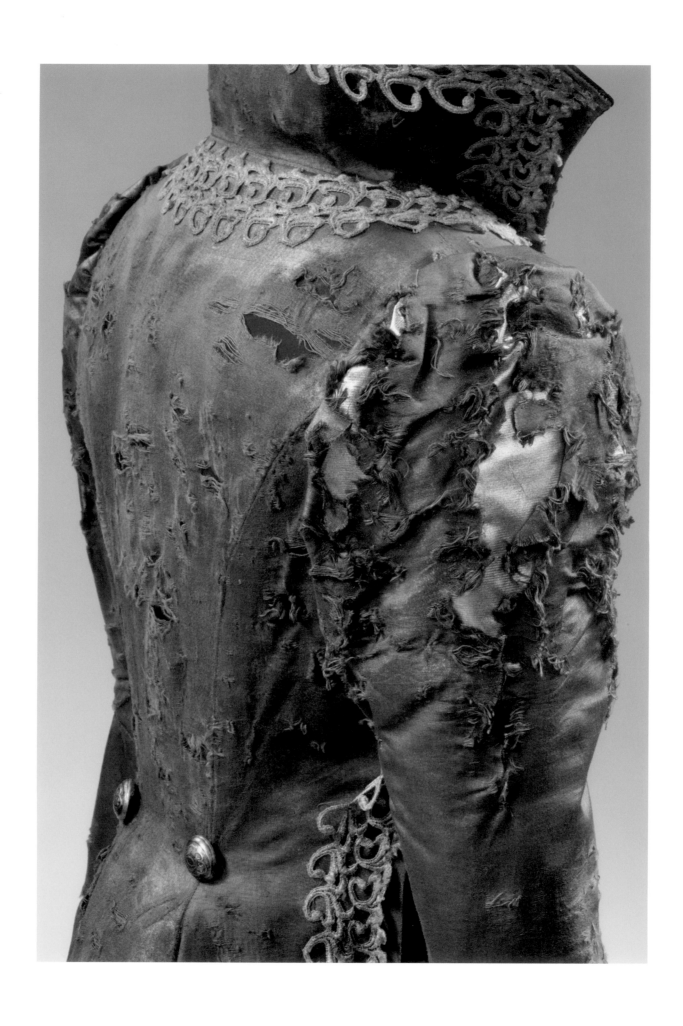

↑→ [190] **ABOVE AND OPPOSITE** ● Distressed frock coat, 1997 ●
Designed by David Bowie for The Fiftieth Birthday Concert ●
THE DAVID BOWIE ARCHIVE

↑→ [191] **ABOVE AND OPPOSITE** • Brogues and 1920s suit • Photographed for
the *Heathen* album cover • THE DAVID BOWIE ARCHIVE

←↑ **[192] OPPOSITE AND ABOVE** ◦ Blue silk suit, 2002 ◦ Designed by
Hedi Slimane for Dior for the Heathen tour ◦ THE DAVID BOWIE ARCHIVE

↑→ [193] **ABOVE AND OPPOSITE** • Distressed tailcoat and ensemble, 2003 •
Designed by Deth Killers of Bushwick for the Reality tour • THE DAVID BOWIE ARCHIVE

←↑ **[194] OPPOSITE AND ABOVE** ◦ Distressed frock coat and trousers, 1995 ◦
Designed by Alexander McQueen for the Outside tour ◦ THE DAVID BOWIE ARCHIVE

DAVID BOWIE IS RESEMBLING HIMSELF

BUT WHO ARE WE

SO SMALL IN TIMES SUCH AS THESE

DAVID BOWIE THEN ... DAVID BOWIE NOW ...

A roundtable discussion with educationalist and writer Sir Christopher Frayling,
writer Philip Hoare and film-critic and broadcaster Mark Kermode, chaired by
Geoffrey Marsh, Director of Theatre & Performance Collections at the V&A.

[GM] Christopher, you were born on Christmas Day 1946, two weeks before David Bowie, and in south London as well, so your life has tracked Bowie's over five decades. Could you give an overview of how you see his relationship with this country has evolved over those years?

[CF] Well, there's south London, which wasn't hip, which was out of town, which seemed very isolated and a very long way from the metropolis – that element of taking the train in and going to clubs, and interesting cinemas, because that's where the action was.

There's America, the whole discovery of American culture in the early 1950s, when the 'grown-ups' were saying that America was Tastee-Freez, and [that it was] smothering English culture – Leavis, Orwell, and T. S. Eliot and *Brideshead Revisited*. Suddenly one way out was America: American pop music, American films and American clothes. I think it's interesting that Bowie's name references the Bowie knife, and Richard Widmark's character 'Jim Bowie' in John Wayne's film *The Alamo*. I remember all that very well, but in particular the sense of isolation, of living out in the sticks – and that the way 'in' was America. And parents hated that – all the talk about how the Americans came in to the War far too late – and how Hollywood claimed that they won it for us.

I started getting involved in art schools a bit later but, of course, Bowie didn't go to one; he went to Bromley Technical High School, where he was fast-tracked to take the art A-level at 16. Peter Frampton's father Owen was his art teacher, and he must have been talking about what was in the ether. I didn't dress up as a youngster – much too conventional – but one of the ways out was to challenge the stereotypes of gender, as well as class. One of the things that Bowie did at that time was change the debate from class to gender; we were going on about class – Marx, demonstrations and all that – but he was talking about something else.

[GM] Philip, you were born 10 years later, so you were a teenager at school when Bowie was making many of his key records. How do you remember it?

[PH] Like Christopher says, Bowie was this creature of the suburbs – but in a way he transcended mortal experience. And growing up in suburban Southampton, from a lower middle-class family, for me seeing Bowie fellate Mick Ronson on stage was concomitant with Nijinsky wanking in *L'après-midi d'un faune*. Bowie's ability to travel through time and bring together all kinds of subversion resembled Wilde's. He commoditized decadence for the suburbs, and Aladdin Sane is Dorian Gray – as is Ziggy Stardust.

My first introduction to Bowie was in my bedroom on a very bad cassette recording of *Ziggy Stardust* that I taped from someone else, and playing it illicitly in my box bedroom in Southampton, and hoping my parents wouldn't hear. And then looking at photographs of David Bowie that were akin to pornography … he represented an extraordinary sense of enablement. It's with me still. It defines me.

I was at a monastery school run by De La Mennais Brothers in Southampton, and I would arrive with a fur-collar coat and a trilby hat – in tribute to Bowie. That sense of being 'other', in a place like Southampton that had no sense of connection to any cosmopolitanism, although it's a port – he created a pattern that one could follow, which was, as Christopher says, not about class, but about gender. But it was beyond that, because he was beyond homosexuality.

He showed that the way one looked could be a statement of identity at a time of incredible greyness and brownness – everything was brown in the early 1970s, as you remember. To go out wearing a woman's jacket and high-heeled shoes, with a pair of pink-satin Oxford bags that my mother had made from a pair of curtains, and then falling down the stairs of the number three bus in the middle of Southampton: you could believe you were David Bowie.

[GM] And did you discuss it with a group at school?

[PH] My best friend and I were only friends with people who liked David Bowie. You couldn't really talk to anyone else. Being in a monastery school gave a particular piquancy to it all. I remember opening up the first Roxy Music album in a classroom and a monk steaming in, hitting the cover from our hands, saying, 'I don't look at pictures of girls, I look at pictures of men.' And the irony was that we were looking at the gatefold inside, which of course was pictures of men – it was Bryan Ferry and Eno. So that whole era – I can't say legitimized, because that's the wrong word – is what Bowie gave me access to. It was an entire other universe.

[GM] And Mark, you came to it slightly later. What was your take when Bowie crossed your horizons?

[MK] I was born in 1963, so I first became aware of Bowie in the early 1970s, almost entirely through cinema. It's interesting you said that Southampton wasn't at all cosmopolitan, which it wasn't, but it did have a massive number of cinemas. Ken Russell remembers growing up there and not being able to throw a stone without hitting a cinema. I first became aware of Bowie because at an early age I went to see *2001: A Space Odyssey*, and so *Space Odyssey* and 'Space Oddity' became connected in my mind. I remember what would have been the re-release cover of *Man of Words/Man of Music* [the album originally released in the UK in 1969 as *David Bowie*] as *Space Oddity* with that picture of David Bowie with the spikey-up hair, which was in the record stores around that time. There was that, *The Man Who Sold the World*, *Ziggy Stardust* and *Aladdin Sane* – and that was back in days when record shops would display album covers in the windows, so you'd get all those albums displayed together.

I called him 'Boughie' back then. And there's an interesting discussion to be had about how you pronounce his name in relation to how you think of him. On 'Future Legend' on *Diamond Dogs* you very clearly hear a voice saying 'Boughie, Boughie', and in the early 1970s he was, as far as I was concerned, David Boughie, becoming Bowie later on. More like the Bowie knife.

I know there's a whole subculture that refers to him as 'Bow-ee'. But to me, he was Boughie, and was connected with science-fiction films, and he was initially scary. He looked like his dress sense came from *A Clockwork Orange*, there was clearly a whole thing about the mixture of bovver boots and gender-neutral clothing, which was in itself strange. You look at the early pictures of Malcolm McDowell from *A Clockwork Orange* with that very, very coiffed hair, but part thug, part effete, and non-specific gender. So my first memory was, 'Wow, that's really scary.' I promised Christopher I wouldn't say this, but around the same time *The Exorcist* was having the same effect on me, which was: 'It's really scary, so I'm interested in it.' There is a connection, which is that anything that was worrying your parents, which was creating scandal, was inevitably very alluring. So I remember being interested because Bowie's image was like science fiction, it was like something that looked scary, and also your parents didn't like it. You look at a film, not so long ago, like *Velvet Goldmine*, which Bowie isn't involved with in any way – but there's that fantastic scene where the teenager is pointing at the television and saying, 'That's me, that is, that's me.' That strange sense of recognition.

And then, not so long after that, only a few years later, you get *The Man Who Fell to Earth*, which of course is his defining role, not just in cinema but across all these cultural references. Obviously it's based on a very respectable book by Walter Tevis, and it's a film that's grown in stature over the years – but that's what he *was*. He himself once said in an interview: 'I was the man, no, I was the androgyne for the time.' That was it. The sense was that he was genuinely a space alien who had somehow ended up on earth, and ended up making recordings of bizarre extra-terrestrial poetry. That's why Nic Roeg casting him in that film was so brilliant. He didn't have to act it. You just thought that it was exactly what he seemed to have been.

So he was a spaceman, living on earth, being a bit scary and therefore interesting, working in records and films, both of which we had been told were slightly debased, slightly rebellious art forms that you probably shouldn't concentrate on too much. Consequently, you end up completely obsessing about them – and him.

[CF] I remember the great debate about Bowie among earnest cultural studies professors – another invention of the late 1960s – was whether the alien image, the *A Clockwork Orange* image and later the Isherwood Berlin image of the early 1970s were actually an escape from the 'real stuff' – you know, that we should be on the streets protesting; we should be doing the things that people did in the 1960s. But he kept stepping out of that commitment – all sorts of commitments, actually: the commitment to gender, sexuality, personality – to anything. He was such a fluid personality that a lot of the heavy mob in cultural studies never really forgave him; they thought he was copping out. I'd argue that actually he was doing something even more radical by redefining gender roles and all these other things we've touched on. He was moving the debate on from the crude Marxism of the 1960s into the politics of identity. But at the time critics wanted their rock'n'roll to be *authentic*, they wanted Springsteen, a sort of blue-collar guy who wears his heart on his sleeve, and it's all about him and *his* life. And Bowie was completely different, he was standing aside from all that and creating all these roles and being very detached, like a Pop artist manipulating all these signs. A singing Warhol. They didn't like that, having to ask, 'Where is he, in all this?'

[PH] It's because he's not serious. He's a very typical English artist in that he doesn't take it seriously. He's almost amateur in the way he approaches things – what annoyed those musos is the fact that he's not Springsteen, and he's not Jimmy Page ... he's always playing, always playing with you. And he's always picking out things and stealing stuff. He's a vampire, a creature of the night. People talk about this sense of vampirism, a transsexual vampire.

The Man Who Fell to Earth is such a key point in the Bowie universe because it exists *sui generis* – it's completely of its own. It could be a science-fiction film made by Powell and Pressburger. You have the way he looks in it, inspired by that great scene in 'Cracked Actor', the Alan Yentob 'Arena' documentary, when Bowie is being driven in a limousine through the desert, and he's making a joke when he sees a wax museum, saying 'You'd think it would melt, wouldn't you?' The man is transfixed by cocaine. You can almost feel it boring through his brain. And he's skeletal thin. He has been reduced to the essence of Bowie-dom. And the translation of that to *The Man Who Fell to Earth* is almost nothing; there's just a thin membrane between the two. The way he looks in the film just takes on that step of always being *beyond*.

Noel Coward said that when David Lean asked him how he'd managed to survive through so many periods that it seemed centuries, Coward's retort was: 'Always pop out of another hole.' Bowie always seems to confound expectation, and I think he really does that intensely in *The Man Who Fell to Earth*.

[CF] I was surprised that the V&A's *Postmodernism* exhibition didn't include that clip of *The Man Who Fell to Earth* of the alien sitting there with a hundred television channels all going at once, and this channel-hopper just vacuuming in all this material. It's such a key image of that 'culture of quotations' moment. It would have distilled much of the exhibition: breadth rather than depth; moving horizontally through information; life in inverted commas; no more grand narratives.

[MK] The interesting thing about that image from *The Man Who Fell to Earth* is not only that it depicts how people watch television now – and it's a common image – but also that it seems to be the distillation of Bowie's entire image. It's significant to point out that the cover images of both *Station to Station* and *Low* are taken from the film (pls 138 and 139). For *Station to Station*, you wonder why he's putting his head through a bunch of black cones, and then you realize it's him putting his head into the space cabin from *The Man Who Fell to Earth*. The *Low* cover was pretty close to a publicity image for *The Man Who Fell to Earth* and on the second side of *Low* we find the song 'Subterraneans' that he had written for *The Man Who Fell to Earth* that ended up not being used in the film – according to Nic Roeg, because someone stiffed him on the money. Being slightly completist, a while ago I took *The Man Who Fell to Earth* and put some of the *Low* music on to it. It works brilliantly! Clearly that's what it's the soundtrack to.

The interesting thing with the film is that it's hard to imagine anybody else getting away with that role, because there are a lot of things about that film that in anybody else's hands would have just appeared clunky and ridiculous. There is no surer way of making a fool of yourself than to be asked to act like you're extraterrestrial and not human. Actors consistently drop the ball doing that because it's so hard to do. The genius of casting Bowie was that he didn't appear to be acting at all. In fact, the one moment in the film when it doesn't ring true is when they stick him in the space-lizard make-up. Then he just looks like a bloke in space-lizard make-up.

[CF] Nic Roeg said that he saw the 'Cracked Actor' documentary on TV, and when he met Bowie it was as if someone was walking towards the part. He just had to *be*, really. I think that Bowie's best film performances are when he just has to be. When he's Warhol in *Basquiat*, when he's Tesla in *The Prestige* or when he's Mr Newton, I think he's astonishingly charismatic and enigmatic. But he's not an actorly actor ... he just is. Casting Bowie was quite a risk, when you think about it. He'd made a few records and in the pop world was very successful, but in film terms – Hollywood – 'Who's he?'

[GM] How do you feel about an exhibition about Bowie at the V&A? Do you think it is part of the myth-making that is going on? Is it appropriate? It's the UK's National Museum of Art, Design and Performance; clearly fashion and popular culture are things that audiences are interested in. In the 1970s, Bowie would probably have thought the V&A was a very grey and dusty place.

[PH] I think Bowie was the Ballet Russes for my generation. When I saw the V&A's Ballet Russes exhibition and saw the backcloth for *Le Train bleu*, it was unbelievable. It suddenly threw you back to the astonishing multimedia effect that the Ballet Russes had at that point. I think it is the same thing for Bowie. Having seen Joseph Beuys and Bryan Ferry lecture at the V&A, I don't think, in true Bowie tradition, that there is a barrier there.

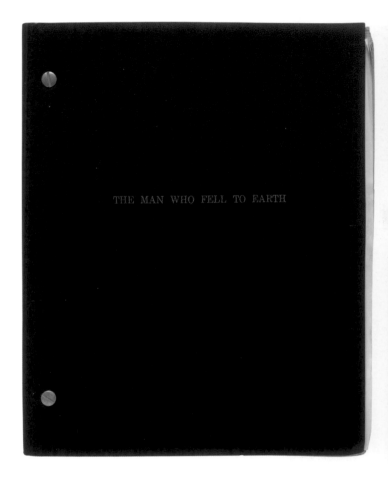

[MK] I think there are very few pop stars who, if you heard they had an exhibition at the V&A, you wouldn't laugh. But in the case of Bowie, to sneer would be ridiculous. It is always really difficult when you talk about anybody who first made their mark in pop music; to then talk about them doing anything outside that field automatically invites derision. Nobody wants to see pop stars act in films because they're rubbish. No one wants to see a pop star's screen prints because they're rubbish. Nobody wants to see a pop star's volume of poetry because it's rubbish. We all 'know' that.

But the fact of the matter is, when you consider Bowie's work in pop music you inevitably start thinking about all the other areas – you think about the music, you think about the videos, you think about the fashion, you think about the political or non-political statements, you think about the films ... you go from gender identity in the 1960s and 1970s through to the after-effects of 9/11. Clearly it would be absurd to think anything but that it is completely justified.

My only thought when I heard about the exhibition was, 'How big is the room?' Literally, where are you going to put it all? You take any five- or ten-year period within his career and there is more than enough to fill one exhibition. What I hope the exhibition won't do is to focus just on 1970–80, and do that to the exclusion of everything else. I would shy away from the idea that that is the only significant period, because I think his cultural significance is, if anything, more now than it was then – because he has passed into the ether. I can't think of many people I obsessed over in the 1970s whose name would be instantly recognizable to the average teenager now. But if you ask a 13-year-old 'Do you know who David Bowie is?', they'll say yes ... and actually the chances are that they saw him in *Bandslam*.

[CF] At the opening of the V&A's Kylie Minogue exhibition in 2006, this diminutive girl stood there by the microphone and said: 'Look, there's me, Kylie Minogue, I'm here tonight, and there's the other Kylie Minogue, who belongs to the history of culture, and the history of art and design. And this exhibition isn't about me, the little girl from Australia, it's about culture, and the history of design.' I thought that was a wonderful thing to say and explained why that exhibition was happening.

In 1910, 85 per cent all recorded music was classical music, now less than ten per cent of recorded music is classical. You can't say the V&A is just there for the ten per cent; it's there for the 90 per cent as well, and actually it's the soundtrack to our lives now, and you have to accept that.

Another point is the high-low issue. Bowie radically stood for breaking down the distinction between, on the one hand, Dada, Duchamp, Baudelaire, Oscar Wilde, you name it – and on the other hand, Tin Pan Alley. Bowie broke down those distinctions, and I think that that's part of the new role of the V&A. It used to embody those distinctions, and it now has to learn how to break them down, and get into the bloodstream of culture. To interpret visual culture across the spectrum.

[MK] The high-low thing is embodied in *A Clockwork Orange*. It inspired so much of Bowie's early stage work, and combines the bovver boy with the person who listens to Beethoven. There was, from the earliest breakout of Bowie's pop career, the idea that you didn't have to be either an aesthete or somebody that worked in a factory.

[GM] Let's fast-forward to 2012. A few months ago a commemorative plaque to Ziggy Stardust was unveiled in Heddon Street for the fortieth anniversary [of the release of *The Rise and Fall of Ziggy Stardust and the Spiders from Mars*]; it's one of only three plaques in London to imaginary characters. It struck me that if Ziggy Stardust walked down Regent Street today nobody would blink an eyelid – but if he walked through a lot of other capital cities, Ziggy might have a lot of problems. How do you see his overall impact looking back over 40 years?

[PH] Where do you start? Like you, I went down to Heddon Street to see the plaque, which is deeply disappointing, I think. In 1912 on the same street where the plaque was erected was the Cave of the Golden Calf, which was probably one of the most decadent clubs ever devised in Britain. Visitors were greeted by a golden calf carved by Eric Gill that was coved in gold, a phallic symbol, and it was worshipped by people to the soundtrack of 'nigger music', which was what jazz was called then. There were men walking around with nail varnish on ... So that sense of what Bowie means now is inflected by what he would have meant a hundred years ago. When you see that image of Ziggy Stardust, he might have been teleported there by Diaghilev or Warhol, as much as from a century in future. And he lives on in that way because of the strength of the image he created, and the strength of the myth that he created, and the strength of the narratives of his songs, which are universes in their own right in a way ... They're timeless, because he was trying to deal with the future. Nothing dates so much as the future from the past, but Bowie seems to have escaped that.

I last saw him at Glastonbury in 2001, when he just rendered everything else around him – and everything that had gone before – to be almost an opening act for what he was. Specifically, when you look at the progress of music, he has been influential throughout. Punk wouldn't have happened without him. The Bromley Contingent were in the audience when I first saw David Bowie, on the *Station to Station* tour in 1976. I saw Siouxsie Sioux and Steve Severin walking out. They were Bowie's children. A generation later at the Taboo club, Leigh Bowery was a bloated Bowie from the Antipodes. There's this transgenic influence being passed from generation to generation through the people who worship Bowie, from Joy Division to Lady Gaga. Tilda Swinton channels him, brilliantly, in fashion shoots. And my 12-year-old nephew knows all the lyrics to 'Ziggy Stardust'.

[CF] I'm not sure that the music in and of itself will be what survives with Bowie, but the music in relation to everything else. The videos are *so* important as extra information being overlaid over the lyrics of the songs. Whereas for the Beatles, I think that some of the songs will long outlive them, I'm not so sure that will happen musically with Bowie. But when you put the videos with the songs, then there's something extraordinary going on: the verbal and the visual, the fashion element, the construction of celebrity ... All these things are happening visually. As long as we can find a way of conserving videos, in 50 years I suspect that will be what goes into the archive – the mixture of the two. Then there will be the legacy, the rock family tree, and who he influences. I would say that Michael Jackson is a good example of someone who completely changes his image and act as part of the backwash from Bowie.

[MK] I slightly disagree with you on the music issue. If, after all these years, you can still listen to 'Cygnet Committee' and think 'Blimey!' ... I had that album [1969's *David Bowie*] when I was about ten or 11, and I still listen to it and am amazed at how much is going on. 'Memory of a Free Festival' is the same.

The thing about his musical influence is that it's actually harder to think of something that he *hasn't* influenced. On the radio the other day, someone was doing a retro thing and playing a track by Suede – and for the first bit you think, 'Oh, it's Bowie. Oh, no, sorry. It's not, it's Suede *doing* Bowie.' One of the funniest moments in any David Bowie film is that moment in *The Hunger* when he walks into a club and Bauhaus are in a cage playing 'Bela Lugosi's Dead'. It must be an intentional gag: Bowie not looking at Pete Murphy, who has got to where he is by doing a David Bowie impression, yet doesn't notice Bowie walking past him.

There's a recent film I mentioned earlier called *Bandslam*, aimed at 13- or 14-year-olds, a story about young wannabe rock musicians. It ends with David Bowie picking them up on the internet and ringing them up and saying, 'I've seen your video and I'd like to produce you.' I saw that film with my daughter, who admittedly grew up in a house with all the Bowie albums around her, but of course she knows who David Bowie is – and the makers of that film must have understood that his role as an icon even to teenagers is big enough that the gag will work. At the end, they'll think, 'Oh yeah, I know him.'

As far as the connection between the music and the videos is concerned, I absolutely agree that the videos are really important – we all remember where we were when we saw 'Ashes to Ashes', or when someone said, 'Wow, he's made a little feature film called "Jazzin' for Blue Jean", it's like a pop video but it goes on for ages.' That drew comparison with John Landis doing Michael Jackson's *Thriller* – people said, 'They've spent *how* much money making it?' There was that crossover. But I think that the music stands up on its own, because it's uncanny how many pop movements have come, like punk, that wiped out all the old dinosaurs – but of course not Bowie. Then along comes techno, and all the New Romantic bands, who all look like they're trying to be David Bowie with tea cloths over their shoulders.

He had worked with German electronic bands long before everybody had a Kraftwerk album. He played the icon in *Christiane F.* ages before anybody thought, 'Oh actually, that's where the future is.' And then the disco thing happens ... the drum sound that he develops on *Low* is the drum sound that you then hear for the next ten years in every dance record. It's easier to pick out the music that hasn't been defined by him – even if the people who made it would shudder at the thought that actually what they're doing is recycling Bowie. And that ties in with the idea of being a magpie, a thief, of stealing things. Of course he did; the genius of what he did was exactly that. He has got an extraordinary sense of history ... who wouldn't have, when the first records you make are mod records and you go on television and complain about being chased down the street because you've got long hair, and the next thing is that you're doing Anthony Newley? By the time he arrived at what we think of as the early 'proper' hits – 'Space Oddity' – he's got a whole career in musical theatre behind him.

[GM] So what other people and ideas do you see when you think of Bowie, his image and his relationship to culture?

[CF] There are lots of other traditions alongside what we've been talking about. Can I quote Oscar Wilde? 'I was a man who stood in symbolic relationship to the art and culture of my age. There was nothing I said or did that didn't make people wonder.' I think that's spot on.

[PH] On the 'dress sleeve' of *The Man Who Sold the World* he's channelling Wilde, via the Aesthetic movement, only bringing it forward into the twenty-first century.

↖ **[200] TOP LEFT** ● Poster for the UK release of *Merry Christmas Mr Lawrence*, 1983 ● Directed by Nagisa Oshima ● THE DAVID BOWIE ARCHIVE

↑ **[201] TOP RIGHT** ● Poster for the Japanese release of *Merry Christmas Mr Lawrence*, 1983 ● Directed by Nagisa Oshima ● THE DAVID BOWIE ARCHIVE

← **[202] LEFT** ● Poster from *Basquiat*, 1996 ● Directed by Julian Schnabel ● The original poster, featuring Andy Warhol and Jean-Michel Basquiat, promoted their joint exhibition in 1985 ● This replica made for the film shows David Bowie and Jeffrey Wright in character ● THE DAVID BOWIE ARCHIVE

↑ **[203] ABOVE** ● David Bowie as Andy Warhol on the set of *Basquiat*, 1996 ● THE DAVID BOWIE ARCHIVE

→ **[204] OPPOSITE** ● David Bowie as Andy Warhol on the set of *Basquiat*, 1996 ● Photograph by Eric Liebowitz ● THE DAVID BOWIE ARCHIVE

[CF] Let's rewind to the moment of his formation as a performer: he's just left school, in 1963/64, then after that, 1965–72 … The things that were in the ether that I think he distilled: you've got *Mythologies* by Roland Barthes, so there is the language of signs and manipulating signs, and nothing is natural or given, it's all manufactured and in someone's interest. Then you've got Warhol saying the same things about celebrity, and that's absolutely hitting England in about 1966. Then there's Georges Bataille writing about transgression and taboo, and that one of the ways you define yourself is in finding society's taboos and exploiting them. There's some Nietzsche, 'Start your rebirth tomorrow and do what thou wilt', arguing that remaking yourself is the way to refresh your life. All of these theoretical contribtutions are in the ether, and somehow he picks up on them. And on the Oscar Wilde-Aubrey Beardsley revival. He's not at art school, unlike Lennon, and Eric Burden, and Pete Townshend and Freddie Mercury, he's actually at the technical college down the road, but somehow he picks up on all this. I think his significance long-term is the distillation of that moment when visual languages were beginning to be understood, and our art was becoming concerned with referring explicitly to signs – New York was taking over from Paris. He embodies the symbolic relationship to the art and culture of the age in a very visual and aural way. That's extraordinary. People will also look back on his beauty as we do at great Hollywood stars. Stills of Bowie will be like latter-day Hollywood studio portraits.

[MK] He always thought of himself as Marlene Dietrich – and on the cover of *Hunky Dory*, he is being Dietrich, he does look like her.

[PH] He's a romantic figure in the tradition of Byron or Keats or Shelley. It's a shame that he has to change … When he went to America he became something that he ought not to have become, commoditized, the same time as he signed to EMI. There's this ten-year miraculous period where he's this lodestone, a lightning conductor for all this amazing stuff that's going on, and he introduces us to Jean Genet, and Burroughs, and Man Ray. Just that sense of something which is beyond his control, almost.

[MK] I would be very careful about imagining that there was a golden age that stopped. I think that we need to be careful, because this conversation is about what David Bowie is now, and there is a sense that he transcended pop in the 1960s and 1970s, but in fact he's been active since then. What happens after *Scary Monsters*, *Let's Dance* and *Modern Love*, when he was massive, is that he moves into other areas, whether that's art, or film, or the internet, or stage production. I saw *The Elephant Man* on stage not with Bowie [in 1980], but with David Schofield, and I thought it was brilliant. But for Bowie, the idea that he would lay himself bare, when he's got everything to lose, is interesting.

On the Internet Movie Database (IMDb) there's a note of what he's 'known for'. Two of the films listed in that section are *Se7en* and *Inglourious Basterds*. Now, for *Se7en* it's because of 'The Hearts Filthy Lesson', and *Inglourious Basterds* because of 'Putting Out Fire', which of course is the theme from *Cat People*. There is a whole body of work that is more significant to a generation who think that Bowie started with *Let's Dance*, who remember buying 'Modern Love' and think that everything before that is the preamble to the point at which he became danceable and mainstream. It was really interesting for me, who has always considered *The Man Who Fell to Earth* as the most definitive thing he's done, that the IMDb says that the most important thing is the theme to *Se7en*.

I think that the Bowie movie legacy is better than many people think it is, because people remember the scene in *Merry Christmas Mr Lawrence*, which I don't like as a film, where he pretends to shave, and everyone says, 'Oh yeah, he studied with Lindsay Kemp', and that's pompous, pretentious and boring. Also there's the tragedy of *Just a Gigolo*, which is a disastrous film and he shouldn't have had anything to do with it. What people forget is that he's really good in *The Prestige*, where he has a pretty good go at [the Serbian-American] Tesla's complicated accent. You watch it and think, 'Sorry, what accent is that?' but apparently it would have been exactly that.

[CF] Nikola Tesla is such an interesting character. There's a famous photo of him in a metal cage with all this electricity being chucked at him – it's now known to be a fake, but it was very influential. Had a huge influence on the creation sequence in James Whale's *Frankenstein*. It's perfect that Bowie plays Tesla.

[MK] He's great in that. He has a brilliant cameo in *Into the Night* in which he's used by John Landis to play a really hard killer. It's only a brief role, but he's really good in it. He's great in *The Hunger*, which as a film is basically MTV on the big screen. I'm not a fan of the film, but he does a vampire – and you mentioned the vampire in connection with the music – and he's perfectly cast. The problem is that people remember like this: *The Man Who Fell to Earth* – great. *Just a Gigolo* – terrible. Followed by *Merry Christmas Mr Lawrence*, which actually nobody liked (other than for the score) but you went to see because it was Oshima. And then they forget that the significant roles are in other movies, whether it's providing music for *Se7en* or being in *The Prestige*, which is the most underrated Nolan movie. It's terrific. Or it's appearing in *Christiane F.*, which at the time was such a controversial film that the censors beat themselves up about it for ages. I remember going to see it and being astonished because I'd never seen a film that dealt with drug addiction in such a visceral way. The idea of putting Bowie right in the middle of that was very bold.

[PH] It's his version of Sinatra and *The Man with the Golden Arm*.

[CF] And not forgetting *Basquiat*, where he at last plays Warhol and actually wore Warhol's wig, and his clothes, and carried his handbag. That must have been a great avatar moment for him. Like Warhol himself using a double in a wig for media interviews.

[PH] Bowie was Warhol's Frankenstein's creature. Without Warhol Bowie couldn't have existed. He was the product of that new attitude to commodification and to art, where Bowie, a musician, could be an artist – a fine artist. That's where the notion of him being in films, films that aren't completely under his control, which aren't an extension of his unreal personality, almost don't work for me. I respect what you say about those films, Mark, but they don't interest me because they're not actually about David Bowie, they're about another character.

The Man Who Fell to Earth works because he's playing David Bowie. That part was written for him before he arrived. There's this sense of things going on around him as this creature falls to the earth; it's the same as Jay Gatsby standing on the end of his Long Island dock. This person who is completely ahead of his era, and is leading the era, and is an avatar that is untouchable. He symbolizes something that is unattainable for us all.

I was talking to a friend about David Bowie the other day, and he said: 'What does he do now? Do you think he has any friends?' I don't think that David Bowie has ever had 'friends'. How could you be 'friends' with David Bowie?

[GM] There is this idea that Bowie, like some other artists such as Blake and maybe Derek Jarman, has this habit of ranging across different art forms and as a result there's an element of discomfort in critical circles …

[PH] The nearest cultural figure to him is William Blake.

[CF] …except that William Blake was utterly incapable of commercializing himself in any possible way, and that Blake believed in his mythology so deeply that he couldn't produce anything that anyone wanted in his own lifetime.

[PH] *Au contraire* – Blake printed his own books so that he'd have complete control over them. I think commercialism defeated him in his age.

[CF] But he wasn't a commodification man, at all.

[PH] But I don't think David Bowie is, really – even the Bowie Bonds, when they come later on.

[CF] Bowie Bonds in the mid 1990s were a very New York phenomenon. There was an economist who reckoned that David Bowie caused the entire banking crash, because he gave everyone the idea of producing bonds out of thin air against the royalties of the future that might or might not happen, which created a trend for inventing financial services living on nothing. 'If you want a single cause of the banking crisis,' the economist said, 'look no further.' Wow!

Even in 1972/73 he was casting the audience in the role of young consumers rather than angry teenagers. At that time the role of the hero in the movies, in rock music, changes from being a crusader – something you believe in, something you root for, which is very Blake – to something that's a style statement. The focus changes into a projection of someone's dreams rather than a model to emulate; that's absolutely Bowie, I think. You don't want to be him because of what he believes in or because of what he's fighting for. You want to be him because you like his style – and that turns the audience into consumers, and that's not Blake, at all. More like Henry Fuseli if you want to go back to that period; Fuseli, who sold lots of pictures and really played the game. In universities in the 1960s, there was the Marxism and sociology, the idea of 'us against the world, we don't like commodification'. I think Bowie really picked up on the idea that there's no shame in commodifying yourself. Actually, it doesn't ruin the art – in some ways it enhances it.

[PH] That's only because he's being interested in Warhol. It's an artistic statement, not a commercial one. His commercial stuff, after he signed to EMI – you feel as though he's doing it to pay tax bills. When he's really doing something, he never thinks about the money. Pop was just a convenient platform for what he wanted to do. There's a great irony that he's Ziggy Stardust, this person who is killed by his fans. He's inviting that. He brings it upon himself and then he feeds off it. He is created by that energy.

[CF] We keep talking about Bowie, and actually we're talking about the 'myth of Bowie'. I'm not sure even he knows who he is anymore – rather like some actors. It's an odd comparison, but for Woody Allen or Clint Eastwood, because they've played the same parts so often, we confuse them with the person they are playing. Bowie has played lots of parts, but we always talk about him as if they exist. I don't know what lies behind those parts. All I know about is the myth, because that is what we are presented with.

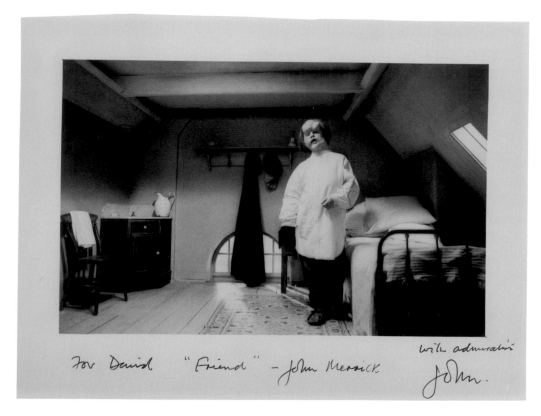

For David "Friend" - John Merrick with admiration John.

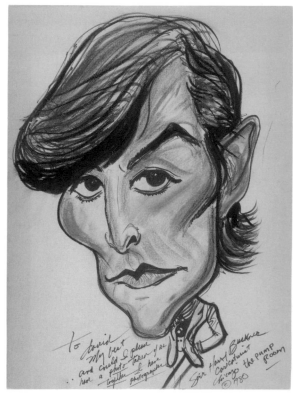

PLAYBILL
THE BOOTH THEATRE

THE ELEPHANT MAN

Richmond Crinkley Elizabeth I. McCann Nelle Nugent
cordially invite you to
the Broadway Debut of
David Bowie
in
"The Elephant Man"
at the Booth Theatre, 222 West 45th Street,
Sunday September 28th, 1980
and to a party in honor of David Bowie
immediately following the performance
57-59 East 11th Street.

Please R.S.V.P to: Harriette Vidal 935-9041 for your tickets.
Curtain is at 7:00 P.M.

↖ **[205] TOP LEFT** ⚫ Signed photograph from John Hurt, 1980 ⚫ THE DAVID BOWIE ARCHIVE

↑ **[206] TOP RIGHT** ⚫ Caricature of David Bowie in Chicago, 1980 ⚫ THE DAVID BOWIE ARCHIVE

← **[207] LEFT** ⚫ Playbill for the Booth Theatre, New York production of *The Elephant Man*, 1980 ⚫ THE DAVID BOWIE ARCHIVE

↑ **[208] ABOVE** ⚫ Invitation to David Bowie's Broadway debut, 1980 ⚫ THE DAVID BOWIE ARCHIVE

→ **[209] OPPOSITE** ⚫ Promotional poster for *The Elephant Man*, 1980 ⚫ Directed by Jack Hofsiss ⚫ THE DAVID BOWIE ARCHIVE

[GM] Moving on to the twenty-first century: although Bowie wasn't in New York on 9/11, he was close by. Some argue that 9/11 was planned as the ultimate piece of media theatre to maximize its international news impact. Do you think that it actually out-Bowied Bowie? That it's one of the few things that has not overlaid Bowie, but gone further?

[CF] That's a very theoretical, post-structuralist, Baudrillard-type position. People died. There were atrocities. They happened. It's NOT a movie, where we're all in the society of the spectacle, and it's all spectacle, and it all evens out at some level. In the end Bowie's an entertainer, and he's in a particular world, and inside that world his innovations that we've been talking about have been fantastic. But outside that world, there's all this history going on. I can't bear Derrida and Baudrillard saying that war is actually a spectacle, or that Vietnam didn't really happen in the accepted sense because we all watched it on television. I don't buy that all. People died. It's not the same as the entertainment business, unless you're talking about the television coverage.

[PH] Frank Kermode talks about how we live through disconfirmed apocalypses, and that they're a trope of modern culture, but that they're a trope of medieval culture as well. Bowie's landscape is post-apocalyptic, from 'We've got five years, stuck on my eyes', it runs all the way through his work. He inhabits *The Wasteland* – which is why Joy Division can inhabit the same wasteland in industrial Manchester in the 1970s and early 1980s. What Bowie represents culturally is that the apocalypse has already happened, that 9/11 has already happened. As soon as I saw the photographs of the ruined twin towers, I opened the gatefold of *Diamond Dogs*, and it's the same image.

[GM] Bowie opened the Concert for New York at Madison Square Gardens, six weeks after 9/11, with [Simon and Garfunkel's] 'America' followed by 'Heroes'. As a Londoner, I thought it was extraordinary to see an Englishman, someone from the suburbs, being a lightning rod for New York's grief. Was there something about him, as a migrant to America, that allowed him to hold an American audience that night?

[CF] It was a very strange moment. I was there a week later, putting on an exhibition in Grand Central Station about the best of British design. We were going to cancel it because we thought it was appalling taste to encourage people to be consumers at this dreadful time, but someone came up with a new slogan, 'UK in NY: Shoulder to Shoulder'. So we put that on the front of the exhibition and suddenly it seemed very emotional, very *right*. The Guards Band was playing Gilbert and Sullivan on the Rockefeller Center garden – in scarlet uniforms – all these greatest hits of British design were in Grand Central Station and Bowie doing the concert – it was a very odd moment. People were wearing badges with Union Jacks and the Stars and Stripes next to each other, saying, 'You're our only friends in the world. You're the only people we can trust.' Blair and Bush. Bowie and Paul Simon.

[MK] If I can add just two things: I feel very uncomfortable about 9/11 ever being talked about as anything other than a hideous terrorist atrocity. You get into very dangerous territory when you start comparing it with spectacle or exhibition for obvious reasons. However, more significant for me in this is that I don't think of Bowie as living in America at all.

I've been convinced for years, whether fact or not, that he lives in Switzerland – because it seems more appropriate that he *should* live in Switzerland. He always seems to me to be someone who should live outside of time and place, and Switzerland – my grandmother's from Switzerland – seems to be the perfect place. A place where you live in a hermetically sealed world that isn't part of the normal world, neutral in wars and with a banking system that's isolated from everyone else. It seems to have arrived from outer space. You made a very good point before about whether you can imagine him ever having 'friends'. I was thinking, 'What – you mean earth friends?' In my head he lives in Switzerland.

Also, he was doing BowieNet very early on, and Bowie Art [bowieart.com is Bowie's on-line gallery], and all those things seem to exist without national boundaries. For me, although I think of him absolutely as British, and I think that the Bromley thing is very important, he does seem to exist in the world without being of a specific country. Which is why if you listen to *Aladdin Sane* it makes sense, because it's about travelling through areas but not being connected with them. It's why in the 'Cracked Actor' documentary the key scene is him in the limousine looking through a glass window, being in the world but not of it. It's why when people say 'He lives in New York', you think, 'Does he?' – because that doesn't make any sense.

[GM] We have over 20 books here about Bowie and there must be at least double that published, with more on the way, apart from all the countless magazine articles. Why does he continue to fascinate writers?

[CF] It is partly because he acts as a lightning rod for all these theoretical concerns at the moment – critics love deconstructing things, and running down theoretical rabbit holes. Partly it's the mystery, the enigma: who is Bowie behind all this? Is he the Invisible Man? That's intriguing for a biographer. Partly I think it's because there are so many unreleased videos, takes and records, and there are these myths of all the material out there – and people think, 'Why won't he release it?' Biographers love to talk about all this intrigue: where are all the versions of the record? Who helped to record it? Where is the master tape?

[GM] You haven't been tempted to write something, Phillip?

[PH] No, I wouldn't. Or only if he asks me! Bowie has never written a book; he doesn't need to write: all of those song-stories are extraordinary narratives. Also, I don't want Bowie to interpret himself. I don't want him to write his autobiography. It's already there. It's in the albums, it's in the videos and it's in the films.

[CF] Well, the myth is. The traditional role of the biographer is to peel that aside, and to try to and find this intelligence, but you can't do that with Bowie; there's an empty room. Like in those sci-fi films where the hero finally breaks into the centre of intelligence – and there's no one there.

[MK] There is a Bowie biography from the early 1970s, written I suppose around the time *Aladdin Sane* was out. It relied very heavily on the idea that once Bowie's father died, things fundamentally changed for him. It was one of those little paperbacks that were popular at the time. That was 40 years ago. One of the problems is, as the plethora of books about him demonstrates, that the changes have been so dramatic. Think about the ten years between 1969 and 1979, think of all the phases he goes through. Think about the ten years that Oasis were together and all the changes that they singularly didn't go through.

Any one period of Bowie's life would more than occupy a biographer. The temptation is always to imagine that all the interesting work was done in the 1970s, but I would contest that. I think there are other periods that are equally interesting. Crucially, the thing I remember about that book I mentioned was reading it as a teenager – because obviously as a teenager you think, 'I want to find out what's behind Bowie' – and you get to the bit where it says, 'It's to do with the death of his father, then everything changes'. But I got there and thought: 'That is utter rubbish, or, if it's not utter rubbish, I don't want to know it. I don't care. What I care about is the fictional invented character.'

[CF] Part of the game with Warhol was inventing your CV; a part of the celebrity thing is to invent. An early press release about Bowie said he went to Bromley Art School, because they felt he ought to have done. It begins there, and people have latched on to certain biographical moments – for example, his stepbrother's mental health problems, the father dying, guilt about the family. Does this help to define Bowie? They latch on to the two or three things they think they *know* about his biography, because of all the smokescreens.

One of the dangers of the celebrity approach to autobiography is that people will believe things that are barefaced lies, but that is part of the joke, in a way. In Bowie's case people have made much too much of tiny little biographical snippets, because they are desperate to know more, and it's all they have. It would be more interesting to write a fictional autobiography. In so far as there are biographical snippets, they all come out of promotional interviews, while he is promoting his work. The famous 1972 'I am gay' statement was from a promotional interview. In fact he made some really quite prescient comments about internet culture a lot later, talking about how people tend to skim and go sideways – horizontal thinking rather than depth thinking – long before that became a fashionable thing to say. Again, that was said in a promotional interview for a record.

[PH] Everything he said was a lie anyway. His statements about his sexuality were fantastically ambiguous. To be ambiguous about something that is already ambiguous – my God! How can you do that?

[PH] I know, but he always retracts those statements. He has retracted that by his existence since, because, as far as I know, he has not had a relationship with a man since …

[PH] Of course it was opposed! All the role models for gay people before Bowie were so extraordinarily … patronizing, I suppose is the word. Because it allows people to put you in a box, and then along comes this person that opens the box, and says, 'You can do any of it'.

[CF] There was that famous interview in *Melody Maker* in January 1972 where he said: 'I am gay, and I always have been gay, even when I was David Jones I was gay.' And that's quite something … at least the first time somebody says it.

[CF] But it was brave because no one had publicly outed a British pop musician, ever. Because it was opposed …

ESCHER SEQUENCE — SCENE

SHE EMERGES ONTO A PLATFORM

CLOSER — SHE LOOKS DOWN ..

" AND IS HORRIFIED

SHE GASPS ..

JIM HENSON

Dear David,

This is the present shape of the script. It is still rough and needs quite a bit of polishing - but you can see where we're going.

I'm looking forward to hearing your reactions.

You would be wonderful in this film.

Sincerely,
Jim

← [210] OPPOSITE • Storyboard for *Labyrinth*, 1986 •
Directed by Jim Henson • THE DAVID BOWIE ARCHIVE

↑ [211] ABOVE • Letter from Jim Henson to
David Bowie, 1986 • THE DAVID BOWIE ARCHIVE

→ [212] RIGHT • Promotional poster for *Labyrinth*, 1986 •
Directed by Jim Henson • THE DAVID BOWIE ARCHIVE

[MK] I think it is interesting to also acknowledge Duncan Jones' career at this point, again as we are talking about Bowie now. Duncan Jones, who turns out to be a brilliant director, and who kept his tinder dry for a very long time and worked, as far as anyone can tell, deliberately not in the shadow of 'my famous father'.

The first film he makes is *Moon*, which is a very 1970s science-fiction movie, and in interviews he talks about him and his dad making little movies together. And of course this is around the time that Bowie was doing all the things we are talking about, and Bowie was obviously influenced by *2001*, *Silent Running*, *Solaris*, all those great movies from the 1960s and early 1970s. Duncan Jones' career is fermented in that. It's interesting that one of the things that shows the ongoing influence of Bowie, now, is that he clearly raised a kid who grew up being very cine-literate, and having a very, very wily take on *how* and *when* to talk to the media.

I was listening to *Hunky Dory* and there is a song on there, 'Kooks', about a kid who then grew up to make a film that I really like, and you don't immediately connect those two things. I think there is something very impressive about the fact that Bowie's influence on his son has not only inculcated a love of cinema and a love of science fiction and all of that, but also clearly he has learnt that the media is something that you deal with very carefully, and at arm's length.

[CF] In supreme irony, he was actually asked about this recently: 'Why don't you move back to London?' He said that 'the trouble is the celebrity culture, they hound you; the paparazzi are everywhere'. That is a supreme irony in his life, but he is right, no one would leave him alone. With all these discussions about bugging and hacking, Bowie would be everywhere. Maybe in New York it isn't like that. And spiritually he was always closer to Warhol's Factory than to Bromley.

[PH] I think that his London is a fictional, fantastical London. He was, trans-chronologically, the spirit of all the subversive Londons that have ever existed – and may ever exist. That's what that image of Ziggy Stardust is about. He is this fairy sprite, almost holographically projected on to London. So his existence in London is always here and not here at the same time.

[PH] I can't think of a single question to which I'd receive a satisfactory answer or, indeed, one I'd want to hear. I mean, where do you start, when faced with someone who is responsible for your alternative education, for opening up the world to you? It would be like Blake talking back to the angels on Peckham Rye.

[GM] As we began our discussion about London, I would like to bring the discussion full circle. London has reinvented itself in last 15 years, and the 2012 Olympics brought the focus of the world on the capital. Bowie could live anywhere in the world, but he chooses to live in New York; clearly whatever transformation has taken place in London, in parallel to his career, is not sufficient to bring him back here.

[MK] He always said that he liked that about New York, the anonymity, the idea you could walk around in New York and nobody bothered you.

[GM] Finally, to end, if Bowie had been with us today, what would you like to have asked him?

[CF] 'What irritates you most about critics writing about you?'

[MK] I'd want to ask him, 'What now?', because, in a way, everything that's happened up until now has been so pored over and so personalized that it doesn't matter what he thinks anymore. It doesn't matter what he meant when he wrote 'Heroes', and it doesn't matter what he thought when he did the cover photography for *The Man Who Sold the World*. It doesn't matter because those things are in the public domain. I think we own the Bowie back catalogue more than he does.

But I think that as somebody who has done so much over that relatively short period – and has reinvented themselves so many times and been so significant not just in the world of music but also the world of cinema and popular culture, and who seems still to be active, on the internet – the question is, 'What now?' The reason is, in my mind he is still a spaceman who – when he is on Earth – lives in a limousine looking at the world from behind a sheet of glass. And he probably doesn't age, and he probably, like Dr Who, has two hearts. And in the end he will go back to whichever planet it is he's come from. And as he is still here, he hasn't finished. So then, what now?

I think it comes back to *The Man Who Fell to Earth* quintessentially summing up what he is. I saw him at the end of *Bandslam* and I thought how young he looked, but of course he looks young, he's a spaceman moving on a different time continuum.

So that would be the question: 'What now?'

DAVID BOWIE IS FAMOUS AND THINKING ABOUT SOMETHING ELSE

→[213] OPPOSITE • David Bowie and Iman at
the Metropolitan Museum of Art Costume Institute
Annual Gala, 2008 • Photograph by Stephen Lovekin

302

DAVID BOWIE IS PHOTOGRAPHIC

NICHOLAS COLERIDGE

Has any rock star collaborated with a wider range of important creative photographers, over a longer period, than David Bowie? The trajectory of his image, and its projection across four decades, tracks the history of photography during the period. Brian Ward, Bruce Weber, Brian Duffy, Masayoshi Sukita, Lord Snowdon, Frank Ockenfels, Anton Corbijn: all played a role in amplifying, refining and sometimes even defining the Bowie image, as surely as Holbein's portraits of Henry VIII or Van Dyke's of Charles I did for their respective patrons centuries earlier. From the very beginning, Bowie had an unerring instinct for who to entrust with his album covers and collateral publicity; over time, he sought out the most interesting, modish and often challenging photographers to interpret each new phase of his journey as an artist.

Of course, it helped that he is good looking and photogenic. In the entire archive of Bowie portraits and stage shots, running to tens of thousands of images, almost none are unflattering. As early as the mid-1960s, when his career had scarcely begun, the photographs that survive show him poised and cool. I have always loved Doug McKenzie's 1966 'mod look' shot of a 19-year-old Bowie, which somehow, in its brooding existentialism, presages the whole later period of his life in Berlin; it could have been taken in the Unter den Linden. It already has the hallmark Bowie look to it, staring into the camera lens through narrowed eyes, somewhat intense, somewhat sceptical, a little bit vulnerable, a little bit camp. You see the same look in Frank Ockenfels' sitting for the *Reality* album cover 37 years later, and the same floppy fringe, come to that.

Although Bowie's status as musical genius would be intact if he'd never been photographed at all, if he'd been as ugly as sin and a lifelong recluse, we diehard Bowie fans were far from indifferent to the photographic images. Brian Ward's cover shoot in the Heddon Street telephone box for the Ziggy album remains an iconic image of the age; I work in the Soho area and never to this day miss an opportunity for a quick Heddon Street detour, on my way back from meetings. But it was Ward's earlier portrait for the *Hunky Dory* album session that touched me first: the androgynous Pre-Raphaelite, fuzzy and soft-focus, which always makes me think of Virginia Woolf's Orlando.

If I had to choose my favourite Bowie image of all time, it would be Masayoshi Sukita's 1972 'Backstage by Door' shot, taken at the height of the Ziggy Stardust period. I love everything about it: posed but not over-posed, grungy but glamorous, seedy but chic, the three blocks of backstage typography ('To Stage' with the arrow and the two 'Exits') satisfyingly juxtaposed with the shoulders of his jacket. And, obviously, one covets the trousers too.

It was striking, when selecting my 16 all-time best Bowie images, how often one reverted to Sukita. Perhaps it took a Japanese eye to do justice to the high-gloss veneer and ironic nihilism of the unfolding Bowie *œuvre*. Nobody recorded the Ziggy and Aladdin Sane eras better than Sukita (the 1972 portraits with red guitar and in Yamamoto costume and, perhaps most of all, the 1973 hand-on-thigh pout-shot against red background, are all classics) but his style evolved in sync with the artist to produce the defining images of the "*Heroes*" period and beyond. I have frequently pondered on the 1978 Tokyo subway shot, with David Bowie strap-hanging on a late-night tube train; one senses he wasn't a frequent public transport-user at this point in his career. But it has a peculiar magic.

I admire Bruce Weber's 1977 portrait with Bowie's face in shadow, because it comes from a completely different place aesthetically, harder and American, with no lingering Ziggyisms. Only the cigarette survives Bowie's late-1970s style transformation. And I like the bravery – the impertinence – of obscuring his face. It would be disallowed as a passport shot, but you know who it is immediately by the body language.

I have selected two strongly stylized portraits by contrasting photographers, the Dutch-born Corbijn and very British Snowdon, which nevertheless bear some artistic resemblance: Corbijn's *Elephant Man* shoot of 1980, with diagonal shafts of light across Bowie's face, and the almost Beatonesque 1995 portrait by Lord Snowdon, in which Bowie poses in a white tuxedo and looks disconcertingly like David Beckham. Both sittings are meticulously stage-managed and artificial, but express important aspects of Bowie's personality and allure. Similarly, the 1980 Brian Duffy 'Ashes to Ashes' image demands inclusion, since it encapsulates a decisive transition point in the Bowie aesthetic; with half a nod back to the late 1960s mime-class days of Lindsay Kemp, but foretelling the impending era of Tin Machine.

My final choice is neither a studio portrait nor even a performance action picture, but a red carpet pap shot by Stephen Lovekin taken of David Bowie and his wife Iman arriving at a New York fundraiser. I include it because, unlike every other rock star in the world with the exception of Bryan Ferry, Bowie still looks great and cool and trim and enviably young, 43 years after the first photograph in this portfolio was taken. There is something gratifying and optimistic in this fact, in knowing that one's heroes don't have to grow old.

Nicholas Coleridge CBE is President of Condé Nast International, and a Trustee of the Victoria and Albert Museum.

DAVID BOWIE IS MAPPING NEW TERRITORIES

Despite redevelopment, much of the central London David Bowie knew in the 1960s and early 1970s still survives. On leaving school in 1963, aged 16, Bowie started at an advertising agency in New Bond Street but left after a year to become a full-time musician and songwriter. Travelling in by train from his Sundridge Park home, Bowie would arrive at Charing Cross station (1). Often he would head up Charing Cross Road, lined with second-hand bookshops and home to Dobell's Record Shop (2), which was crucial for rare or imported records before the advent of mail order.

The Saville Theatre (3), owned by the Beatles, was a key live music venue – and Bowie saw Jimi Hendrix perform there. Further, beyond Saint Martins School of Art (4), is Denmark Street (5), then the centre of the UK's music business with publishers, agents, studios, hustlers and press such as *NME* and *Melody Maker*. Aspiring musicians, including Bowie, would hang out at cafés such as the Gioconda waiting for leads. Across Charing Cross Road, is Soho proper, home to the film industry, run-down flats housing prostitutes and bohemians such as artiste Lindsay Kemp (6), clubs like Tiles (7) and publishers Essex Music (8).

The cutting-edge Trident Studios (9) was a critical venue, where Bowie recorded five early albums including *Space Oddity*. Around the corner was Wardour Street (namechecked in 'The London Boys'), with the famous Marquee Club (10), where Bowie often played. Pubs and cafés, such as the 2i's (11) where musicians and journalists gossiped, as well as mod clubs the Flamingo (later the Wag Club, 12) and Scene (13), were also nearby. Past the clothes shops of Carnaby Street (14) was Heddon Street (15), where in 1972 the photograph for the *Ziggy Stardust* cover was taken. Ziggy's 'death' was celebrated at a party at the Café Royal (16) after a concert at the Hammersmith Odeon on 3 July 1973.

1. London Charing Cross Station
2. Dobell's Record Shop
3. The Saville Theatre
4. Saint Martins School of Art
5. Denmark Street
6. Lindsay Kemp's flat at Bateman's Buildings
7. Tiles nightclub
8. Essex Music publishers
9. Trident Studios
10. The Marquee Club
11. The 2i's coffee bar
12. The Flamingo / The Wag Cub
13. The Scene nightclub
14. Carnaby Street
15. Heddon Street
16. Café Royal
17. Electric Garden nightclub
18. Drury Lane Arts Lab
19. The UFO nightclub
20. The Boop-A-Doop nightclub

DAVID BOWIE IS REFERENCED

ASTRONAUT OF INNER SPACES:
SUNDRIDGE PARK, SOHO, LONDON … MARS
GEOFFREY MARSH

1   The road shown in the video of 'The Buddha of Suburbia' (1993) is not where Bowie lived, or indeed typical of his home area. St Matthew's Drive, Bromley, a cul-de-sac of bungalows, was chosen because it could be easily shut off for filming.

2   Mostly short visits to Germany and Holland to record TV appearances, but also a ten-day trip to music festivals in Malta and Italy in the summer of 1969, and three weeks in the USA promoting his third LP, *The Man Who Sold the World*, in early 1971.

3   When Bowie was born in January 1947, London was still, just, an imperial capital. India and Pakistan were granted their independence at midnight on 15 August 1947.

4   Interviews with Thomas Frick, *The Paris Review*, c.1984 and 30 October 1982, in *Re/Search* (1984), no. 8/9.

5   These houses still form 20 per cent of the UK's current housing stock.

6   Frozen in the mid-twentieth century by the creation of the Green Belt by the Green Belt (London and Home Counties) Act, 1938, enhanced by the Town and Country Planning Act, 1947.

7   The existing Sundridge Park House was designed by John Nash in 1797. Although much of the grounds were sold off for housing in the 1930s, the core remains as a golf course and tennis courts: more 'Miss Joan Hunter Dunn' than 'Inner City Blues'.

8   David 'Bowie-to-be' Jones was born on 8 January 1947 at 40 Stansfield Road in Brixton, south London. When he was six, the family moved close to Bromley in Kent, then just outside the official boundary of London. The Jones family moved twice before settling at Plaistow Grove. The first two houses were more modern and larger. At Plaistow Grove, the Joneses were in a Victorian terrace '2-up, 2-down'.

9   Ethnically, almost 100 per cent white. It is estimated that in 1939, 30 per cent of British families lived in a house built in the last 20 years, the highest proportion in the last hundred years.

10 In 1956, only 25 per cent of middle-class households had an electric fridge – see M. Young and P. Willmott, *The Symmetrical Family: A Study of Work and Leisure in the London Region* (1973), Table 2. For comparison, 42 per cent had a washing machine and 52 per cent a television. The comparative figures for working-class households were 4, 13 and 35 per cent respectively. As late as 1970, 75 per cent of middle-class residents in outer London still wanted to move further out and, prior to inner-city 'gentrification', only 10 per cent wished to move into inner London.

11 It is often noted how many leading musicians of the 1960s, from bands like the Who, the Kinks, the Rolling Stones etc., had suburban upbringings, but little research has been done to analyse the detail of this phenomenon and how it shaped their music. From the mid 1970s, inner-city gentrification increasingly offered a lifestyle alternative to suburbia and by the 1990s predictions began to be made of suburbia becoming 'slumurbia'.

12 Terence 'Terry' Guy Adair Burns (1937–85) was Bowie's half-brother and lived with him until he was six. He was the son of David's mother, Margaret Mary 'Peggy' Burns (1912–2001). In 1968 Bowie said: 'My father tries so hard but his upbringing was so different that we can't communicate. He and all his friends were in the army during the war – an experience I can't imagine – and he takes naturally to iron discipline.' See S. More, 'The Restless Generation: 2', *The Times*, 11 December 1968.

13 See interview with Bowie in the TV programme 'David Bowie: Sound and Vision', produced as part of the 'Biography' documentary series by the A&E network in the United States, November 2002.

14 Kevin Cann, *Any Day Now: David Bowie, The London Years: 1947–1974* (London, 2010), p.22.

15 See interview with Bowie in the TV programme 'David Bowie: Sound and Vision', produced as part of the 'Biography' documentary series by the A&E network in the United States, November 2002.

16 Kevin Cann, *Any Day Now: David Bowie, The London Years: 1947–1974* (London, 2010), p.19. Dates quoted in this essay are largely drawn from his book, which provides an exhaustive analysis of this period.

17 John Jones (1912–69) was orphaned at a young age and does not seem to have had a particularly happy childhood in Yorkshire. Prior to the massive expansion in social services in the late 1960s, such employment by a charity was much more unusual than it would be today.

18 £3,000 would have bought six new semi-detached suburban houses in London – which in the mid-1930s sold for £495 upwards. It is tricky to translate this sum into modern values, but using average wages (£4 per week in 1933; £725 in 2009), it would be equivalent to £400,000–600,000. It is difficult to envisage how John could have lost so much so quickly unless he was the victim of fraud or extortion.

19 Hilda Sullivan (1908–1900) was of Irish-Italian parentage. Her mother, an acrobat, was killed in a circus accident when she was five. She was brought up in France by her grandmother and was a talented pianist and singer. In March 1933, as Hitler came to power in Germany, the Austrian Chancellor Dollfuss became dictator. Nine months later, John married Hilda, on 19 December 1933. They divorced in August 1947.

20 Named after Helen Cane, the famous American singer, known as the 'Boop-Boop-a-Doop Girl' and the original source of the cartoon character Betty Boop, created in 1932 and subsequently the cause of a long-running court case. The song 'Don't Take My Boop-Oop-A-Doop Away' first appeared in the film *Musical Justice* (1931). I am indebted to Kevin Cann for the location of this venture. Soho nightclubs at this time were no place for the unwary. Although Kate Merrick, who ran the infamous 43 Club in Gerrard Street, had just died, violence, vice, protection rackets, corruption and the police were never far away, see Judith R. Walkowitz, *Nights Out: Life in Cosmopolitan London* (New Haven, 2012), p. 209–52, which explores the role of such clubs in developing jazz. Following a court case in 1932, many 'bottle party' clubs opened in 1933–4. Bowie recalls stories of wrestlers congregating at his father's club, following the relaunch of the sport in 1930 and prior to its ban in the late 1930s. The London *Schweizerbund* was founded in the late nineteenth century in what was then one of the main German areas of London. It survived until after World War II and the building is still a club, although currently boarded up.

21 During the following decade, as a result of major changes in childcare methods, Dr Barnardo's Homes began closing its famous children's homes and the organization changed its name to Dr Barnardo's in 1966.

22 Bowie had to slow it down with his hand to play 45s. His father picked out rare records from among donations to Dr Barnardo's.

23 The Grafton was a UK brand developed in the late 1940s. At £55, it was a significant investment, about a tenth of the price of a new car such as a Cortina. Although half the price of a brass sax, it was used by many professionals, notably Charlie Parker, John Dankworth and Ornette Coleman. John gave careful, cautious but consistent support for his son's ambitions in the entertainment world, including maintaining his financial records.

24 See interview with Bowie in the TV programme 'David Bowie: Sound and Vision', produced as part of the 'Biography' documentary series by the A&E network in the United States, November 2002.

25 Ibid.

26 Now Ravens Wood School, sometimes confused with the separate Ravensbourne Art College. Twenty years earlier, Sir George Martin had attended the Grammar School, now Ravensbourne School.

27 Owen Frampton was the father of musician Peter Frampton (b. 1950) of Humble Pie fame, who also attended the school and later played with Bowie.

28 The two were close but Bowie has admitted mythologizing Terry's influence. It is not clear what music venues they visited together, prior to Bowie going to the new R&B clubs in west London in 1962 with his friend George Underwood. The main shift of clubs from jazz to R&B took place in 1962–3, symbolized by the change of the former Cy Laurie Jazz Club/Mac's Rehearsal Rooms (from 1948 to 1950 Ronnie Scott's Club 11 – supposedly the location of the first recorded arrest in the UK for cannabis possession) in Ham Yard/41 Great Windmill Street, to The Scene, one of the key mod venues over the next few years.

29 The novel *The Buddha of Suburbia* (1990) was written by Hanif Kureishi (b. 1954), who attended Bowie's school a decade later – in itself, an indicator of the changes to south-east London in the 1970s.

30   The second of the group's first three singles, all of which made number one, a feat not repeated until Frankie Goes to Hollywood in the early 1980s.

31   Andy Warhol had, of course, started in advertising, working as a commercial illustrator from 1949. For an amusing account of working in a film commercials company in the mid 1960s in New Bond Street, see Jeremy Scott's account of James Garrett and Partners in *Fast and Louche* (London, 2003), pp. 167–86.

32   This is also the period when Marshall McLuhan's ideas on the media and the gobal village began to spread. Bowie discussed McLuhan in an interview with Patrick Salvo in the May 1971 issue of *Circus*. By this time McLuhan's influence, massive in the 1960s, was beginning to decline.

33   See for example Bowie's flair for publicity in creating the fictitious International League for the Preservation of Animal Filament, then renamed the Society for the Prevention of Cruelty to Long-Haired Men, which garnered coverage by Cliff Michelmore on the topical magazine show *Tonight*, broadcast on the newly launched BBC2 on 12 November 1964.

34   Dobell's Records was located at 75 and 77 Charing Cross Road. Doug Dobell started selling records in 1946 after he was demobbed. Shops such as his were crucial in the 1950s and '60s for supplying rare records and imports. The shop closed in 1980.

35   Berwick Street declined after 1940 due to clothes rationing and bomb damage. John Stephen opened His Clothes, the first boutique in Carnaby Street, in 1958.

36   The City Of Westminster Plan, published in 1946, proposed the comprehensive clearance of 130 acres in central London, including the whole of Greek, Frith, Dean and Old Compton Streets – see Judith R. Walkowitz, *Nights Out: Life in Cosmopolitan London* (New Haven, 2012), p.289–91. In 1962, Lord Holford's scheme for redeveloping Piccadilly Circus proposed the complete demolition of the eastern side and the construction of three towering office blocks. At this period, the Government also commissioned Sir Leslie Martin, architect of the Royal Festival Hall, to plan the complete redevelopment of Whitehall. His scheme, which would have left the Banqueting House on a traffic island, was finally abandoned in 1971.

37   The architect of Centre Point was Richard Seifert, who also designed the cylindrical Space House, off Kingsway, at this time. The 17-storey Kemp House tower block in Berwick Street, completed in 1962, gives a good idea of what the whole of Soho might have become. These flats replaced the heart of the pre-war clothing district, which had been flattened by a landmine.

38   See, for example, the London County Council's huge Alton Estate at Roehampton (1958/9), inspired by the planning ideals of Le Corbusier, which even appeared on a British stamp in 1964. By 1966 François Truffaut's film *Fahrenheit 451* was already using these buildings as backdrops for a future dystopian state where books are banned. In 1963, work started on the vast Aylesbury Estate in Southwark, designed for 10,000 people. During Bowie's daily commute into central London, he would have passed through an entire swathe of inner south London being re-planned with council estates.

39   For a good indication of the seedy appearance of Soho at this time, see the street scenes in *The Small World of Sammy Lee*, starring Anthony Newley, released in 1963. According to George Tremlett in *David Bowie: Living on the Brink* (London, 1996), Ken Pitt, Bowie's manager, had worked on the film and kept out-takes of Newley, which he later showed to Bowie.

40   Rank's short film *Look at Life – Eating High* (1966) presents the tower's newly opened revolving restaurant, managed by Billy Butlin, as the place for the modern successful businessman to eat. Bowie dined there in March 1967, after seeing Cliff Richard in *Cinderella* at the London Palladium. One wonders if he looked down below at the site of his father's failed nightclub, a couple of streets away. The restaurant features in the trendy spy thriller *Sebastian*, released in 1968. The director, David Greene, also specifically used the new complex of office blocks along London Wall, previously included in Antonioni's *Blow-Up* (1966), to communicate a new-look London to American audiences. Wilson gave his famous speech at the 1963 Labour Party Conference. In October 1964 he became Prime Minister.

41   Rank's short film *Look at Life – Coffee Bar* (1959) shows the venue's basement. The short inspired the feature film *Beat Girl* (1960), starring Adam Faith, which was promoted with the line 'Hop-Head UK School Girls Get in Trouble'. The music for the film was composed by John Barry and became the first British film soundtrack to be released as an LP. In a neat summary of shifting generational conflict, the wayward daughter is a student at Saint Martins School of Art, while her architect father is designing a Le Corbusier-inspired high-rise *Ville Radieuse* for a British ex-colony. See also Andrew Ings, *Rockin' At The 2i's Coffee Bar* (Brighton, 2010).

42   On 10 May 1970, Bowie received a Novello Award at the Hippodrome for 'Space Oddity'. The BBC broadcast the ceremony on Radio 1, but it was shown on television in the US and on the continent, and the footage survives.

43   Paul Raymond (1925–2008) had started in show business after World War II, touring nude revues. By September 1955, his show *Burlesque*, featuring the Sex Appeal Girls, was at the Chelsea Palace, King's Road, one of London's fine Edwardian inner-city music halls then sliding downwards towards demolition.

44   The new Marquee Club also included a small recording studio made famous by the success of the Moody Blues' 'Go Now' (1964). Recording work in Soho expanded in 1967, when the Sheffield Brothers opened their state of the art eight-track Trident Studios, across the road at 17 St Anne's Court. This become one of London's key studios, and Bowie recorded five albums there, beginning with *Space Oddity* in 1969.

45   On 26 September 1968, theatre censorship was abolished in the UK. The following evening the American rock musical *Hair* opened at the Shaftesbury Theatre. Other 'permissive' legislation included the Abortion Act of 1967, which came into effect in April 1968, and the Sexual Offences Act of 1967, which partially decriminalized homosexual activity. The latter only applied to England and Wales.

46   See Jon Savage, 'Oh! You Pretty Things', pp.99ff.

47   Recorded at Decca's main studios in Broadhurst Gardens, West Hampstead, now the rehearsal rooms of English National Opera – but not much changed.

48   The show regularly had an audience of 12 million. It was Bowie's TV debut, but the BBC wiped the tape, a common practice in the 1960s that also accounts for the loss of most early recordings of 'Top of the Pops'.

49   Now the Giaconda [sic] Dining Rooms. In 2012 a short section of film turned up showing Bowie and the Manish Boys walking into the café in 1965. Both *Melody Maker* and the *New Musical Express* had their offices in Denmark Street. There was also the Tin Pan Alley Studio (TPA) from 1954, mostly used for demos, and from the early 1960s, Regent Sound Studios was at number four, one of the first independent studios in London. The Rolling Stones recorded their first album there early in 1964. Music publisher Dick James (1920–86), who signed the Beatles and founded Northern Songs with Brian Epstein, worked around the corner in Charing Cross Road. A fascinating Pathé Film survives of the street in 1951 and the Kinks immortalized it in 1970 in 'Denmark Street': 'Down the way from the Tottenham Court Road/ Just round the corner from old Soho/ There's a place where the publishers go/ If you don't know which way to go/ Just open your ears and follow your nose/ 'Cos the street is shakin from the tapping of toes/ You can hear that music play anytime on any day/ Every rhythm, every way/ You got to a publisher and play him your song/ He says "I hate your music and your hair is too long/ But I'll sign you up because I'd hate to be wrong."'

50   The show was produced by Associated Television (ATV), controlled by Lew Grade (1906–1998). An indication of ATV's power in the 1960s is that the company bought the Beatles' catalogue with the purchase of Northern Songs in 1969.

51   The three LPs of 'The Black and White Minstrel Show' all made number one between 1961 and 1963, the first for nine weeks. Robert Luff's stage version at the Victoria Palace Theatre, which ran from 1960 to 1972 was, with 6,477 performances, the longest-running musical in the UK until *Cats*.

52   See, for example, the career of Cilla Black in the 1960s.

53   Oldham (b. 1944) was manager and producer of the Rolling Stones aged 19. Epstein (1934–67) became manager of the Beatles aged 27. See also Joe Boyd, *White Bicycles: Making Music in the 1960s* (London, 2006) for a good account of the development of the music business at this time.

54   It is often forgotten how much performing Bowie was doing. In 1965–7, he averaged over 60 appearances a year.

55   See Radio London interview at the Marquee Club, 1966.

56   Bowie's single 'Rubber Band'/'The London Boys' was the seventh single released by Deram. The label was established in 1966 to exploit Decca's new Deramic Stereo Sound (DSS) audio system, which was made redundant by the introduction of eight-track recording in 1968. Among Deram's first successes was the Moody Blues' concept album *Days of Future Past*, including 'Nights in White Satin'. Other early signings included Cat Stevens, the Move and Amen Corner. From 1967 to 1970, Deram was releasing a single a week.

57   *Sgt. Pepper* spent 21 weeks at the top of the UK album charts. Clinton Heylin's *The Act You've Known For All These Years* (Edinburgh, 2007) provides exhaustive detail on the album and its time, including the impact of the cover designed by Peter Blake.

58   Brian Aldiss, *My Country 'tis not only thee – A Story of the World after the Vietnam War* (1987).

59   The event prompted a famous cartoon in *Private Eye*

(22 November 1968, no. 181, p.8), the satirical magazine founded in Soho in 1961, targeting the builders, Taylor Woodrow, who sued.

60   The complementary shift was the growing love affair with Victorian architecture, symbolized by the 'saving' of St Pancras station from demolition in 1967. The film *Smashing Time* (1967), written by George Melly as a satire on swinging London, shows the filthy condition of the station at the time. In 1972, Equity launched a campaign to save London's Victorian Theatreland, ignited by the threatened demolition of 16 theatres, including the Lyceum and the Coliseum. By the late 1970s a massive heritage boom was taking place across the UK – see Robert Hewison, *The Heritage Industry: Britain in a Climate of Decline* (London, 1987).

61   J. G. Ballard, 'Time, Memory and Inner Space', *The Woman Journalist Magazine*, 1963. The term inner space was first used by W. H. Auden in 1940 and J. B. Priestley in 1953, see John Baxter, *The Inner Man: The Life of J. G. Ballard* (London, 2011), p.120. Ballard set out his views in 'Which Way to Inner Space?', *New Worlds* (May 1962), No.118. *Astronauts of Inner-Space: An International Collection of Avant-Garde Activity – 17 Manifestoes, Articles, Letters, 28 poems & 1 Filmscript* was published in San Francisco in 1966. It included contributions by William S. Burroughs, Allen Ginsberg, Marshall McLuhan and others.

62   See John Baxter, *The Inner Man: The Life of J.G.Ballard* (London, 2011), pp.172–9. Burroughs wrote the preface to *The Atrocity Exhibition*. Part of the book – 'The Assassination Weapon' – was produced as a multimedia performance at the ICA, produced by Stewart McKenzie, on 11–16 August 1969. John Cage had explored chance in composing after receiving a translation of the *I-Ching* in 1951 – see also his music/art composition *Chess Pieces*, created for the Imagery of Chess exhibition organized by the Surrealists in New York in 1944. From 1953 onwards, Cage worked with his partner Merce Cunningham on such ideas in dance. Terming it the 'mosaic approach', Marshall McLuhan used a similar technique in writing about the media – in separated essays – as early as *The Mechanical Bride: Folklore of Industrial Man*, published in 1951. He based the title on the work of Marcel Duchamp. His book *The Medium is the Message: An Inventory of Effects* (1967) attempts to convey his thesis through the actual design.

63   William S. Burroughs (1914–97) lived in London from 1966 to 1973. His took part in a joint interview with Bowie on 17 November 1973, just before his return to America. Published in *Rolling Stone* magazine on 25 February 1974, 'Beat Godfather Meets Glitter Mainman' is one of the key texts recording the development of Bowie's ideas prior to his leaving the UK. Burroughs' *Naked Lunch* (1959) was cleared of obscenity charges in Massachusetts in 1966, the last such trial in the US.

64   Brion Gysin (1916–86) joined the Surrealists after arriving in Paris in 1934, but was expelled from the group in 1935.

65   Jeff Nuttall (1933–2004) was one of the founders of *International Times* (IT), the magazine of the UK counter-culture, which was launched on 14 October 1966 at the Roundhouse, London, at a gig featuring Pink Floyd. His book *Bomb Culture* (1968) is important for its examination of contemporary culture in the

context of the threat of a nuclear strike. In 1966 he also founded *The People Show* theatre group, a key part of the alternative theatre movement.

66   The work was created from chopped-up film originally shot in 1961–5 for a planned documentary entitled *Guerrilla Conditions*.

67   See Burroughs' introduction to *Man at Leisure* (1972), a book of poems by Alexander Trocchi (1925–84). See also Fred Kaplan in *1959: The Year Everything Changed* (New York, 2010), pp.26–40, who seems to suggest that Burroughs used the phrase in 1959. The conference was organized by Jim Haynes and Sonia Orwell, among others, personalities who later were to feature significantly in Bowie's career.

68   Quoted in Eric Mottram, *William Burroughs: The Algebra of Need* (London, 1977), pt 1, ch. 1.

69   Kevin Cann, *Any Day Now: David Bowie, The London Years: 1947–1974* (London, 2010), p.116.

70   This just preceded Nam June Paik's video-art experiments. Both were made possible by the introduction of the first consumer video equipment, notably the Sony Portapak, which slashed the costs of making films and provided instant viewing. Warhol used a Norelco machine – for a detailed discussion of this piece and its broader importance in portraiture and identity, see Callie Angell, 'Doubling the Screen: Andy Warhol's Outer and Inner Space', *Millennium Film Journal* (Spring 2002), No. 38. In November 1966, Ken Pitt, Bowie's manager, visited Warhol at the Factory and brought back a test pressing of Lou Reid's *Velvet Underground and Nico*, which he gave to a fascinated Bowie.

71   See *Children of Albion: Poetry of the Underground in Britain*, an anthology published by Penguin in 1969, with its strong nod to William Blake, whose 'Glad Day' is on the cover. For the overall context of this interest see Rob Young, *Electric Eden: Unearthing Britain's Visionary Music* (London, 2010), pp. 327–350. The first Glastonbury Festival, celebrating Midsummer, was held in 1970. Bowie appeared at the second – and much larger – festival in 1971.

72   The first battles about saving entire areas, rather than individual buildings, were beginning to gear up in Covent Garden and Tolmers Square in Euston.

73   In January 1966, John Lennon had acquired a copy of Leary's book from the Indica bookshop, opened by Barry Miles, John Dunbar and Peter Asher the previous November, and subsequently wrote 'Tomorrow Never Knows'. LSD was, of course, legal in the USA and UK until Autumn 1966.

74   There was also considerable interest in Scientology. Burroughs took up Scientology in 1967/8 but subsequently rejected it. See 'I, William Burroughs, Challenge You, L. Ron Hubbard', *Mayfair* (January 1970), vol.5, 1.

75   Peter Brook, *The Empty Space* (London, 1968). The controversy over Edward Bond's *Saved*, produced at the Royal Court Theatre in London in November 1965, was key in the abolition of theatre censorship by the Theatres Act, 1968. In 1968, Thelma Holt founded the Open Space Theatre in Tottenham Court Road and Léonie Scott-Matthews moved Pentameters, founded in August 1968, to the Three Horseshoes, its current home in Hampstead, in 1971, leaving Dan Crawford the honour of opening London's first pub theatre at the King's Head, Islington, in 1970. For detailed

information of the many companies that started at this time, see the Unfinished Histories website (www.unfinishedhistories.com). For the parallel story in New York, see Stephen J. Bottoms, *Playing Underground: A Critical History of the 1960s Off-Off- Broadway Movement* (Michigan, 2004).

76   Haynes had previously helped establish the UK's first paperback bookshop and the Traverse Theatre in Edinburgh.

77   No new theatres had been built in the West End since the 1930s and the first was the New London, opened in 1973, based on the Total Theatre designed by Walter Gropius. Performance, therefore, largely still meant sitting in a typical Victorian theatre with a proscenium arch design. The trustees of the new National Theatre, still in the planning stages during the 1960s, did not consider a 'studio' space appropriate, although the future Cottesloe Theatre was slipped into the design as a storage area. The Inner London Education Authority built the first fringe venue, the Cockpit, at Paddington in 1969–70. This was designed as a theatre in the round.

78   At least once on 6 December 1968, as Feathers, although Bowie may have rehearsed and played there on other occasions.

79   See 'final letter' dated 28 October 1969, announcing the closure of the Arts Lab. See also Jim Haynes, *Thanks for Coming* (London, 1984). The Arts Lab showed work by many artists/writers, including Yoko Ono, Steven Berkoff and Roelef Louw. It also provided a home for the London Film-Makers' Co-Op and was the first place in Britain to show Warhol's *Chelsea Girls* in August 1968. This was advertised by the famous Alan Aldridge poster, commissioned at Warhol's request, of the nude 16-year-old actress Clare Shenstone, photographed by Don Silverstein. It was designed at Ink Studios. A New Arts Lab was established in Robert Street, Camden, in October 1969 and in April 1970 it was the location for the infamous exhibition Jim Ballard: Crashed Cars, originally planned for the ICA in 1968. Bowie never performed at the ICA. The Arts Lab movement reflected the massive loss of city-centre commercial theatres (particularly ex-music halls) and cinemas during the late 1950s and '60s as television killed off the last remnants of live variety.

80   The opening of the ICA on The Mall was followed by the Hayward Gallery, which opened in July 1968 as part of the major expansion of the Southbank arts complex. Performance also moved into mainstream art. In 1967, while at Saint Martins School of Art, Richard Long created 'A Line Made by Walking', which distilled his earlier experiments with land art into a single line – recorded by a black-and-white photograph.

81   Kemp opened his show *Clown Hour*, using Bowie's album as the interval music, at the Little Theatre, Garrick Yard, on 4 August 1967. At the time he was living above a strip club in Bateman's Buildings, Bateman Street, a run-down alleyway in the middle of Soho.

82   Following quotes from Kevin Cann, *Any Day Now: David Bowie, The London Years: 1947–1974* (London, 2010), p.112.

83   A few weeks later on 25 September 1967, Gilbert and George met for the first time at Saint Martins School of Art – 'it was love at first sight'. However, it took them some time to develop their total living sculpture.

84   Kevin Cann, *Any Day Now: David Bowie, The London Years: 1947–1974* (London, 2010), p.112.

85 Bowie's documented music performances dropped off during late 1967 and '68, but George Tremlett believes he was undertaking engagements without telling his manager, see George Tremlett, *David Bowie: Living on the Brink* (London, 1996), p.83. His first theatre work with Kemp, *Pierrot in Turquoise*, opened on 28 December 1967 at the New Theatre, Oxford, before moving to the Mercury Theatre, Ladbroke Road, in London. However, Bowie was still interested in music, Marc Bolan recalling the hours spent discussing the contemporary scene.

86 Bowie's membership number was 57135. He subsequently appeared in *Spotlight*, the casting directory, where he was categorized in 1969 as 'Juvenile and Juvenile-Character Men'.

87 The initial impact of *Hair*, with its on-stage nudity, has faded over the years. However, it was significant at the time not just because of its story, but because it was a product of the New York fringe. Its director descibed it as an opportunity to create 'a theatre form whose demeanour, language, clothing, dancing, and even its name accurately reflect a social epoch in full explosion' – for more details, see Scott Miller, *Sex, Drugs, Rock & Roll, and Musicals* (Boston, 2011), pp.60–83. Jules Fisher, the show's designer, subsequently designed Bowie's Diamond Dogs tour in 1974. In 1969 Kenneth Tynan launched his nude revue *Oh! Calcutta!*

88 Including *Cabaret*, with Judi Dench starring as Sally Bowles, on 5 April 1968.

89 Bowie auditioned for the film but was unsuccessful. *Oh! What a Lovely War* was filmed by Richard Attenborough and Brian Duffy in the summer of 1968 on the West Pier, Brighton, and nearby. One only needs to look at Bowie's performance of 'Rubber Band' in the promotional film *Love Me Till Tuesday*, recorded in February 1969, to see the connections. Five years later, Duffy took the photographs of Aladdin Sane. Farthingale subsequently appeared in another four films, including MGM's *The Great Waltz* (1972), one of the last films released in Cinerama. She also appears, in a cloud, in the top left-hand corner of the back cover of *David Bowie* (released November 1969), which includes the song 'Letter to Hermione'.

90 This Arts Lab, 'Growth', took place on Sunday evenings at the Three Tuns, 157 High Street, Beckenham, from 4 May 1969 until 5 March 1970, when the venue changed into a folk club. 'Growth' organized the Beckenham Free Festival on 16 August 1969 – the Saturday of the Woodstock Festival in the USA. In an interview with Chris Welch in *Melody Maker*, published in September 1969, he extols the talent available in suburban Beckenham and describes Drury Lane, then about to close, as 'tripe' and on another occasion as 'pretentious'. It may just be that the main organizers at Drury Lane, who were a good decade older, experienced and strongly opinionated, ignored the interest and ideas of the 21-year-old Bowie. Ironically, Jim Haynes was a colleague of Sonia Orwell, George Orwell's literary executor, and lived in the basement of her house when he moved to London. In 1973, she turned down Bowie's request to make a musical of Orwell's *1984*, a project that changed into *Diamond Dogs*. For another view of the Arts Lab, see also Stuart Home, 'Walk on Gilded Splinters: In Memorandum to memory 13 April 1969 – Alex Trocchi's State of Revolt at the Arts Lab in London' for a flavour of events there. Some footage of this chaotic evening, organized by a young Lynne Tillman, is included in Jamie Wadhawan's *Cain's Film* (1969).

91 Stanley Kubrick's film *2001: A Space Odyssey*, released in the UK on 10 May 1968 (in the middle of the Paris riots), had a significant impact – not least on Bowie, who saw it at the cinema several times. At the end of Kubrick's ambiguous film, 'the Star Child turns to consider the Whole Earth floating in front of it, both glowing a bright blue-white. The two appear as newborn versions of Man and Earth, face-to-face, ready to be born into a future of unthinkable possibilities' – see Robert Jacobs, 'Whole Earth or No Earth: The Origin of the Whole Earth Icon in the Ashes of Hiroshima and Nagasaki', *The Asia-Pacific Journal* (28 March 2011), vol. 9, issue 13, no. 5. The film *Barbarella* (1968) is another reminder that space was viewed in many ways at the time, from the deadly serious to the high camp and comic.

92 See Robert Poole, *Earthrise: How Man First Saw the Earth* (New Haven, 2008). The 24 December 1968 broadcast was the most watched TV programme in history up to that time. The three astronauts recited Genesis, verses 1–10, concluding their message with 'and from the crew of Apollo 8, we close with good night, good luck, a merry Christmas – and God bless all of you, all of you on the good earth.' *Life* magazine selected the image as one of its 100 most important photographs of the twentieth century. A similar image appeared in autumn 1968 on the first issue of the *Whole Earth Catalog*, created by the radical writer and ecologist Stewart Brand. This is cited by Steve Jobs as one of the key milestones in the evolution of the information age. However, it seems doubtful that Bowie would have seen this US publication by early 1969. Brand had led a campaign to get NASA to release images of Earth taken from unmanned spacecraft, as he felt it would help develop a new environmental sensitivity.

93 It was included as an insert since *The Times* was still printed in black and white at the time. There is a photograph of this insert at www.photo-transport. co.uk/moon/moon

94 Bowie had been urged by his manager Ken Pitt to compose a new song for a promotional film planned for German TV and elsewhere. The popularity of such promotional films was driven by the successes of the Beatles and the Moody Blues. In December 1968, the Rolling Stones made *Rock and Roll Circus*, also planned for TV (but unreleased until 1996). Bowie's promotional film was not released at the time, but was eventually issued as *Love Me Till Tuesday* in 1984. 'Space Oddity' was recorded at Morgan Studios, Willesden, on 2 February 1969 and filmed four days later at Clarence Studio, Greenwich.

95 A key, but often overlooked, factor in the creation of 'Space Oddity' was that in January 1969 nobody, including Bowie, knew that Apollo 11 would land on the moon in July. Obviously, this was NASA's objective, but the Apollo missions 8, 9 and 10 were to test manned capsules. If anything had gone wrong, as had happened with Apollo 1, 6 and 13, the programme would have been rescheduled, although NASA was desperate to meet Kennedy's 1961 deadline to achieve a landing by the end of the decade.

96 Ironically, the song came to prominence as a result of the release of a new recording, made on 20 June 1969 at Trident Studios, Soho, to coincide with Apollo 11 landing on the moon on 20 July. It was also played over the PA system at the huge, free Rolling Stones concert in Hyde Park on 5 July. The song peaked at number five at the start of November, a literal case of *per ardua ad astra*. Bowie was not unique in this approach. J. G. Ballard had rejected space travel in the 1960s; see *Memories of the Space Age* (Wisconsin, 1988), which collects stories dating back to 'The Cage of Sand', originally published in 1963. This is discussed in Gary Westfahl, 'The Man Who Didn't Need to Walk on the Moon: J. G. Ballard and "The Vanished Age of Space"', *Internet Review of Science Fiction* (July 2009). NASA reformed its strategy as Mission to Planet Earth in the 1990s.

97 See Dominic Sandbrook, *Seasons in the Sun: The Battle for Britain 1974–1979*, (London, 2012).

98 Bowie first travelled to the USA from 23 January to 18 February 1971 to promote *The Man Who Sold the World*. Because of work permit issues, he did not perform on this trip. Bowie first mentioned the idea of Ziggy Stardust while in Los Angeles.

99 And a new level of income: George Tremlett estimates that in October 1969, Bowie earned more than in the whole of 1968. See *David Bowie: Living on the Brink* (London, 1996), p.102.

100 *The Man Who Sold the World* was released in the US in November 1970 and on 10 April 1971 in the UK. The history of the cover is complicated by censorship – see Kevin Cann, *Any Day Now: David Bowie, The London Years 1947–1974*, pp.210–13. The eventual UK cover was photographed in September 1970 at Bowie's new marital home at Haddon Hall, Beckenham.

101 Photographer Keith 'Keef' Macmillan was the same age as Bowie and well established, with a string of successful album covers for artists such as Black Sabbath and Rod Stewart for the progressive Vertigo Records and others. He went on, from 1975, to be a pioneer of music videos, working with Kate Bush, and eventually became a successful TV producer.

102 See John Beck and Matthew Cornford, 'Home Counties Surrealism', *Eye: The International Review of Graphic Design* (Summer 2008), no.68 (eyemagazine.com; accessed 29 April 2012).

103 Bowie was photographed in two different Mr Fish 'man-dresses' – originally for the inside of a gatefold album sleeve. The setting is sub-Christopher Gibbs – see his designs for *Performance*, filmed in 1968 but released in summer 1970. Bowie knew of Mr Fish's shop, opened in 1966 at 17 Clifford Street, just off Savile Row, as his school friend Geoff MacCormack worked for him. The shop often featured in films about 'Swinging London' and can be seen in the film for 'Sell Me a Coat' in Bowie's promo film *Love You Till Tuesday*, recorded early in 1969, but only released in 1984.

104 The image on the back cover is from a set using the second man-dress, and he holds the King of Diamonds. This card is called 'Caesar' by French playing-card manufacturers, who name each of the court cards. The King of Spades is 'David'.

105 Bowie has appeared on all of his studio-album covers, apart from *Tin Machine II*.

106 The origins of glam are complicated and lie outside this essay. However, the start is conventionally linked to the success of Marc Bolan's 'Hot Love' in March 1971 and his appearance on 'Top of the Pops'.

107 The image was considered by Mercury too provocative for the American public and Bowie's concept for the sleeve was revised, without him knowing, for the album's November 1970 US release.

108 A confidence, strengthened if needed, by the impact of the Warhol-driven 'play' *Pork* at the Roundhouse in August 1971, which caused a scandal in the UK media. All the elements for offending middle-class suburban sensibilities were there – see George Tremlett, *David Bowie: Living on the Brink* (London, 1996), pp.150–4. Bowie also saw the 'shock-rock' American Alice Cooper perform at the recently opened Rainbow Theatre, Finsbury Park, on 7 November. In 1971, Brian Ward photographed Bowie in a full Egyptian outfit, a look also used by the occultist Aleister Crowley (1875–1947), who was popular with rock musicians at the time. This was before the hugely successful Tutankhamen exhibition at the British Museum in 1972.

109 The background and iconography of this photograph is discussed in detail in Rob Young, *Electric Eden: Unearthing Britain's Visionary Music* (London, 2010), p.326.

110 See Larry Schweikart, *7 Events that made America America* (New York, 2010), which argues for the role of Western pop music in undermining Communism.

111 John Walsh, 'Me, Ziggy and the passion of pure fandom', *The Independent*, 29 March 2012: 'it makes no sense, but it means everything'.

112 See Jonathan Haidt, *The Righteous Mind: Why Good People are Divided by Politics and Religion* (London, 2012).

THEATRE OF GENDER: DAVID BOWIE AT THE CLIMAX OF THE SEXUAL REVOLUTION
CAMILLE PAGLIA

1 'TopPop', television programme, The Netherlands, October 1977.

2 Interview with Jools Holland on 'The Tube', Channel 4, March 1987. Bowie: 'If I'm writing and recording, I find I don't need to paint. But if I'm not doing very well, and I can't write, and there's a kind of block or a blank there, then I revert to painting, and it opens up like a watershed of ideas and associations and things.' In an interview recorded on 16 May 1978 in Cologne, Germany, for the BBC2 documentary series 'Arena', Bowie told Alan Yentob that when he returned to Europe after living in Los Angeles, painting helped him 'get back into music'. He described his painting style as 'a form of Expressionistic Realism'.

3 Bowie said he had 'a Pre-Raphaelite kind of look' on *Hunky Dory*. Interview with Ian 'Molly' Meldrum for 'Countdown', a weekly Australian music television programme, taped in October 1980 in a Japanese restaurant in New York during Bowie's run in *The Elephant Man* on Broadway.

4 'I was so lost in Ziggy, it was all a schizophrenia.' 'Cracked Actor', BBC documentary filmed in 1974 and first aired on 26 January 1975.

5 Bowie about Ziggy Stardust: 'I wanted to define the archetype "messiah/rock star" – that's all I wanted to do.' Interviewed by musicians Flo and Eddie of the Turtles and Mothers of Invention for '90 Minutes Live', CBC, 25 November 1977. In the 1978 Yentob interview for BBC2, Bowie said about his stage characters, 'They're all messiah figures.' Bowie about Yamamoto in an interview for NBC's 'The Today Show', April 1987: 'I wanted the best of the contemporary fields working with me, kind of like Diaghilev did when he was doing ballets.'

6 Craig Copetas, 'Beat Godfather Meets Glitter Mainman', *Rolling Stone* magazine, 28 February 1974. Conversation between Bowie and William S. Burroughs the prior November at Bowie's London home. Bowie reveals he had taken the name of American frontiersman Jim Bowie, inventor of the massive Bowie knife, because 'I wanted a truism about cutting through the lies.' In a 1996 interview with Avi Lewis for the Canadian television programme 'The New Music', Bowie said that 'however many critics were saying how important the Beatles were' at the time, 'the artists' were talking instead about the Velvet Underground: 'Tomorrow's culture is always dictated by the artists … The artists make culture, not the critics.'

7 Bowie about Major Tom: 'He was my own ideal of what I wanted to do, somebody totally in his own world … He was a hero to me but an antihero – he didn't have any social contacts [laughs].' (Interview in 1980 with Ian 'Molly' Meldrum for 'Countdown', an Australian television programme.) In a 1979 interview with Mavis Nicholson, Bowie recalled putting himself in 'dangerous situations', specifically 'areas where I have to be in social contact with people, which I'm not very good at doing.' ('Afternoon Plus', Thames Television, recorded 12 February 1979.)

8 'Dinah!', CBS talk show, 15 April 1977. Iggy Pop sat on the couch between Bowie and Dinah Shore, the motherly blonde host. Bowie's pelvic thrust punctuating his analysis of Iggy's method drew a faux naïf response of 'I wonder what he means by that! Gee whiz!' (producing audience laughter) from the other guest, Rosemary Clooney, a veteran big-band singer, like Shore. Despite his gentlemanly British manner, Bowie had managed to break the code of American television, then very strict on daytime programmes directed at homemakers.

9 'The Dick Cavett Show', ABC, recorded in New York on 2 December 1974; aired 5 December 1974. Cavett asked Bowie about his mother: 'Does she have any trouble explaining you to the neighbors?' Bowie replied, 'I think she pretends I'm not hers [laughs] … We were never that close particularly. We have an understanding.' In a remote-camera interview from London, Russell Harty condescendingly probed Bowie (in Burbank, California) about his mother; Bowie coldly replied, 'That's really my own business.' ('The Russell Harty Show', BBC, recorded 28 November 1975.) Cavett asked Bowie what he was reading: 'What would we find on your coffee table in your apartment?' Bowie responded, 'At the moment, mainly pictures. I bought Diane Arbus's book of photographs, a photographer I like very much.'

10 Bowie on the making of the 'Ashes to Ashes' video: 'We went down to the beach, and I took a woman there who looked like my mother. That's the surrealistic part of making movies.' ('David Bowie Weekend' on MTV, 4 and 5 April 1993.) The actress was Wyn Mac, wife of comedian Jimmy Mac, who played Warwick on the BBC sitcom 'Are You Being Served?'

11 David Bowie and Mick Rock, *Moonage Daydream: The Life and Times of Ziggy Stardust* (New York, 2005), p.140.

12 Charles Shaar Murray, 'David Bowie: Gay Guerrillas & Private Movies', *New Musical Express*, 24 February 1973.

13 Aretha Franklin can be heard singing a smash hit from *Lady Soul*, '(You make me feel like a) Natural Woman', in the limousine crossing the desert in the 1975 BBC documentary 'Cracked Actor', where Bowie drinks milk from a large carton and is questioned by Alan Yentob. (Aired 26 January 1975.) It was this sequence which convinced director Nicolas Roeg to cast Bowie as the alien star of *The Man Who Fell to Earth* (1976).

14 Introducing his version of 'Wild is the Wind', Bowie said, 'During the mid-1970s, I got to know Nina Simone, whom I've got incredible respect for as an artist and a composer and a singer.' Even though she had not written this song, her 'tremendous' performance of it had 'affected' him greatly: 'I recorded it as an *hommage* to Nina.' ('David Bowie Weekend' on MTV, 4 and 5 April 1993.)

15 'Dinah!', CBS talk show recorded in Los Angeles, 24 February 1976. Dinah Shore's other guests were Nancy Walker and Henry Winkler. Earlier Bowie says about his continual openness to and influence by other performers and styles, 'I'm usually saturated.'

16 Interview with Alan Yentob, recorded 16 May 1978 in Cologne for the BBC2 documentary series 'Arena'.

17 Ibid.

18 'Parkinson', BBC1 chat show, recorded 27 November 2003. Michael Parkinson asks, 'What was Ziggy about?' Bowie replies, 'It was about pushing together all the pieces and all the things that fascinated me culturally – everything from kabuki theatre to Jacques Brel to Little Richard to drag acts. Everything about it was sort of a hybrid of everything I liked.'

19 Interview at Stadthalle, Vienna, 1996. Bowie says, 'I was trying to pinpoint a tradition of ritualizing of the body.' He cites as a 'semi-nihilistic equation' André Breton's definition of the ultimate Surrealist act as shooting a pistol randomly into a crowd (from the Second Surrealist Manifesto of 1930). Bowie calls it 'as potent an image' as Duchamp's urinal in presenting the body as 'a ritualistic way of articulating twentieth-century experience'. (In the first Surrealist Manifesto of 1924, Breton compared 'the modern mannequin' to 'romantic ruins' in exemplifying the 'marvellous', a central Surrealist principle.) Bowie mentions as an antecedent the Romantic writer Thomas DeQuincey's 1827 essay, 'On Murder Considered as One of the Fine Arts'. In the same interview, he says that he liked Expressionism since he was 'a kid' and that he had especially admired Gustav Klimt, Egon Schiele and the Blaue Reiter group.

20 In a 1987 interview, Bowie said, I was always very seriously affected by my dreams … I found the dream state magnetic. It just captured everything for me.' When he saw the films of Dalí and Buñuel and the paintings of de Chirico, he thought, 'Yes, that's exactly how I want to write. How do you work like that?' ('Day In, Day Out', MTV special during Bowie's Glass Spider tour.)

21 'Cracked Actor', BBC documentary filmed in 1974 and first aired on 26 January 1975.

22 In an Australian television interview, Bowie said of Little Richard, 'He was my idol' (28 November 1978). Elsewhere Bowie said, 'I wanted to be a white Little Richard at eight – or at least his sax player.' ('David Bowie: Sound and Vision', A&E network's 'Biography' series, 6 October 2002.) Bowie told ABC's '20/20',

'I fell in love with the Little Richard band. I had never heard anything that lived in such bright colours in the air. It really just painted the whole room for me.' (13 November 1980.)

23 *Art Talk: Conversations with 15 Women Artists*, ed. Cindy Nemser (New York, 1975; revised edition 1995), p.252.

24 'Watch That Man', *BUST* magazine, Fall 2000.

25 Craig Copetas, 'Beat Godfather Meets Glitter Mainman', *Rolling Stone* magazine, 28 February 1974. Bowie tells William S. Burroughs that 'All the Young Dudes' refers to the 'terrible news' collected by Ziggy Stardust, who is torn to pieces on stage by the 'black hole' of the 'infinites'. This news, Bowie says, appears in 'Five Years', his first song on the *Ziggy Stardust* album: 'News had just come over, we had five years left to cry in … Five years, that's all we've got.'

PUTTING OUT FIRE WITH GASOLINE: DESIGNING DAVID BOWIE

VICTORIA BROACKES

1 The A-level was taken early, at 16. Bowie's school was focused on arts subjects. It is sometimes reported that Bowie has only one O-level, but this is not the case – which has been confirmed by The David Bowie Archive.

2 Kevin Cann, *David Bowie, Any Day Now: The London Years: 1947–1974* (London, 2010), p.29.

3 *Inspirations*, 1997. Directed by Michael Apted, Argo Films, Clear Blue Sky Productions.

4 Quoted in Richard Cromelin, 'David Bowie: Darling of the Avant-Garde?', *Phonograph Record* magazine, January 1972.

5 Sometimes known as the Konrads, the band appear as 'Kon-rads' on their drum kit, as seen in Roy Ainsworth's photographs. It is likely that (as with the pronunciation of Bowie), the name and spelling did change. See Peter Doggett, *The Man Who Sold the World: David Bowie and the 1970s* (London, 2011), p.31.

6 Quoted in David Buckley, *Strange Fascination: David Bowie: The Definitive Story* (London, 2005), p.291.

7 Nicholas Pegg, *The Complete Bowie* (London, 2009), p.10.

8 Craig Copetas, 'Beat Godfather Meets Glitter Mainman', *Rolling Stone* magazine (28 February 1974). Reprinted in Elizabeth Thomson and David Gutman (eds), *The Bowie Companion* (Cambridge, MA, 1996), p.108.

9 'Cracked Actor', 1974. Directed by Alan Yentob, first shown on BBC 2 as part of the series 'Omnibus', 26 January 1975.

10 Quoted in Jon Pareles, 'David Bowie: 21st Century Entrepreneur', *New York Times*, 9 June 2002.

11 Jonathan Barnbrook interviewed by Victoria Broackes, March 2012. Interview at www.vam.ac.uk/channel/

12 Bill Janovitz, *The Rolling Stones' Exile on Main St, 33⅓* (London, 2005), p.1.

13 Information supplied by the The David Bowie Archive.

14 Henry Edwards and Tony Zanetta, *Stardust: The Life and Times of David Bowie* (London, 1986), pp.112–13.

15 David Bowie and Mick Rock, *Moonage Daydream: The Life and Times of Ziggy Stardust* (London, 2005), p.12.

16 Ibid., p.192.

17 Ibid., p.248.

18 Jonathan Barnbrook interviewed by Victoria Broackes, March 2012.

19 Ibid.

20 Nine of Bowie posing in front of 23 Heddon Street (taken from different angles); nine under a tall lamppost; four under a sign marking the premises of furriers K. West; six of him leaning against the building, holding a guitar; 12 in the alley; two outside a telephone box and 12 close-ups.

21 Gary Kemp interviewed by Victoria Broackes, April 2012.

22 For an extended analysis of this period of Bowie's career, see Peter Doggett, *The Man Who Sold the World: David Bowie and the 1970s* (London, 2011).

23 Ibid., p.10.

24 Elizabeth Thomson and David Gutman (eds), *The Bowie Companion* (Cambridge, MA, 1996), pp 105–17.

25 Nick Stevenson, *David Bowie: Fame, Sound and Vision* (Cambridge: Polity Press, 2008), p.67.

26 For a detailed discussion of the album's development see David Buckley, *Strange Fascination: David Bowie: The Definitive Story* (London, 2005), pp.181–90.

27 Henry Edwards and Tony Zanetta, *Stardust: The Life and Times of David Bowie* (London, 1986), p.176.

28 Nick Stevenson, *David Bowie: Fame, Sound and Vision* (Cambridge: Polity Press, 2008), p.179.

29 David Buckley, *Strange Fascination: David Bowie: The Definitive Story* (London, 2005), p.184.

30 Michelangelo Antonioni's 1966 film *Blow-Up* captures the glamour and celebrates the innovatory spirit of this new generation of photographers.

31 The book at Bowie's feet is a novel by Walter Ross, *The Immortal* (1958). The main protagonist, Johnny Preston, is said to be based on James Dean. An alternative dust jacket (not the one shown in the *Diamond Dogs* portrait) was designed by Andy Warhol.

32 Dylan Jones, *Haircuts: fifty years of styles and cut* (London, 1990), p.67.

33 Nicholas Pegg, *The Complete Bowie* (London, 2009), p.471.

34 Jules Fisher's previous work included the first American tour of *Tommy* and the Broadway production of *Jesus Christ Superstar*.

35 For further analysis of the Diamond Dogs set see Nicholas Pegg, *The Complete Bowie* (London, 2009), p.471 and David Buckley, *Strange Fascination: David Bowie: The Definitive Story* (London, 2005), pp.199–203.

36 See pl.82. Detailed storyboards illustrated and annotated by Bowie feature 'mealcaine' as food, as well as rollerskating youths, film notes, set models and character sketches.

37 For further discussion of Bowie's London influence, see Geoffrey Marsh, 'Astronaut of Inner Spaces', pp.27–67.

38 Fifteen roadies, supplemented by a 20-man crew recruited at each venue. Nicholas Pegg, *The Complete Bowie* (London, 2009), p.473.

39 In the light of Bowie's appropriation of Guy Peellaert from the Stones, this counter-exchange seems to neatly complete the creative circle.

40 Visconti previously solo-produced the albums *Space Oddity*, *The Man Who Sold the World* and *David Live*.

41 David Buckley, *Strange Fascination: David Bowie: The Definitive Story* (London, 2005), p.333.

42 Mallet went on to collaborate with Bowie on several other music videos including 'Let's Dance' and the censored 'China Girl' in 1983, and 'Hallo Spaceboy' in 1996, in addition to the documentary films of Bowie's performances, *Glass Spider* (1988) and *David Bowie: Black Tie White Noise* (1993).

43 Nicholas Pegg, *The Complete Bowie* (London, 2009), p.28.

44 Jonathan Barnbrook interviewed by Victoria Broackes, March 2012.

45 *David Bowie: Sound and Vision*, 2002. Produced and directed by Rick Hull. Researchers: Mai-Ly Nguyen and Karl D. Ring. Van Ness Films, Inc. For Foxstar Productions. 20th Century Fox Film Corporation.

46 Nicholas Pegg, *The Complete Bowie* (London, 2009), pp.30–1.

47 Ibid., p.29.

48 See Clinton Heylin, *All the Madmen: Barrett, Bowie, Drake, Pink Floyd, the Kinks, the Who and the Journey to the Dark Side of English Rock* (London, 2012).

49 Bowie in interview, *Musician* magazine, July 1990

50 J. G. Ballard discusses what he means by inner space in the essay 'Time, Memory, and Inner Space' – see pp. 34–5 of this book, Geoffrey Marsh, 'Astronaut of Inner Spaces'. The full article is at www.jgballard.ca/nor_fiction/non-fiction.html

51 Quoted in Nicholas Pegg, *The Complete Bowie* (London, 2009), pp.333 and 359–60.

52 Scary Monsters Interview (RCAD|LI–3840), 1980 (US). Bowie talking about the 'Ashes to Ashes' video.

53 Interview, backstage footage after performing 'Heroes' on 'TopPop', 13 October 1977, Avro TV, The Netherlands.

54 *Inspirations*, 1997. Directed by Michael Apted for Argo Films and Clear Blue Sky Productions.

55 Eliot, T.S., "Philip Massinger," *The Sacred Wood*, New York: Bartleby.com, 2000.

FOR 'WE ARE THE GOON SQUAD': BOWIE, STYLE AND THE POWER OF THE LP COVER, 1967–1983

CHRISTOPHER BREWARD

1 Peter York, *Style Wars* (London, 1980), pp.113–4.

2 For this reason I dedicate this essay to my friend Mark, who among my childhood friends got to Bowie first.

3 Peter Doggett, *The Man Who Sold the World: David Bowie and the 1970s* (London, 2011), p.45.

4 John Gill, *Queer Noises* (London, 1995), p.106.

5 Hanif Kureishi and Jon Savage (eds.), *The Faber Book of Pop* (London, 1995), pp.391–4.

6 Gill, p.107.

7 Kureishi and Savage, p.391.

8 Kureishi and Savage, pp.456–64.

9 Hugo Wilcken, *Low* (New York, 2008), p.28.

10 Christopher Breward, 'Camp and the International Language of 1970s Fashion' in Maria Luisa Frisa and Stefano Tonchi (eds.), *Walter Albini and his Times* (Venice, 2010), pp.15–17.

11 Wilcken, p.79. See also Glenn Adamson and Victoria Kelley (eds.), *Surface Tensions: Surface, Finish and the Meaning of Objects* (Manchester, 2012).

12 Wilcken, p.15.

13 Wilcken, p.127.

14 Doggett, p.307.

15 Glenn Adamson and Jane Pavitt (eds.), *Postmodernism: Style & Subversion 1970–1990* (London, 2011), p.94.

16 Doggett, p.325.

17 York, p.241.

18 York, p.243.

19 York, p.244.

CHANGES: BOWIE'S LIFE STORY

ORIOLE CULLEN

1   Mark C. O'Flaherty, 'Men's wear ch-ch-changes', *Financial Times* [online], 23 September 2011, www.ft.com/cms/s/2/c395d1b0-e075-11e0-bd01-00144feabdc0.html, accessed 27 February 2012

2   Richard Nicoll, email exchange with Oriole Cullen, 25 April 2012.

3   Janice Miller, *Fashion and Music* (Oxford, 2011), p.1.

4   Ibid, p.2.

5   Dean Mayo Davies, 'The Sound of Style: Tim Blanks', *AnOther Magazine* [online], 14 June 2011, www.anothermag.com/current/view/1161/Tim_Blanks, accessed 17 April 2012

6   In recent years, the fashion world has anointed Bowie's fellow South Londoner Kate Moss as the embodiment of Bowie-style. A model who shot to fame by bringing an androgynous look to the era of the supermodel, with an edge of the 'English rebel' and her own standing as something of an icon, she is the perfect vessel to channel Bowie. While she is known for her own style – and for the various relationships she has had with rock musicians – her role as a model has always been to provide a blank canvas from which to project the creations of designers/stylists and photographers, she does this so deftly that her persona does not infringe in anyway on the Bowie mystique but simply ads a hint of contemporary glamour. In October 2003, Q magazine published 'Clash of the Titans', an interview with David Bowie by Kate Moss accompanied by photographs by Ellen von Unwerth.

7   David Bowie and Mick Rock, *Moonage Daydream: The Life and Times of Ziggy Stardust* (London, 2005), p.86.

8   '20 questions to David Bowie about his image', *Mirabelle* magazine, January 1974.

9   Simon Frith, 'Only Dancing: David Bowie Flirts with the Issues' in Angela McRobbie (ed.), *Zoot Suits and Second-Hand Dresses* (London, 1989).

10   Paul Raven, 'Popping the question: David Bowie', *Mirabelle* magazine, September 1972.

11   Kevin Cann, *Any Day Now: David Bowie The London Years 1947–1974* (London, 2010), p.20.

12   'Teen-Age Page', *Nashua Telegraph*, 4 November 1974, p.14.

13   Nik Cohn, *Ball the Wall: Nik Cohn in the Age of Rock* (London, 1989), p.309.

14   Michael Watts, 'Oh You Pretty Thing', *Melody Maker*, 22 January 1972.

15   'Teen-Age Page', *Nashua Telegraph*, 4 November 1974, p.14.

16   Cameron Crowe, 'Candid Conversation: An outrageous conversation with the actor, rock singer and sexual switch-hitter', *Playboy* magazine, September 1976.

17   Garry Mulholland, 'Stardust Memories', *Uncut* magazine, April 2012, p.28.

18   David Iztkoff, 'The Fashion Rocks Q&A', *Lucky* magazine, October 2005.

19   Garry Mulholland, 'Stardust Memories', *Uncut* magazine, April 2012, p.31.

20   David Bowie and Mick Rock, *Moonage Daydream: The Life and Times of Ziggy Stardust* (London, 2005), p.17.

21   Ibid.

22   Garry Mulholland, 'Stardust Memories', *Uncut* magazine, April 2012, p.28.

23   Adrian Deevoy, 'Boys Keep Swinging', *Q Magazine*, June 1989.

24   Michael Watts, 'Waiting for the Man', *Melody Maker*, July 1972.

25   'The Kansai Yamamoto Show!!!', *Harpers & Queen*, July 1971, p.47.

26   David Bowie and Mick Rock, *Moonage Daydream: The Life and Times of Ziggy Stardust* (London, 2005), p.17.

27   Ibid., p.80.

28   Kevin Cann, *Any Day Now: David Bowie The London Years 1947–1974* (London, 2010), p.285

29   Ibid., p.289.

30   David Iztkoff, 'The Fashion Rocks Q&A', *Lucky* magazine, October 2005.

31   David Bowie and Mick Rock, *Moonage Daydream: The Life and Times of Ziggy Stardust* (London, 2005), p.38

32   Dylan Jones, *Haircults: fifty years of styles and cut*, (London, 1990), p.67.

33   Ibid., p.72.

34   'David Bowie's Make-up Do's and Don't's', *Music Scene*, November 1973.

35   Charles Shaar Murray, 'The Byronic Man', *The Face*, October 1984.

36   Suzy Menkes, 'Gucci does David Bowie glam rock', *New York Times* [online], 22 February 2006, www.nytimes.com/2006/02/22/style/22iht-rmilan23.htm, accessed 27 February 2012

37   *Mirabelle*, 14 July 1973.

38   Kevin Cann, *Any Day Now: David Bowie, The London Years 1947–1974* (London, 2010), p.304.

39   Alexandra Shulman, *Vogue*, May 2003.

40   Mark C. O'Flaherty, 'Men's wear ch-ch-changes', *Financial Times* [online], 23 September 2011, www.ft.com/cms/s/2/c395d1b0-e075-11e0-bd01-00144feabdc0.html, accessed 27 February 2012

41   Cally Blackman, email exchange with the author, 18 April 2012.

42   'People Who Turn Me On', *Fan* magazine, October 1974

43   Correspondence with the author, 2012.

44   Godfrey Deeny, 'The Paris men's wear shows', *Financial Times* [online], 28 January 2011, www.ft.com/cms/s/2/f3b343ac-2a61-11e0-804a-00144feab49a.html, accessed 6 March 2012

45   Ben Edmonds, 'Ol Orange Hair is Back', *RAM*, March 1976.

46   Diane Solway, *W* magazine [online], August 2011, www.wmagazine.com/fashion/2011/08/tilda-swinton-cover-story-fashion, accessed 3 April 2012

47   Ibid.

48   Tim Blanks, 'Tim Blanks Recommends: The Bowie Look Revisited', Fantastic Man [online], 21 October 2011, www.fantasticman.com/#/recommendations/tim-blanks-recommends-the-bowie-look-revisited/accessed 10 February 2012.

49   Charles Shaar Murray, 'Sermon From the Savoy', *New Musical Express*, 29 Sept 1984.

50   Correspondence with the author, 2012.

51   David Iztkoff, 'The Fashion Rocks Q&A', *Lucky* magazine, October 2005.

52   'Fashion: turn to the left. Fashion: turn to the right', *Dazed & Confused* magazine, issue no.26, November 1996.

53   Ian Buruma, 'Tell A Man by his Clothes', *Anglomania: Tradition and Transgression in British Fashion* (New Haven, 2006), p.19.

54   David Iztkoff, 'The Fashion Rocks Q&A', *Lucky* magazine, October 2005.

55   Ibid.

56   Dean Mayo Davies, 'The Sound of Style: Hedi Slimane', *Another* magazine [online], 14 May 2010, www.anothermag.com/current/view/243/Hedi_Slimane, accessed 3 April 2012.

57   Tim Blanks, 'Tim Blanks Recommends: The Bowie Book', *Fantastic Man* magazine [online], 17 October 2011, www.fantasticman.com/#/recommendations/tim-blanks-recommends-the-bowie-book/, accessed 12 April 2012.

58   David Iztkoff, 'The Fashion Rocks Q&A', *Lucky* magazine, October 2005.

59   Mark C. O'Flaherty, 'Men's wear ch-ch-changes', *Financial Times* [online], 23 September 2011, http://www.ft.com/cms/s/2/c395d1b0-e075-11e0-bd01-00144feabdc0.html#axzz1tGAgnALV, accessed 27 February 2012.

ACKNOWLEDGEMENTS

It is the case with pop culture subjects generally and pop music in particular that the world is full of genuine experts: from individuals such as David Buckley, Kevin Cann and Nicholas Pegg, whose books we have consulted on a daily basis, to the non-published Bowie fans, who not only know a huge amount, but also have a passion for their subject that is unparalleled in more traditional V&A exhibition subjects. We have received assistance of every kind: intellectual, practical and personal. We would like to thank the many friends and new contacts, within and outside the V&A, for their continuous interest and offers of insights and material which has meant that we have completed the project with our fascination growing. The broader art, design and performance community has also been remarkably generous in supporting our efforts.

Profound thanks go to Dr Kathryn Johnson, the project's assistant curator, whose contribution has helped us every step of the way; and Sandy Hirshkowitz of The David Bowie Archive, who has been with us from the outset, alerting us to the best material and acting as one-woman conduit to the delights stored in the archive. Their contributions have been both extensive and crucial. Thanks to Bill Zysblat for making it possible. Equally deep thanks go to the rest of the core project team: our wonderfully inventive exhibition designers 59 Productions working with Real Studios, graphics and lighting specialists; Eleanor Townsend and the Exhibitions department; external advisors Jonathan Barnbrook, Kevin Cann, Howard Goodall, Paul Morley and Jon Savage; cost consultants; our editor Tom Windross and the team at V&A Enterprises, Davina Cheung, Clare Davis, Mark Eastment and Vicky Haverson. We are grateful to Alexandra Stetter, our copy-editor, and Jonathan Abbott.

We would also like to thank all the contributors to this book, who added their own diverse perspectives and broadened the scope of literature on Bowie. Their articles not only informed our own understanding of the subject but also influenced the content of the exhibition. Thanks also go to the photographers who have allowed us to show their work.

Countless external people have contributed: Oliver Bradbury, Brian Croft, Chris Duffy, James Hyman (The James Hyman Pop Culture Magazine Archive), Dr Elizabeth Kehoe, Gary Kemp, Geoff McCormack, Ewan O'Neill, Helene Thian, Francis Whately, Kansai Yamamoto. At the V&A others have also contributed hugely to the project. Space does not permit us to mention everyone, but we would particularly like to thank: Richard Davis, Alan Derbyshire, Liz Edmunds, Lara Flecker, Tom Grosvenor, Adair Harper, Diana McAndrews, Richard Mulholland, Gesa Werner and Anna Wu.

We benefited greatly from the assistance of interns throughout the project. We would like to recognize them all here, and thank them for their time and energy: Jasmine Aslan, Edie Campbell, Lauren Fried, Claudia Goss, Holly Harris, Ben Jefferson, Sara Nuzzi, Amanda Pajak, Evie Prichard, Louise Rytter, Dzmitry Suslau.

The V&A Research and Theatre & Performance Departments have been stimulating environments in which to develop such a project, and we are grateful to our colleagues for their advice and support. On behalf of everyone at the V&A we would like to thank Mark Jones, former Director of the Museum, Ian Blatchford, former Deputy Director, and Damien Whitmore, Director of Public Affairs, who had the confidence in the idea and us to commit the Museum to the project.

PICTURE CREDITS

DAVID BOWIE IS INDEXED

↑ **[214] ABOVE AND FRONT COVER** ● David Bowie ●
Photograph by Brian Duffy

↑ **[215] ABOVE AND BACK COVER** ● David Bowie, 1995 ●
Photograph by Gavin Evans

DAVID BOWIE
IS THE END